FOOD AND BEVERAGE MANAGEMENT

FOOD AND BEVERAGE MANAGEMENT

Edited by

Amrik Singh Sudan

ANMOL PUBLICATIONS PVT. LTD

NEW DELHI-110 002 (INDIA)

ANMOL PUBLICATIONS PVT. LTD.

Regd. Office: 4360/4, Ansari Road, Daryaganj,
New Delhi-110002 (India)
Tel.: 23278000, 23261597, 23286875, 23255577
Fax: 91-11-23280289
Email: anmolpub@gmail.com
Visit us at: www.anmolpublications.com

Branch Office: No. 1015, Ist Main Road, BSK IIIrd Stage
IIIrd Phase, IIIrd Block, Bangalore-560 085 (India)
Tel.: 080-41723429 • Fax: 080-26723604
Email: anmolpublicationsbangalore@gmail.com

Food and Beverage Management

First Edition, 2001

Reprint, 2010

ISBN 81-261-1069-4

PRINTED IN INDIA

Printed at Mehra Offset Press, Delhi.

Contents

Preface

Hotel industry has close relation with tourism industry. With the flourishing of international tourism, Hotel industry has also gone drastic changes and has grown leaps and bound. In the current age of globalisation and liberalisation it is growing rapidly—having cosmopolitan touch. In true sense, hotel, hospitality and catering are enthusing the feeling of international integration, thus the world as a global village.

The present work is intended to bring together authentic information on diverse aspects of hotel, hospitality, and catering management such as—hotel management, restaurant management, housekeeping management, hospitality marketing, food and beverage management, and foodservice operations. The entire information is logically organised under above titles. The concepts and developments are supported by facts and figures.

To make the work comprehensive we have gathered the information from various sources. We are grateful to all the scholars whose writings are cited or substantially made use of in the present venture. I am also thankful to my colleagues and friends who have assisted me in one way or other while preparing the manuscript. Last but not the least, I am indebted to Mr. J.L. Kumar, Managing Director, Anmol Publications Pvt. Ltd., New Delhi for his constant moral support and also for bringing out this work within a short span of time.

—Editor

1

Consumer Needs

A foodservice system is activated by in mind and needs. A successful manager always keeps consumer needs performs all duties with these needs in mind. Although preliminary market and site analysis provide important demographic information, it is imperative to understand the types of consumers and what they actually want. The easiest way to assess consumer needs is to question why a particular consumer, or a group of consumers, is or should be availing themselves of the foodservices provided by an operation.

Consumers might be interested in the menu, convenience, atmosphere, entertainment, discounts, service, or other factors. The base line remains the fulfillment of consumer needs and their satisfaction.

Once consumers and their needs are identified, it becomes important to know what they like and dislike, whether it be related to food and/or foodservice. There are relatively few publications emphasizing the needs and wants of consumers availing themselves of various types of foodservices. Since consumers represent various segments of the population, their needs can be considered from two aspects:

(1) types of consumers utilizing foodservices and

(2) types of foodservices serving specific consumers.

Types of consumers

Since consumers represent all age groups, their needs and wants are subject to individual variations, which may be physiological or sociological in origin. Some consumers may avail themselves of a foodservice in order to meet their nutritional needs or requirements; others may use them as status symbols or for exhibiting affection. Therefore, it is important to understand what particular consumers want; this should be the first step in setting up any type of a foodservice system.

From the consumer-needs point of view, various consumers may be categorized as follows: (1) children, (2) adolescents, (3) adults, (4) senior citizens, (5) students, (6) shoppers, (7) workers, (8) travelers, and (9) patients. Although there is a certain amount of overlap in these groups, there is still a definite distinction in the types of foodservices and foods that individuals in each of these groups prefer.

Children

Children are a very important and special group of consumers since they are the major influence when families eat out. Although this fact was not given much importance by the foodservice industry in the past, recently more emphasis has been placed on attracting this category of consumers, particularly by the fast foodservices.

Children are very easily influenced by advertisements and are fascinated by special gift offers. Their needs and wants should be given high priority by any foodservice planning on attracting families and groups. Foodservice chains have attracted this category of consumers by providing special offers backed by large-scale national publicity. In addition, many food chains have attracted children by providing playgrounds, birthday parties, and special gift packages.

Some facilities even provide such entertainment as games, animated cartoon characters, videogames, and other means to keep the children busy while the food is being served. These attractions are for adults as well and are a means of supplementing income for the owners of the foodservice operations.

Fast-food restaurants are preferred by families with children because of their convenience, informal atmosphere, and low prices. Also, since the service is relatively fast, the problem of children becoming impatient is solved. Foodservice managers must always remember that families particularly the larger ones-are looking for economy and bargains when they eat out with their children. The latter, in turn, attach particular significance to eating out since they consider it a special occasion and a treat. Therefore, they prefer food items that are not frequently served at home. Also, it is important to remember that the children themselves-not their parents-make decisions on what they want, which should be considered when planning menus.

Although children seldom accompany their parents to fine restaurants, they may frequently go to medium-priced restaurants. Special menu planning and advertisements are therefore essential to attract these target groups of consumers. The menus should feature foods that are attractive, interesting, filling, and preferably accompanied by special beverages like milk shakes, ice sherbets, ice creams, and carbonated drinks.

Adolescents

This is a very special group of consumers, one that is passing through a stage of the life cycle in which physiological changes are taking place and social awareness is developing. Adolescents often become "calorie-conscious" at this stage so that salads, vegetables, and low-calorie menu items are particularly preferred by them. For many foodservice managers, dealing with the diverse needs of this group of consumers is a challenge and at times an unrewarding experience. Also, it is very hard to please this category of consumers, particularly those who eat at an institutional type of foodservice. The very fact that the recipes are standardized in foodservices compared to "home" food which has day-to-day variability in taste-may be a reason for their displeasure.

Since adolescents are becoming more and more influenced by the food provided by the fast-food chains, there is a growing trend in many institutional foodservice operations to include foods that are similar to those served by local fast foodservice chains. Among this group of consumers there is a small subgroup that prefers special foods due to different food beliefs. Also, special dietary foods like skim milk, yogurt, vegetarian dishes, and other low-calorie items are gaining in popularity. In addition, teen-agers buy a great deal of machine-vended food and drinks. Both alcoholic and nonalcoholic beverages, particularly carbonated ones, are very important for these consumers. On occasion, this category of consumers may visit fine restaurants, particularly when dating or for exhibiting self-esteem. Special entertainment is also an important attraction for these consumers.

Adults

This is a very broad category, the food preferences of which are based on the marital status of its members. Thus, the needs of single, widowed, divorced, and married consumers are very much different. Singles who are largely independent often cat away from home, as they do not care to cook or clean up after meals. Also, they may prefer to eat at fast-food restaurants where they will not feel lonely, as they often do at relatively fine restaurants. Singles often look for a variety of food choices in addition to fast service. Ethnic foods that are hard to prepare at home, like Chinese or Mexican foods, are preferred by consumers within this group. Singles also buy a great deal of take-out food. Since marital status greatly affects the economical status of individuals, the frequency with which married couples eat out depends on the total income of the family, the time available for outings, and family size. Most families prefer occasionally visiting midpriced foodservice operations, mainly for economic reasons. Such drinks as beer, wine, and cocktails are very popular among Individuals within this category.

Senior citizens

This group of food consumers represents a very special group and is an ever-growing market for the foodservice industry. Among the many factors that affect their food habits and preferences are (1) loneliness, (2) diminished taste and olfactory sensitivity, (3) physiological changes, (4) anxiety, (5) depression, (6) dental problems, (7) rigid food habits, (8) lack of mobility, (9) lack of nutritional knowledge, (10) socioeconomic status, and (11) resistance to change. These factors seldom operate singly and so are very much interrelated and complex.

Consideration should be given to these factors while planning menus and foodservice facilities intended for the elderly. Unfortunately, there is a considerable lack of information about their food likes and dislikes. They directly or indirectly are frequent consumers availing themselves of different types of foodservices. Some senior citizens may reside at home, while many are in nursing homes or convalescent centers, thereby using institutional foodservices. For senior citizens, eating out is more often a social rather than a physiological need. Eating out can therefore eliminate boredom, pass time, and provide a change of atmosphere since they are often isolated or may be required to spend numerous hours with a spouse, roommate, or colleague. Food thus becomes an important reason for them to dress up and spend come time outside the residence.

Many are tired of eating home-cooked food, leftovers, or institutionally prepared foods. Also, they prefer convenience and do not feel like cooking or cleaning up. Their main concern, however, is economy since they are often on a limited income. They prefer easily chewable and tasty food, probably due to a diminishing sense of taste and dental problems. Senior citizens avail themselves of special offers, coupons, early-bird specials, "buy-one-get-one-free" offers, and other bar gains.

Often, these food bargains may prove to be less expensive than fixing meals at home. They may prefer a variety of foods and at times complete meals while eating out. Since cost is a primary consideration and since these older food patrons prefer staying on for long periods of time, the foodservices often frequented by this group of consumers include coffee shops, cafeterias, and food counters within malls or shopping centers. These places provide a perfect atmosphere for them since they get an opportunity to socialize over a cup of coffee and some of the soft textured foods (cakes and toast, for example) that go very well with that coffee. There are several aspects that need to be considered while serving patrons in this group. One of them is the size of the food portion. Medium-to-small servings are normally preferred by the elderly consumers, and therefore the emphasis should be on small serving sizes with more variety.

Heavy meals are generally avoided by these consumers, particularly for dinner or supper; their big daily meal is usually at lunch time. Therefore, nutritious and filling meals should be planned for lunch. Fried foods and dairy products are generally avoided by individuals in this group. They like foods cooked simply with less spices and prefer such semiliquid foods as soups, stews, or casseroles. It also is advisable to add fresh fruits and vegetables to their meals, whenever possible. Comfort can be cited as the single most important factor in the selection of a foodservice by these consumers. Comfort may be derived from such factors as accessibility, a pleasant atmosphere in a dining area with bright lighting, less congestion and traffic, no waiting lines, an easy-to-read menu, provision of ambulatory facilities, vicinity of malls and shopping centers, good heating and/or air conditioning, cordial service, light entertainment, television, and newspapers. In other words, elderly patrons are looking for a place where they are welcome and feel at ease.

Senior citizens usually have food habits that are very much set and are very difficult to change at this stage of life. Frequent criticisms of the contemporary meal patterns may be expected. Foodservice managers should realize that senior citizens are their most loyal customers and as such should be expected to return on a recurring basis.

On the other hand, they are also very hard to please since they often get frustrated very easily. However, it should be understood that their feelings may stem from physical or socioeconomic reasons rather than displeasure with the food. Residents in such institutions as nursing homes often take out their anger (from other sources) on food and/or foodservices. Food frequently becomes an easy target for anger. The elderly should be considered as important potential clients for a foodservice operation, since they represent an increasing segment of the population in the United States. Some of them have special dietary needs, which should be taken into account when planning meals for them. Most of them prefer cafeteria-style foodservices, giving older patrons the option to regulate portion sizes arid to make their selections from a variety of displayed foods. As mentioned earlier, they like a relaxed and leisurely eating atmosphere.

In older to accomplish this, they may also prefer visiting at slack periods of business to avoid crowds and to have time for socialization. These customers often develop an acquaintance with foodservice personnel, particularly waiters and waitresses, which establishes repeat business. Since eating out is influenced by we other conditions, the season may play an important role in their decision and frequency to eat away from their place of residence.

Students

School and college students represent a very hard-to-please category of consumers, as they often complain about the food provided by school or college foodservices. Common complaints include that the food is starchy, nonnutritious, loaded with calories, or monotonous.

Menu planning thus becomes a challenge for school and college foodservice managers. Students often prefer convenience when selecting food-serving places, mainly because they may lack the time, the motivation, or the facilities to prepare meals. A limited student budget can be expected to influence their selection of places to eat out. They often visit local foodservice establishments, particularly on weekends.

Since some residence hall foodservices do not provide meals on weekends, college students find it necessary to eat out. Lack of transportation causes this group to patronize eating establishments that are close to campus- Likewise, school students prefer eating lunch out at places close to their school. Several studies have shown that breakfast is the most common meal skipped by this group of food consumers. There is a growing tendency for them to select low-calorie or vegetarian foods, since they are becoming more calorie conscious- Salad bars are also becoming popular among these consumers.

Carbonated beverages and certain alcoholic beverages tire also very popular and are commonly preferred items by tire majority of college students. School students mainly prefer soft drinks, since they are below the age limit for alcoholic beverages.

Students generally prefer eating on campus-in sororities, fraternities, or dining halls-mainly because of the conveniences of living and eating they provide. Lack of time or incentive are the common reasons for selecting this type of foodservice for regular meals.

On-campus foodservices should consider satisfying these consumers by providing menu items that are generally preferred by students. Inclusion of a large variety of foods should be the main consideration when planning menus for the consumers in this group. Students are also very much value conscious and seriously consider the quality and quantity of foods provided for the price. These reasons make it advisable to include students in the menu-planning process so as to take into account their opinion and food preferences.

Frequent use of standardized recipes becomes too monotonous for them, and variations in the preparation methods may be desirable. Consideration should be given to the fact that students love to eat out after supper or late at night, particularly during examination periods. Also, they may have to eat at times other than the scheduled meal hours, because of class schedules. For these reasons, residence halls often provide continuous foodservices for the major part of the day.

Shoppers

This is a new category of consumers, on that is growing in proportion with malls and shopping centers. Many franchise-type foodservices and cafeterias are expanding their operations to provide foodservices to this category of consumers. Since shopping is their primary motive, food becomes secondary to these consumers, although at times shopping and dining may be combined. Since these consumers are interested in shopping, convenient locations of the foodservice operations are highly desirable.

Many retail stores have their own foodservices, such as cafeterias or lunchrooms, and provide a limited to an extended menu. It is recognized that a "dining experience" is not the intended motive of these consumers, since they are primarily interested in refreshment and a diversion from shopping.

Fast service becomes an important consideration, particularly during peak shopping hours and holiday seasons. Therefore, the menu should include items that can be prepared and served as quickly as possible. Families with children most often use these types of foodservices, since the children get restless while shopping with their parents.

Foodservices in shopping centers are very unique in the sense that they provide opportunities for informal chats with acquaintances, a place to rest and become refreshed, a place for meeting, and, more important for some, a place to sit and watch the crowds. Location, therefore, plays a very important role in the selection of foodservices by these patrons.

In addition to shoppers, people who work in or near these shopping centers also avail themselves of these foodservices, particularly at lunch time. The foods commonly provided by these places include cakes, salads, desserts, doughnuts, pretzels, ice cream, and popcorn. Senior citizens also prefer to visit these places if conveniently located, since they provide an opportunity for them to meet each other and to watch many people and observe the "moving scene" of the market.

Workers

Both blue- and white-collar workers represent a very loyal and growing class of consumers for any type of foodservice. Many businesses and industries are realizing that establishing their own foodservices for their employees may result in direct or indirect benefits. An example of an indirect benefit is the comfort and satisfaction provided by on-site meals and the resulting increase in the motivation and productivity of the workers.

On-premise foodservice operations may be considered one of the fringe benefits provided by the employers. As with other groups, convenience from the consumers' viewpoint is an essential component for the success of such foodservice operations.

Company cafeterias should preferably be relaxing and have very quick, efficient service, since there is a need to unwind quickly from the tension caused by work. Employers also prefer that the service be fast so that employees will not lose work time. Most employers provide, for a very low price, good food that can range from a snack to a whole meal.

For many workers, the food served at the company foodservice may be the main meal of the day, since they may not have the incentive to cook at home after long and/or irregular hours on work shifts. Also, many prefer to eat hot meals rather than a cold "brown-bag" lunch. The company lunch also provides for socialization with friends and co-workers. An added attraction of company cafeterias is that they are very convenient in severe weather, because they are usually under one roof or in one complex.

Machine-vended foods also are purchased by this group of consumers. Blue-collar workers may be in need of nutritionally sound diets, and company foodservices may be the means of providing good nutrition to these consumers, particularly if the meals provided represent the main meal of the day.

Many businesses and industries that provide on-site foodservices also emphasize a pleasant dining atmosphere primarily for two reasons: (1) a good, quiet atmosphere is needed ' as a change from noisy work places, and (2) management executives use these facilities for meetings and get-togethers.

Many companies now have executive dining rooms that provide an opportunity to present a positive image of the business to visitors, clients, prospective employees, and the press. The food and decor in these dining areas are therefore planned to be attractive and of a superior quality. Since many of these companies are not related to foodservices, outside contractors may be hired to run the company dining areas.

Foodservice establishments in businesses and industries benefit from serving a large number of employees. Thus, the foodservice is largely dependent on a large employee work pool and works best when there is on-going employment and overtime work. On the other hand, the foodservices are affected by the retrenchment of the employees, slack periods, or by shutdowns.

Most of these places provide a variety in menu items, charging considerably lower prices to consumers, since meals are partially or wholly subsidized by the employers. The company cafeteria may also have a large salad bar, sold by the ounce, or a variety of sandwiches. Some foodservices may even have "all-you-can-eat" offers, particularly in jobs where heavy physical work is required or where situations demand temporary isolation from families as in the case of oil rigs, coal mines, and offshore drilling plants. The quality as well as quantity of food is very important to workers of all types. The food habits of these consumers are influenced by frequent consumption of fast foods, and therefore the menus provided should preferably include items that are normally served by the fast-food restaurants.

Many of the fast-food chains are trying to attract this category of consumers for breakfast and lunch by offering special items that are often discounted. More breakfast items are being offered by fast-food operations for this group of consumers, since it is very convenient for workers to have a prepackaged breakfast available in a relatively short time on their way to work.

Traveller

People are always on the move in the United States, whether it is for business, leisure, or for family visits. These travels are at a peak during special vacations, conventions, national holidays, or other important events. Travel may be by car, trailer, truck, bus, train, ship, or plane and may vary in duration.

Certain travelers, like truck drivers, are constantly on the move and are therefore a continuous source of income for the foodservice establishments on or near highways. As far as travelers are concerned, the main incentive is to get rest, and a fine dining experience is not their motive. Likewise, atmosphere is usually not the primary consideration as long as the service is fast and efficient. Nevertheless, cleanliness and uncrowded conditions are still required. Also, such facilities as adequate washrooms and dining areas, are considered by consumers when selecting food stops while traveling. Many prefer franchised fast-food restaurants, since they are familiar with the type of food they offer and know they will be served quickly.

Hot foods and cold beverages, mostly carbonated, are preferred by most of these consumers. Most of the items selected are medium priced, particularly the foods purchased by those traveling in large groups or with families. Truck drivers are a very important segment of these consumers, since they are normally repeat customers. Many foodservices try to attract these "year-round" customers by providing efficient and pleasant waitress service or discounts. Discounts are also extended by many to bus drivers when they bring in busloads of passengers.

Foodservices at bus stops, train stations, or airports cater to the needs of the passengers, their guests, and transportation personnel. Passengers in transit find these foodservices very handy and convenient, particularly since they often have time between transportation connections; passing time is often the primary motive of these consumers. They may want to sit at a convenient and comfortable spot and refresh themselves while waiting for their next ride or flight. Some might prefer a drink or two to buying food. The crew and staff of the transportation services are among the regular customers of these types of foodservice operations. Also, when flights are delayed or cancelled, most airlines depend on these foodservices to provide food and beverages to the detained passengers. Thus, they have a regular business from the passengers as well as the transportation staff.

Fast foods generally are preferred by the passengers. It is noteworthy that at some places, particularly airports, foodservice facilities are designed either without seating arrangements or with a less comfortable type of seating, since fast turnover is desired by these foodservice operators. Foods selected for use in in-flight meals or on trains are those that can be stored, re-thermalized, and served without any loss of quality or safety.

Patients

Patients represent very hard-to-please foodservice patrons, primarily because they may also have physiological and psychological problems. The very fact that they are ill and hospitalized puts a strain on patients, which may have a considerable impact on their appetite or food preferences. For these consumers, food is more of a curative item than a means for preventing illness. They are more anxious to leave the hospital or to regain their health than to remember hospital food as a pleasant or lasting experience. The anxiety associated with the condition of their health or the physiological tests they might be undergoing often create a great deal of frustration. There are several types of meals served by health-care facilities, and they vary according to an individual's condition. Probably very few other foodservices have as well-planned menus as hospital foodservices.

Food items are very carefully selected and arranged in menu cycles under the constant scrutiny of dietitians as well as health authorities. Meals may have several dietary modifications that range from differences in food texture to caloric and specific nutrient contents. Since there are a large number of individuals who may be on special diets-such as low-sodium, low-calorie, or other modified foods, either permanently or for a prolonged period of time-there is a need for almost any type of foodservice operation to include special items in the menus. Foodservice managers have to carefully plan the menus based on the health status of the patients. The hospital atmosphere itself interferes with the aroma and acceptability of foods.

Most hospitals have cycle menus which normally range from two to three weeks. Although some of the meals may be modified, foods are also prepared for normal patients, medical and nursing staff, and other hospital personnel. Some hospitals provide for cocktails and special dinners for certain occasions and for parents of newborn babies. Special meals are also provided for medical staff members, administrators, and visitors.

Types of foodservices

Foodservices may also be classified in terms of consumer needs, which will help in assessing foodservices from a different viewpoint. For this discussion, foodservice operations may be classified as follows:

1. Fast foodservices
2. Midpriced restaurants
3. Upscale restaurants
4. Take-out foodservice facilities
5. Hotel/motel foodservices
6. Foodservices at leisure facilities
7. Foodservices in health-care facilities
8. Foodservices in business and industry
9. Foodservices in educational institutions
10. Community foodservices

The intent is to present the consumer needs from different angles and to show that there is more than one way of classifying foodservices. In order to avoid duplication, only salient features of each type of foodservice will be discussed.

Fast foodservices

The term "fast" refers to the service rather than to the food; it is a term very commonly misunderstood by many. Fast service does not mean that the quality of food is inferior or loaded with calories. This fact needs emphasis, since there is a lot of misunderstanding among general consumers.

For faster service these foodservices rely enormously on automation. On the other hand, since there is a need for faster service, there is a limitation to the food items and menu choices offered by these facilities. Until very recently, the emphasis was on a single item or on a menu consisting of such specialty items as hamburgers and fried chicken.

However, sophisticated market testing, advances in equipment and facilities, and consumer tastes and preferences have led to a trend whereby these fast foodservices are now offering a variety of food items. Thus, a hamburger chain may also offer chicken, ham, fish, salads, sausages, and several other combinations. There is very keen competition among fast foodservice operations, which has led to the development of a varied menu as well as service. In order to eliminate the misconception about food served by the fast-food chains regarding their caloric or nutritional contents, many foodservices are providing nutritional information or are labeling the foods they offer.

Fast foodservices are also considered as restaurants that are not suitable for special occasions or a fine dining experience. As the name indicates, these places are not designed to provide the elegant lunch or dinner. Their very concept is based on fast service which runs contrary to the leisurely service in a fine restaurant.

The fast service concept is also carried over to the type and quality of seating arrangements, which are obviously planned to facilitate a fast turnover rate. Seating is normally congested with less comfortable to moderately comfortable seats. Cleanliness may be more important than the decor or atmosphere at these places. Patrons usually expect fast foodservice places to have a crowded atmosphere.

Each fast foodservice chain features a fairly distinct type of menu and has a target population, thereby controlling a specific segment of the market. Economy has a direct impact on the popularity and sales among the fast foodservice chains.

Double-income families have resulted in an increased number of consumers using fast foodservice operations. Most of, the fast foodservices are popular for providing quality foods for limited money, in addition to providing fast and efficient service. Probably it is the only segment of the foodservice industry in which coupons, discounts, games, prizes, and other promotions are extensively used with increasing frequency.

Since there are many fast foodservice chains and there is considerable competition, consumers have more flexibility in selecting food at these places. Also, since these places feature fixed menu items, it becomes important to provide special discounts and offers in order to attract repeat consumers. Some of these chains capitalize on the children's market and therefore promotions are directed toward attracting them. There are some places that provide special shows and electronic animated cartoons and characters in order to attract children as well as to keep them busy between placing orders and serving foods. These places are gaining considerable popularity. Children normally regard fast foods as a treat. Birthday parties, gifts, playgrounds, special packages, and calendars are also offered to attract children. Children also bring in adult consumers with them. Fast foods are not just for teen-agers and children, since young families, office workers, business executives, working spouses; in short, people of all ages and sexes visit these facilities.

Normally, lunch is the busiest time, particularly in an area surrounded by offices and shopping centers. Many fast foodservices are attracting workers by providing breakfasts. Long lines are not appreciated by patrons who are going to work or who have limited time for lunch.

Drive-in facilities are considered to be an added convenience offered by fast foodservices. Many patrons prefer taking food out or eating in the car while traveling, which saves a considerable amount of time. Fast service is the top priority of these foodservices. Employees are trained with an emphasis on serving consumers as rapidly as possible.

Management of some fast-food places specify to their employees that a few minutes or even seconds is the optimum serving time per customer. A variety of foods are being offered by fast foodservices, and there is stiff competition among various franchised operations. In order to please diet-conscious consumers, many places are offering special salads and low-calorie items.

On the other hand, certain foods like fried chicken and pizza are the choices of still another group of patrons, since it is difficult to prepare these items at home in small edible quantities in a limited time. One can expect changes and new developments in this segment of the foodservice industry. Many of the franchised fast-food items are very popular in the United

States. Their logos are symbolic of the type and quality of foods served by these establishments.

Midpriced restaurants

This category includes restaurants or foodservices that offer midpriced items, and whose service is not necessarily as fast as that of the fast-food chains. Many "family restaurants" fall into this category. Almost all age groups are among the target consumers of these types of foodservices.

Midpriced restaurants are patronized by customers who want more than what is offered by the fast foodservices. There is a growing demand for a lighter-calorie-wise-type of food, particularly salads, by the consumers visiting these operations.

Since most of these are family-type restaurants, they are frequented by children and therefore a varied menu is necessary. The foods desired by these consumers are of a different nature than those normally cooked at home. Low-cost, economical food items are popular, since it is often difficult to take out the entire family to an expensive restaurant.

A varied menu, a modest decor, and a pleasing atmosphere are important to these patrons. All the above-mentioned factors are important in getting repeat business for these restaurants. Sometimes entertainment is offered at these restaurants thus combining dining with music or entertainment, particularly for special occasions. Dinner is the busiest time for these places, since it is usually then that both spouses have time available for eating away from home. Also, since these restaurants are open until late at night, their hours suit a variety of consumers.

Since this group of foodservices consists of family restaurants, coffee shops, diners, pancake houses, and theme restaurants, the late hours are convenient for those returning from a movie, concert, work, library, or bar to stop for light meals, snacks, or beverages in a quiet atmosphere. The overall nature of these places allows for a congenial and comfortable setting for dining with friends and relatives, or for celebrating special occasions.

Overcrowding is commonly seen in some of the favorite restaurants, and reservations are often required to dine at these facilities. Menus offered include food items suitable for all ages, with specials offered on each day of the week. Special parties and weddings are also catered by many midpriced restaurants. Some people are interested in different foods and would very much like a variety in foods served. Others are attracted by the specialities and/or ethnic foods offered by these facilities. The customers are generally looking for foods other than the typical "hamburger."

A cordial and quiet atmosphere with privacy is preferred by patrons visiting these places. Formal table settings and service are also important to the consumers. They expect to be seated cordially and waited on as a prelude to the dining experience. Special seats or high chairs may be needed by patrons with young children. Music, games, and puzzles are often provided, in order to keep the family members entertained while the food is being prepared and/or served. This type of foodservice operation attracts a considerable number of consumers who are interested in an average type of dining facility where family and friends can get together on an informal basis or for special occasions.

Upscale restaurants

Fine restaurants as well as "theme" restaurants can be included in this category. Consumers visiting these facilities are looking for a dining experience that is unique and memorable. They expect quality in both the food and the service and are willing to pay the price for it. They are particularly interested in menus that include foreign foods and dishes that are either difficult to prepare at home or that require special skills for their preparation.

Most of the consumers visiting these places are sophisticated and have a variety of dining experiences; they are therefore looking for quality. Cocktails and good wines must be served at these restaurants. Since these restaurants are often selected for dining on special occasions, there is a demand for an elegant atmosphere and decor, such as candlelight, antiques, and unusual decorations.

Live entertainment such as an orchestra, singers, or dancers is frequently offered. Shows, special guest appearances, plays, and theme nights are some of the attractions of these restaurants. Elegant preparation methods and presentations of foods from a varied menu are expected. Thus, dining out at fine restaurants can be a form of relaxation, a social event, entertainment, privilege, and fun. These places provide opportunities to go with the special person for a memorable occasion. Married couples may find that dining at such a restaurant offers an opportunity to be alone together and to get away from the children, since patrons rarely bring their young children to such restaurants.

Theme restaurants within this category provide special attractions. If the theme is related to a foreign country, the patrons can imagine that they are in that country. This requires skillful meal preparation as well as presentation. Many places coordinate the decor, music, and entertainment with the particular theme. Tableside food preparation and service are also very common attractions of these restaurants. Patrons of fine restaurants do not like them to be too crowded or too brightly lit; they also do not like loud music.

Colourful arrangements on plates or platters are highly desirable and expected as is elegant service. There is a need for a sophisticated blend of all desirable attributes to make these operations successful. These patrons are willing to pay more or to travel extra miles in order to get what they desire. Some businessmen find these upscale restaurants to be good places to meet with their clients. Red meats, seafood, and a variety of vegetable dishes are normally included in their menus.

Take-out foodservice facilities

Take-out food includes such items as pizza, deli sandwiches, pastas, gourmet salads, special ethnic foods, hamburgers, chicken, and ice cream. It includes practically all food items that are feasible for taking out. These foodservices either do not provide any dining facilities or have very limited dining areas. Some consumers may even prefer buying food from the drive-in and eating it at home. These take-out foodservices are very handy for getting food at times when there is neither the incentive to cook at home nor to eat out.

The increasing popularity of home entertainment, such as videos, electronic games, and cable television, calls for "home eating" of restaurant foods, particularly on weekends and holidays. Also, some consumers, particularly working singles, may not have the incentive to cook and may feel awkward eating alone in a restaurant; this group is a big user of take-out services. Students also find these services very handy at late night hours, particularly during examination periods. Take-out foodservices may also provide home delivery of foods.

Since food has to be carried a certain distance before consumption, the foods most suited for take-out include items that maintain their quality and temperatures for prolonged periods of time. Pizza is the most commonly preferred take-out or home-delivered item. Also, breakfast items, such as doughnuts, cakes, and cookies and beverages such as cokes and coffee are very popular take-out items.

All ages use the take-out foodservices, regardless of their income bracket or marital status. In other words, these types of foodservices provide for meals prepared away from home with the comfort of home and no cleanup or kitchen work. At times these foods may prove less expensive than eating at the restaurant. In addition to quick service the quality of the food offered is particularly important to the consumers.

From the management point of view, menu selection and quick delivery are the most important factors in this type of operation. Special packaging or holding equipment may be an added expense for the foodservice operators. However, these expenses may very well be compensated for by the fact that the consumers are not being waited on and are not occupying seats in the restaurant.

Hotel/motel foodservices

Many hotel foodservices rely not only on in-house customers but also on outside consumers. Of course, the main target consumers are those staying in the hotel facilities. Guests may also order foods by room service, which is an important component of service in a hotel. Breakfast is the meal most often eaten in the room while staying in a hotel. Room service of foods requires attention to ensure desired temperature and quality of foods. Rapid service is highly desirable whether it is room service or in the adjoining motel restaurants, since travelers are normally on a very tight schedule. Toast, scrambled eggs, sausage, and hot breads are very popular breakfast items; the continental breakfast is also popular. Guests staying in hotels and motels usually do not eat lunch at the facilities since most plan to be away during that time. However, special dinner events are well attended. The foodservices in hotels are very busy during conventions, meetings, or holiday seasons. Cost is not often a major factor while eating out by these consumers, since dining is either on a business account or is considered to be a single-occasion expense. Courteous service is an amenity expected by hotel customers. Convenience is the primary reason for preferring services at the same location.

Competition may be intense if the hotels are located in busy industrial or business areas. Special meals, breakfasts, and brunches are offered by hotels in order to attract in-house guests as well as local customers. Parties are also arranged at times by these facilities. These foodservice operations profit considerably during conventions and large banquets, which are often booked several years in advance. Hotels located in larger cities, resorts, vacation, and recreational areas offer variety in meals and services. Larger hotels often have several theme restaurants and cocktail bars on their premises to attract guests and give them ample choices. Carts are also used to dispense foods and beverages for the convenience of patrons in lobbies of larger hotels. Foodservices provided by hotels may be very elaborate and foods are usually prepared under the direction of skilled and well-trained chefs.

Foodservices at leisure facilities

Amusement parks, zoos, sports arenas, resort areas, vocationlands, and other tourist attractions are places where foods and beverages are very much in demand. From the foodservices point of view tourists represent "captured" patrons since they usually do not want to waste time looking for places to eat. In addition, many of these food facilities do not allow food from the outside, which adds to the business on their premises. Consumers may be of all ages and sexes. Long lines are normally observed at stands at amusement parks or at hot dog stands in a stadium. Fast foodservice is essential, since food is not the major source of attraction and there may be limited time in between activities.

Cleanliness and quick service are very important for repeat business. Consumers are willing to pay more than usual, so cost or variety in foods is riot important to them. Also, the caloric content of the foods is not very important to many, since it is considered to be only a single-occasion deal. They are particularly anxious and willing to try new and exotic food items. The time limitation and the lack of knowledge as to the location of other foodservices have an impact on the selection of places to eat. Carbonated beverages are commonly preferred, particularly on a hot and humid day and in the open-air facilities. Children are very much attracted by the foods and beverages at these places.

Many consumers prefer foodservices that offer snacks rather than a complete meal. Although more variety in foods may be desirable, more choices will increase the serving time since it becomes increasingly difficult for consumers to make up their minds. Consumers have limited expectations from foodservices at these places, except in fine restaurants in resorts and vacationlands. Many resort areas provide for elegant fine dining facilities. They also often offer a variety of theme restaurants and entertainment.

Economy has a great impact on these types of foodservice facilities, since the visits to these places are largely dependent on the available disposable income. When efficiently planned, these services may be very profitable. Depending on the location, weather, kind type of leisure facilities, there may be certain peak periods of business.

Foodservices in health-care facilities

Health-care facilities primarily include hospitals, nursing homes, and convalescent centers. Foodservices provided by health-care facilities represent operations where menus are planned extremely carefully, since there is always a need for specialized diets as well as having to comply with rules and regulations of various regulatory agencies. Hospitals have different food items arranged in cycle menus ranging from one to three weeks' duration. Food often becomes an easy target of criticism for many patients in hospitals and nursing homes. There is a wide difference in food preferences by those in hospitals compared to those in nursing homes because of the length of stay and incentive to eat. The psychological impact of being in a hospital affects appetite, since there may be anxiety due to several reasons.

On the other hand, in nursing homes, residents stay for long periods of time, so that food plays an important role in their daily lives and becomes a frequent topic of discussion. There are chances of complaints of monotony in food items served or that the food is different from what they are used to eating. The residents have considerably less work to do and spend endless hours in socializing with co-residents. It becomes very important to carefully plan menu items for this group. Health-care foodservices are regarded as more or less of a "recession-proof" business. In addition to patients, these facilities also serve the health professionals as well as visitors. Dietitians are specially hired to help in menu planning as well as for consultation on diets.

Foodservices in business and industry

Cafeterias and restaurants in plants and industries are increasing enormously. Worker motivation is the primary reason for providing foodservice facilities to employees by business and industrial employers. These facilities primarily cater to the needs of the workers. Snacks are also consumed to a much greater extent at these locations. Many of these places operate on a 24-hour basis. Economy has both a direct and indirect impact on these types of foodservices. There are nominal charges at many of these places since worker productivity compensates for the subsidized cost of the meals.

Quality, quantity, and costs are carefully assessed by the consumers before using these foodservices. There is a demand for food of high quality in large portions. In addition to providing increased motivation and decreased fatigue for many, these meals are often the main meals of the day. There may also be special dining areas for executives and guests. Since there is very limited time for breaks and meals, quick service is highly desired by the consumers and more so by the employers. Every minute I's important for the industry, which can be interpreted in terms of dollars. Even a few minutes of delay may prove to be very expensive for the employers. Foodservice managers at such facilities are therefore under constant pressure. Variety in the menus offered is also desirable to please the consumers.

Many businesses and industries let contract foodservices manage their foodservice operations. These types of foodservices are primarily limited to the employees and their guests and are not open to the general public. Special meals may also be served on special occasions and parties may be arranged. These foodservices are gaining in popularity and have a potential for future development.

Foodservices in educational institutions

School, college, and university foodservices represent another very important segment of the industry. School lunch programs on a national basis are very important for the health of the growing population. But consumer satisfaction becomes a problem in these types of foodservices. Menus therefore need careful assessment in order to meet the requirements of the agencies as well as to see that they meet the dietary goals.

A variety in menus is essential in these types of foodservices. These consumers have food preferences which are very much different from other age groups. Their selections are affected by the food items normally offered by the fast foodservices, such as hamburgers, pizza, and tacos. More and more foodservices are including these items in the menu to please the consumers within this group. Students eating in residence halls are generally required to participate in "board plans."

This facilitates the production and management within these foodservices since it provides for a predictable sales volume over an extended period of time, such as one semester or one academic year. This helps in reducing costs and offers an attractive package price to students by these services.

Students often miss breakfasts and other meals due to a variety of reasons. There are also some places where the foodservices operate on a continuous basis for a certain period of time which eliminates the possibility of rush and overcrowding. In addition to resident hall facilities, foodservices are also provided by several on-campus sororities and fraternities, as well as student unions and other private operations.

Traditionally, there is a negative image of these foodservices among students, partly because they compare it with food at home or consider it monotonous. Most foodservices have student advisory groups to help in menu planning, These types of foodservices are vulnerable to student enrollment and economy. Federal support to students as well as school lunch programs will indirectly affect the future development of this type of foodservice.

Community foodservices

There are several government-sponsored programs that provide foods or foodservices for special segments of the population or for special occasions. Examples of these types of foodservices include WIC (Women, Infant, and Children) programs, "Meals on Wheels" programs, and other similar programs. The needs and wants of the consumers are different. Most of these consumers belong to a specific socioeconomic group. Other foodservices are also offered by religious and charity organizations. Also, during disasters and emergencies, foodservices are offered by various governmental and nongovernmental agencies.

2

Equipment Selection

Since equipment represents a fixed asset of a foodservice operation, which depreciates the moment it is purchased and installed, equipment selection requires careful planning and decision making. If improperly selected, equipment may tie up much needed cash and lead to the failure of the operation. There is a variety of restaurant equipment available with varying degrees of modifications and a wide price range.

Whether a particular piece of equipment is really needed and whether it is a good investment is the most difficult decision a foodservice manager is faced with. In addition to experience, careful calculations are needed before such a decision is made. The volume of food production and handling, employee productivity, and profitability of a foodservice operation directly depend on the type of equipment available at that facility.

Considering the systems approach, the main process within a foodservice operation is the conversion of raw food into the finished product, based on the organizational objectives. This process is not possible without proper equipment. Thus, the entire operation of a foodservice system is based on the availability of suitable equipment. The factors to be considered in the selection of equipment are discussed in this chapter.

Need

This is a very important consideration since it is obvious that need should dictate the purchase of equipment. Need and planned use of equipment should be evaluated on the basis of whether the purchase or addition of that particular equipment (1) will result in desired or improved quality of food, (2) will result in significant savings in labor and materials costs, (3) will result in increased quantity of finished food products, (4) and/or will contribute to the overall profitability of a foodservice operation. Essential equipment should be given priority and preliminary selection should be based on the basic needs of an operation.

Need for a particular piece of equipment should be assessed from different points of view as, for example: (1) whether the equipment will be used for prolonged periods of time, (2) whether it has the potential for meeting the future needs of the foodservice operation, (3) whether the equipment will require maintenance, (4) whether there exist alternate, less expensive versions of a similar piece of equipment that can adequately meet the demand of an operation.

Cost

There are several costs that are incurred in the purchase, installation, and maintenance of any equipment in any type of foodservice operation. The major costs incurred in the purchase of equipment are (1) purchase or initial cost; (2) installation cost; (3) insurance costs; (4) repair and maintenance costs; (5) depreciation costs; (6) initial financing costs, interest, and other charges; (7) operating costs; and (8) costs of bénefits and losses derived by addition of the equipment. Installation of equipment may require extensive remodeling that may be more expensive than the cost of the equipment itself. Market prices of the equipment vary, based on the type of the equipment, manufacturer, and the utility of the equipment. A comparative assessment of these costs is essential before making any decision regarding purchasing of equipment. Some of these costs are calculated by the manufacturers and are available for consideration before purchasing or making a decision.

Expensive equipment, like dishwashers, requires more careful assessment than relatively less expensive equipment. There are various methods of calculating the profitability of equipment based on costs. A foodservice manager may derive an equation that can be used for calculating the profitability of equipment based on factors most pertinent to that particular foodservice operation. A common equation used for calculations is:

$$E = \frac{A}{B+C+D}$$

where E = calculated value

A = savings in labor over the expected life of the equipment

B = cost of the equipment (including installation) minus the resale value of the equipment at the end of the expected life

C = cost of operation and maintenance of the equipment

D = interest or gains possible from investments instead of purchasing the equipment.

In the above calculations, if the value of E is 1.0 or more, then it is advisable to purchase the equipment, since it should more than pay for itself if the value of E is more than 1.5, it is highly desirable even necessary-to purchase that equipment. However, if the value of E is less than

1.0, it may not be advisable to purchase that particular equipment. Thus, the higher the value, the more potentially profitable it is to buy that equipment.

In the above-mentioned formula, the expected life of the equipment has to be included. Figures for the life expectancy of equipment are available from the manufacturer or the U.S. Internal Revenue Service. Normally, the life of common foodservice equipment ranges from 9 to 15 years. Various modifications of the formula may be made based on the factors directly pertaining to a particular foodservice operation. One such modification would be:

$$H = \frac{L(A + B)}{C + L(D + E + F) - G}$$

where H = calculated value

L = expected life of the equipment in years = savings in labor per year

B = savings in material per year

C = total cost of the equipment, including installation costs

D = cost of utilities per year

E = projected cost of maintenance and repair of the equipment per year

F = annual projected interest on the money in C, if invested elsewhere for the life of the equipment

G = turn-in value at the end of the life of the equipment.

As in the case of tile previous formula, if' the calculated value H is higher than 1.0, it is a "Good Buy"; if it is less than 1.0, it is advisable to say "Good-Bye" to the deal.

Normally, the higher the value of H the more advisable it is to purchase that equipment.

The following example will illustrate the application of the above formula. A restaurant owner is contemplating buying a steam-Jacketed kettle for his operation. The data available indicates:

Expected life of the steam-jacketed kettle	12 years (L)
Projected savings in labor per year due to the purchase of the equipment	\$ 500 (A)
Projected savings in materials per year due to the purchase of the equipment	\$300 (B)
Purchase and installation cost of the equipment	\$3500 (C)
Projected costs of utilities per year to operate equipment	\$ 57 (D)
Projected cost of maintenance per year for equipment	\$ 15 (E)
Annual projected interest on the purchase and installation cost of the equipment (assuming rate of simple interest to be 6%) will be \$3500 X 6%	\$ 210 (F)
Projected turn-in value after 12 years	\$ 200 (G)

The value of H may be calculated by substituting the data in the formula as follows:

$$H = \frac{12(500 + 300)}{3500 + 12(57 + 15 + 210) - 200}$$

$$= \frac{9600}{3500 + 3384 - 200} = 1.44 \text{ ("Good Buy")}$$

The life expectancy of equipment may be much more than calculated, and so tile final value of H may be higher. A conservative figure should preferably be used for the expected life for equipment. On the other hand, equipment may not last as long as expected or may get outdated before the expiration of the projected life period.

Functional attributes

Since the equipment is selected to fulfill certain functions of a foodservice operation, it is necessary to evaluate each piece of equipment based on functional attributes in the light of the desired needs. Performance of the equipment should be assessed based on the cost as well as the availability of other equipment.

Maximum possible functions as compared to the costs should be given preference. The possibility of modifying the equipment by attachments and other changes should be considered as an asset. Both present and future anticipated menu changes will also dictate the type of equipment to be selected. If relatively large sums are being invested in the purchasing of equipment, future changes and development should definitely be taken into consideration. Functioning of equipment is also based on the type of energy required for its operation its well as the extent to which it is planned to be used.

Sanitation and safety

Sanitation and safety are primary considerations in purchasing any equipment for a foodservice operation. Ease of cleaning and sanitation should be given high priority when selecting equipment. No matter how sophisticated a piece of equipment is, if it cannot be cleaned properly, it is not suitable for a foodservice operation. All materials used in the manufacture of the equipment, particularly food-contact surfaces, should be made up of nontoxic materials. Equipment used in food production should be such that safe temperatures can be maintained easily and at all times.

Sufficient accessories such as lights and dials should be integral parts to ensure that the proper temperatures are reached and maintained by the equipment. All parts should be easily accessible for cleaning. Wherever applicable and possible, the parts of the equipment should be able to be disassembled and reassembled easily and quickly to facilitate easy cleanability.

Self-cleaning types of equipment are most preferable. The National Sanitation Foundation (NSF) certifies foodservice equipment that meets defined sanitary standards. If possible, equipment that has been approved by NSF should be given preference.

All equipment selected for a foodservice operation should have built-in safety features. Electrical equipment should be used with the proper voltage and should be free from any hazards. All moving and sharp parts should be properly protected. There should not be any rough or sharp edges on any pieces of equipment.

Safety locks and devices should be used on all equipment wherever possible, such as in steamers, steam-kettles, and carts. Equipment should be free of crevices or holes, which may either harbor insects or microorganisms or hinder its proper cleaning and sanitation. All factors related to sanitation and safety should be checked before making any decision regarding the purchase of equipment.

Size, appearance, and design

The size of the equipment should be such that it can easily be accommodated in the space available in the layout and design of the facility. It may be difficult to place equipment where limited space is available.

Improperly located equipment will be a continuous source of inconvenience and even a hazard. The doors and openings of the equipment should be designed in such a way that they do not cause any problems or hazards. The design and appearance of the equipment should be attractive and should perform the maximum functions with a minimum of problems. Durability of the equipment should be given consideration in the design, since the equipment used in foodservice operations is subjected to constant use and abuse. Although the functional characteristics should be given priority over the design, the latter should be such that it lends to smooth functioning of the equipment.

Foodservice equipment should also be selected on the basis of its overall performance which includes such aspects as quietness of operation, easy mobility, remote control operations, computerized controls, variety of functions, availability of parts, and ease of maintenance. Those pieces of equipment that are known for their superior performance in a desired situation should be given priority when selecting equipment for any type of foodservice operation.

Materials used in construction of equipment

Foodservice equipment may be made from a variety of materials. The cost of the equipment will largely be dependent on the type of materials used in its construction. Some of the most common materials are described below.

Wood

Wood has both advantages and disadvantages for use in foodservice equipment. However, its disadvantages outweigh advantages because one of the major drawbacks associated with wood is sanitation. Since it absorbs moisture and is subjected to cracking from the humidity of the atmosphere, it is unsafe from the sanitary point of view. On the other hand, wood has the advantages of being light in weight, it can be designed into different shapes, it can cushion noise, it can provide beauty, and it is relatively economical. Its use in foodservice is mainly restricted to cabinets, shelvings, handles, cutting boards, and other surfaces that do not come in contact with food.

Metals

Various types of metals are used in the construction of foodservice equipment. Metal sheets, plates, and plates with varying degree of polishing are used in various forms for foodservice operations. Metal sheets and plates are usually specified in a standard measure referred to as "gauge," which indicates the weight of the materials per square footage. Gauge is an indication of the durability of the materials used in equipment.

Electroplating is the most common method used for plating metals. Such pure metals as aluminum, black and cast iron, or copper may be used, though most of the metals used in the construction of the foodservice equipment are alloys, such as stainless steel (steels are iron and carbon in various combinations), brass (copper, zinc, and other metals), and Monel (two-thirds nickel and one-third copper).

The use of pure copper has been practically discontinued in foodservices because it requires polishing, is expensive, is relatively heavy in weight, and it reacts with certain food products.

Nickel is used for equipment trim, cafeteria railings, and counters.

Aluminum is used for utensils, equipment interiors and exteriors, and steam-jacketed kettles. It is light in weight, has high thermal and electrical conductivity, does not corrode easily, is hard and durable, and can withstand pressure at high temperatures. It may be used in combination with other metals to form alloys having higher tensile strength.

Cast iron is used in stands and supports of equipment and other surfaces that do not come in contact with food. Iron is used in pots, pans, griddles, range tops, gas burners, and similar equipment. Brass is used in faucets and shut-off valves. Steel is used for ovens, range interiors, exteriors, shelving, frames, and supports. Galvanized steel and iron, which is steel and iron treated with acid (by pickling) and coated with zinc, is used in dishwashing machines, sinks, tables, equipment legs and supports. Noncorrosive metals formed by the alloys of iron, nickel, and chromium may also be used in the construction of foodservice equipment.

Stainless steel

The extent to which stainless steel is used in foodservice operations and importance justifies its discussion in detail. Stainless steel is preferred in foodservices because it can be easily cleaned, is very bright and attractive, and can be kept sanitary since its bright surfaces show dirt easily.

Like other steels, it is made by the combination of iron and carbon in a proportion that results in a material that is resistant to oxidation or corrosion. Thus, it resists rust and stain formation. It can resist high temperatures, provide a shiny appearance, and is relatively easy to maintain. These desirable attributes have made stainless steel one of the most desirable and expensive materials used in foodservice operations.

Most of the stainless steels used in foodservices have a low carbon content and a relatively' high chromium content. Common stainless steels have 11.5 to 27%

chromium and a low carbon content. A higher chromium level provides a higher degree of hardness. Numbers are assigned to different types of stainless steels to designate their, composition.

The most commonly used stainless steel in foodservices is No. 302, which is composed of 18% chromium, 8% nickel, and 0.15% carbon. Since stainless steel is expensive, thickness is an important consideration in its selection.

As the number of the gauge increases, the thickness decreases. Selection of the stainless steels should be based on their thickness. In general, Gauges 8, 10, and 12, because of their thicknesses, make good supports; and Gauges 12 and 14 make good table tops. Gauges 20 and above are primarily used for facing and exteriors. The cost of the stainless steel is also based on the extent of polishing desired, since polishing requires labor, material, and energy. The extent of polishing is designated by "finish number."

Plastic

The most common advantage of the plastic is that it is available in different forms and can be molded into different combinations. Some of the commonly used plastics are acrylics (used in food covers), melamines (used for a variety of dishes and glassware), fiberglass (used in boxes, bus trays, and trays), nylons (used in equipment and mobile parts), phenolics (used in trays and containers), polyethylene (used in storage containers and bowls), polypropylene (used for dishwashing racks), and polystyrene (used for cups, covers, and packages).

There are many different brand names for plastics, so it is important to select them on the basis of their use and durability. Some of the plastics are very hard and durable. Their sanitary properties should be given consideration in selection.

Table 1
Thickness of stainless steel of various gauges

Gauge	*Inches*	*Milimeters*
8	0.1644 (11/16)	4.1758
10	0.1345 (9/64)	3.4163
12	0.1046 (7/64)	2.6568
14	0.0747 (5/64)	1.8974
16	0.0598 (1/16)	1.5189
18	0.0478 (3/64)	1.2141
20	0.0359 (1/32)	0.9119
24	0.0239 (1/40)	0.6071

Coatings

Coatings are placed on certain base metals to provide desired properties which would be difficult to achieve if only metals are used. They may be enameled, painted, glass-coated, bonded or baked on. Acrylic enamel, baked enamel, and porcelain enamel are commonly used in foodservice equipment. Silicone, which is an intermediate substance between organic and inorganic materials, is primarily used for making nonsticking surfaces, such as ice cube trays and ice buckets. One of the coatings that is becoming very popular is Teflòn, which is a fluorocarbon resin sprayed on oven interiors, pans, griddles, and other surfaces to facilitate good food release from these surfaces.

For foodservice use, selection of materials for equipment should be based on their intended use. Guidelines for material selection based on interior surfaces may be summarized as follows:

— For *food contact surfaces,* materials selected should be smooth, nontoxic, corrosion resistant, stable, nonabsorbent, relatively heat resistant, and easily cleanable. They should not impart any colour, odour, or taste to the foods with which they come into contact. They should not be affected by the PH of the foods and should not interact with any substances commonly present in foods or formed during food processing.

— For *splash-contact surfaces,* materials should be smooth, easily cleanable, corrosion resistant, noncracking, nonchipping, and nonspalling, and resistant to relatively high temperatures. These surfaces should preferably be nonpainted.

— For *surfaces not in contact with foods,* materials should be corrosion resistant, of a noncracking, nonchipping, and nonspalling type.

Table 2
Finish numbers for stainless steels

Finish Number	*Description*
1	Hot rolled, annealed and pickled, dull rough
2B	Full finish, bright, smooth, cold rolled
2D	Full finish, dull, smooth, cold rolled
4	Standard finish for use in foodservices
6	High tampico, brush finish with velvety luster, used for specific tableware
7	High glossy polish with mirror or highly reflective finish

Types of energy and its sources

In the selection of equipment for use in foodservices, energy plays a very important role. With increased emphasis on energy conservation, it is important to select those pieces of equipment that are energy efficient. In order to understand energy, it is necessary to know its common sources as well as the common terminology used for the sources of energy. Energy is available in different forms and can be transferred from one form to another.

The common sources of energy primarily used in foodservices are electricity, gas, steam, and oil. The most important definitions and concepts related to the sources of energy are described below.

Electricity is the most common form of energy used in foodservices. It runs by a flow of electrons in an electric current, which is analogous to the flow of water in a pipe. As in the case of water, electricity can be quantitatively measured by the number of electrons flowing from a particular point at a given time. This flow of electrons per second is measured in amperes (amp or *I*). As the force of water from a pipe can be measured in pounds per square inch (psi), electricity can also be measured in volts (V).

A "volt" can be defined as the force required to push 1 amp of electricity by a given point in one second. Thus, the voltage is indicative of the force with which electricity is flowing. There are different ranges in voltage, such as 110-120 V and 220-240 V.

Voltage requirement is an important consideration in the purchase of any equipment. Also, before plugging in any electric equipment, voltage should be checked, since serious damage may result by using improper voltage. Foodservice equipment is frequently available in different voltages and some comes with dual voltages. A switch is provided to change to the desired voltage.

The force behind the flow of electrical current (V) multiplied by the amount flowing (amp or I) gives the measure of electricity in watts (W). In other words, $W = V \times I$. This is an important relationship and can be used for different calculations pertaining to electricity:

$$W = V \times I$$

$$I = W/V$$

$$V = W/I$$

The required amperage can be calculated using the above relationship. For example, if 2000 W of electricity is on a 110-V line, the amperage requirement would be I/V, or 2000/110, which is equal to 18.2 amp. A 25% safety factor, for possible fluctuations in electric current, should be added to this figure. Thus a 25-amp fuse will be needed for this circuit. In planning electrical outlets for equipment use, these calculations are very helpful. It should be noted that as the voltage increases, amperage decreases.

The watts and volt required for any electrical equipment are specified on a plate affixed to the equipment. For calculating the cost of the electricity, watts used per hour are used. Thus a "watt-hour" (Wh) is one watt of electricity flowing steadily for an hour.

Since there are a large number of watts involved in the use of electricity, a "kilowatt-hour" (kWh) is used, which is 1000 W of electricity flowing steadily for an hour. Costs of electricity are usually given in cents per kilowatt-hour, from which energy costs of any equipment or electrical appliance may be calculated.

Many of the electrical appliances, particularly those used in foodservices, have a grounding system in them. Since electrons in electricity carry a negative charge, they can be attracted toward a positive charge.

Electricity may become free (due to various reasons) and flow to undesirable places. Thus, in order to provide for safety, measures are taken to ground negatively charged electrons by attracting them to a positive charge. It is advisable even necessary-to use a grounding system. Usually the three-pronged plugs have grounding in them. In foodservice operations, all electrical equipment should be grounded for safety reasons. When there is a resistance to the flow of water, there is an accumulation of water. Similarly, when there is a resistance to electricity, it accumulates to form heat. This principle is used when resistance elements are used for heating ovens, fryers, and similar equipment. Resistance (*R*) is set up against electricity by using certain metal wires, such as nickle, chromium, or their alloys. Resistance is measured in "ohms." One ohm is equal to 1 amp at 1 V. Ohms can be calculated as:

$$R = V/I$$

$$I = V/R$$

$$V = IR$$

Electricity may exist as a direct current (DC), or as an alternating current (AC). The type of electricity in the United States is in the form of AC. An AC generator of electricity sweeps masses of electrons that are sent in alternating pulses. Most alternators in the United States set up 60 alternating pulses per second which is referred to as "cycles" (c) or "hertz" (Hz).

Cycles are important for equipment that have motors or revolving parts, such as blenders and recorders. Their speed and performance are affected by the number of cycles. This information is usually provided by the manufacturer and is often placed on a plate on the equipment. For motors, the power is expressed in the form of horsepower (hp). One hp is equal to 746 W. The flow of steam, which is another form of energy, is measured in pounds per square inch. Heat may be measured by the temperature or by the amount expressed in British thermal units (Btu) or calories. A Btu (British thermal unit) is the quantity of heat required to raise the temperature of one pound of water by 1^0F. A calorie is the amount of heat required to raise the temperature of one gram of water by 1^0C; it is equal to 3.968 Btu. This type of calorie should not be confused by the calorie used in nutritional sciences.

Once the energy requirements of all appliances and equipment are known, it is relatively easy to calculate the energy costs or to conduct an audit. In order to conserve energy, it is desirable to conduct energy audits at periodical intervals of time and to conserve energy wherever possible.

Types of food service equipment

In order to select equipment for any foodservice operation, it is necessary to have a complete set of data on the types of equipment available for each category of functions. Long-term durability should be considered in the selection of equipment. A brief description of the factors that should be considered in the selection of commonly used foodservice equipment is given below. Such equipment as refrigerators and freezers are deliberately excluded since they are common household items.

Ranges

The range is the most basic piece of equipment needed by practically every type of foodservice operation; it may be gas or electric. Most ranges are mounted on the floor, and the cooking is done in pots or pans directly placed on the range top. Since ranges are among the most frequently used equipment, heavy-duty framework is preferred. Tops of gas ranges come in a variety of forms, shapes, and arrangements of elements.

Ranges that can be cleaned easily and those that have drip trays that can be removed for clean-up are the most practical. Reflectors are also desirable. Several attachments and modifications are available; for example griddle attachments are often used. Some ranges have ovens below or above. It is difficult to assess the capacity of the ranges desirable for a foodservice operation, since it depends on several factors, including the type of menu and the number of meals to be served. However, for most types of foodservice operations, the number of ranges may be calculated based on the number of meals served per day. The exact requirement will only be possible after assessing the exact needs of the foodservice operation. Modifications and special attachments to ranges are desirable. Their location should be such that they are easily accessible to employees working in the production areas as well as in the service areas.

Conventional ovens

Conventional ovens are also among the most important equipment in any type of foodservice operation. Basically, an oven is a heated chamber in which foods may be cooked at various temperatures. In conventional ovens, the heat may be distributed by conduction, convection, or radiation.

As in the case of ranges, durability is of prime importance in the selection of ovens. The frame, door, exterior, and interior materials should contribute to the longevity and cleanability of the equipment. Several types of attachments are also possible for conventional ovens. Heating elements should be selected on the basis of the desired use.

Since energy conservation is an important consideration, insulation materials and their thickness should be considered. It is desirable to have 4 to 5 m of insulation. Commonly used insulating materials are fiberglass, rock wool, or vitreous fiber. Temperature-regulating controls are desirable, as are panel lights and computerized controls.

In order to save much needed space, ovens may be Installed in decks or stacks. In deciding the requirement for the number of ovens, recommendations as mentioned for the ranges may be followed. The capacity should be based on the type of products for which the ovens will be needed.

The following formula can be used to calculate the number of ovens needed:

$$\text{Required no. of ovens} = \frac{\text{no. of servings}}{\text{no. of servings per pan} \quad \text{no. of pans per oven} \quad \text{no. of batches per hour}}$$

Table 3

Recommended Number of Ranges Based on Meals Served

Meals served per day	*Number of ranges*
Under 300	1
300-400	2
400-500	3
500-1000	4

For example, if a total of 400 servings is desired and there are 24 servings per pan, and the cooking of one batch requires 20 minutes, assuming there are three batches per hour and that two pans can be accommodated per oven, the number of ovens or the number of decks required for an oven may be calculated as follows:

$$\text{Required no. of ovens} = \frac{400}{24 \times 2 \times 3} = 2.8 \text{ or } 3$$

When calculating the capacity, the number of items on the menu and possible staggering of time should be considered.

Convection ovens

The conventional ovens discussed earlier are designed to be heated by an element either at the bottom or at the top or both. The problem associated with this type of heating is that heat is not uniformly distributed within the oven cavity. In order to facilitate uniform distribution of the heat, other methods are used in convection ovens. There are several types of convection ovens, of which the most common are:

— *Forced-air convection ovens,* in which a fan is used to circulate heat in the oven cavity. The velocity of air circulation helps in the uniform distribution of heat.

— *Roll-in type convection ovens,* in which carts or large assembly of racks may be rolled into a large-size oven. Heat is so circulated as to reach all racks, thereby facilitating uniform heating.

— *Pulse-type convection ovens,* in which alternating gusts of hot air followed by cold air are used. The hot air facilitates the baking or cooking of the foods, whereas the cold air helps in the cooling of the products and controlling overcooking of the products.

The advantages of convection ovens are:

1. Since there is a uniform distribution of heat, product quality is greatly improved.
2. Since the surfaces are heated, there is a desirable browning effect.
3. All parts of the oven may be fully utilized so that the efficiency and capacity of the oven are greatly improved.
4. Relatively lower temperatures are needed for cooking food as compared to the other conventional ovens.
5. Less labor and space is required compared to the conventional ovens.

6. They are more energy efficient.

There are certain disadvantages to convection ovens which may be corrected to some extent, and the ovens on the market now have been greatly modified to eliminate or reduce these drawbacks. Some of the disadvantages of convection ovens are:

1. Foods may get overcooked and a thick layer may be formed on top.
2. Surfaces of foods may be cooked more than the lower portions, thus resulting in uneven cooking.
3. Since there is air flowing with certain velocity, batters or soft foods may be blown to one side giving an undesirable appearance.
4. Certain foods cannot be prepared in these ovens due to the circulation of heat as well as the temperature of the air that affects the food surfaces.

In selection of these ovens, the source and type of heat distribution should be considered. Other aspects of their use are similar to the conventional ovens.

Infrared ovens

The use of infrared energy, which is a form of radiant heat, in foodservices is relatively new and innovative. The top as well as the bottom of the oven may be heated depending on the location of the source of energy. A conveyor belt may be used for the introduction and removal of the food products. The advantages of these ovens are:

1. Foods are cooked in a relatively short period of time.
2. The quality of certain foods is improved due to high temperature in a short period of time, and due to the surface and/or bottom heating.
3. The ovens occupy relatively less space.

4. Due to the high temperatures -that can be reached, most of the infrared ovens have self-cleaning mechanisms.
5. Either glass or metal pans may be used.
6. The outside environment does not get heated.
7. Owing to a shorter cooking time, these ovens are energy efficient.
8. Special preparation and flavors may result from this specialized cooking. This is particularly true for such an infrared oven as the conveyorized tube broiler.

As with the convection ovens, there are certain disadvantages to the infrared ovens and the manufacturers are trying to improve these ovens. Low-chamber height is one of the drawbacks in table-top ovens. Since foods are heated to a high temperature, care should be taken to prevent overcooking. The interior of the oven may get very hot and become a safety or fire hazard. Recent improvements have made infrared energy a potentially useful source of energy that can be utilized effectively in the cooking of foods in foodservice operations.

Mechanical and pizza ovens

The mechanical ovens are similar to the other ovens except that they have a larger capacity and certain mechanical parts that help in the movement of the food products within the oven. There are moving trays within the oven that facilitate inspection of the products and provide for benefits of the forced-air convection oven. These ovens may be heated by gas or by electricity. There are several modifications in the mechanical ovens. Some of the common forms of the mechanical and pizza-type of ovens are:

— *Reel oven.* These ovens have trays that travel vertically within the oven. There is an opening and glass door through which food products may be inspected.

— *Rotary oven.* These ovens have circular shelves that rotate horizontally around a central axis.

— *Traveling tray oven.* These are fairly large-sized ovens in which the products are placed in trays that travel through the oven.

— *Pizza oven.* These ovens are very similar to the other types of ovens except that they have more depth and are placed horizontally. This facilitates the placement and removal of pizza trays within the oven.

Mechanical ovens provide special functions which add to the efficiency in quantity food production. The factors to be considered when purchasing these types of ovens are very similar to the other type of ovens.

Microwave ovens

Microwave ovens, like the infrared ovens, are based on the use of addition to cook foods within the oven chamber. Microwaves are very short electromagnetic waves that have a wavelength between the ultrahigh bands and the infrared bands. The wavelengths assigned to microwave ovens are (1) 915 MHz, which are 13 m or 32 cm long, and (2) 2450 MHz, which are 5 m or 12 cm long. Megahertz (MHz) are a million cycles per second (cps). The penetration of a 915-MHz wave is greater than that of a 2450-MHz wave, but the food is cooked slower in 915-MHz wave than in 2450-MHz wave.

There are several advantages and disadvantages of microwave ovens.

Advantages:

1. Foods can be cooked faster.

2. The surrounding atmosphere is not heated.
3. The ovens are very useful for reheating food portions in a very short period of time.
4. There are several applications in foodservice operations which make microwave ovens very useful. For example, they can be used to thaw meats and reheat foods.

Disadvantages:

1. An inability to cook large quantities of foods. This is their greatest drawback from the foodservice point of view.
2. Certain foods are cooked unevenly.
3. Additional cooking, using other types of ovens, is required for browning effects.
4. Special utensils are required.
5. Repair is expensive.
6. Extra care is required since the oven may get damaged easily improperly cleaned.

In order to overcome some of the disadvantages, a combination of convection and microwave ovens being manufactured. An example of such a combination is the Jet-Waveu™. It has electronic digital control, and the extent of cooking by one or both of the ovens can be programmed. In selecting microwave ovens, wavelengths, electrical current requirements, capacity, and safety features should be taken into consideration. There are several special applications of microwave ovens that should be considered from a foodservice operation's point of view; for example:

1. Reheating portions of foods
2. Making sauces and gravies

3. Warming syrups
4. Drying bread crumbs and making croutons
5. Drying hard cheese
6. Heating wet towels for the customers
7. Softening jellies and spreads
8. Crisping potato chips
9. Reheating coffee in cups
10. Decontaminating flour and cereals

Deep-fat fryers

The distinctive flavor and appearance of fried foods make deep-fat fryers one of the most valuable pieces of equipment in many foodservice operations. The Points that should be considered in the selection of deep-fat fryers include:

1. Deep-fat fryers should be made of sturdy materials and noncorrosive metals.
2. Their heating elements should be appropriate for the type of desired frying.
3. Their temperature controls should be located at a place that is free from spattering of fat and which can be reached safely without any contact with the heated fat.
4. They should have an easy and convenient fat-drainage system.
5. They should use fat economically, without contributing to the breakdown or smoking of the fats.
6. They should have a good mechanism for the removal of crumbs and other food particles from fats.
7. They should have an easy to handle or automatically controlled frying basket.

There are a number of different kinds of deep-fat fryers available on the market; these include pressurized deep-fat fryers that reduce the cooking time and improve the quality of the fried products. Fat can be saved and reused if the deep-fat fryer is designed with such features as siphoning and other cleaning devices. Other accessories should be selected, if fried foods are particular specialties on the menu of the foodservice operation.

Fryer basket lift-out devices are highly desirable, since they help to produce products of uniform quality, in addition to their convenience. Other deep-fat fryer accessories include crumb trays, fat filters, thermometers, infrared holding light, and siphons. Determination of the capacity of the deep fat-fryer needed should be based on the number of deep-fried items on the menu as well as its frequency of use.

Tilting skillets

Tilting skillets, also called tilting fry pans, have a variety of uses in any type of foodservice operation. They are one of the most versatile and indispensable Pieces of foodservice equipment. Multiple applications make them very valuable in the restaurant; they also save considerable space.

Most tilting skillets are mounted on the floor or brackets attached to the floor. Their source of heat may be gas or electricity. Since it has multipurpose functions, skillet capacity should be selected based upon possible applications. A tilting skillet may be used for several purposes, including:

1. Griddle cooking, since the frying pan may also be used as a griddle. Thus, such products as hamburgers, eggs, and cheese sandwiches can be easily prepared.

2. Both deep-fat and shallow-fat frying. In general, it is very convenient and safe for shallow-fat frying.
3. Stewing meats and vegetables as well as cooking or steaming vegetables.
4. Sautéeing foods.
5. Holding foods either at room or higher temperatures. This is a special advantage of the tilting skillet.
6. Poaching.
7. Proofing, since the temperature can be adjusted.
8. Preparing sauces, casseroles, mixed foods, baking (to a limited extent), heating water, boiling eggs, and cleaning fruits and vegetables.

Thus the tilting skillet is one of the most desirable pieces of equipment in a foodservice operation, and the decision to purchase it should be based on its potential uses within a Particular foodservice operation.

Griddles

Griddles provide heated surfaces that may be used for a variety of cooking tasks. They are particularly useful for short-order cooking in restaurants and may be heated by gas or electricity. Table space near the griddle is highly desirable in order to place various itemds and equipment. It is useful in cooking meats, particularly patties, pancakes, eggs, steaks, and sausages. If a griddle is not required for frequent use, other equipment that may be substituted for a griddle should be explored, as such equipment could be more versatile.

Broilers

Broilers that are used in dry heat cooking provide a special desirable flavor. Their source of heat may be gas, electricity, or infrared energy; charcoal and wood may also used in certain types. They are available in many shapes and sizes. The charred or smoked flavor in meats is provided by broiling. The principal part of a broiler consists of a grid and a mechanism through which fat drips and is partially burnt to produce a smoked flavor. Broilers may be of an upright or back-shelf type. Their source of heat may be located at the top and/or bottom.

In order to produce a char-broiled effect, charcoal, metal, or ceramic tiles may be used. Infrared energy is used in recently developed broilers. There are conveyorized broilers and rotisserie type of broilers that are suitable for specialized broiling. When purchasing broilers, the source of heat, grid temperatures, safety, fatdrainage system, and efficiency should be checked. The capacity and size of the broiler will be dependent on the extent to which broiled foods are included in the menu.

Steam-jacketed kettles

In any type of foodservice operation, steam-jacketed kettles are indispensable. These kettles are heated by using moist heat within the Jacket. The kettle may be one-third, half-, or full-jacketed. When the steam is let into the jacket, it condenses on the outside of the inner shell thereby giving up its beat to the metal, which is transferred to the foods. Thus, steam does not come in contact with the food being heated.

Steam-jacketed kettles are commonly referred to as "workhorses" in foodservices and are very useful in cooking foods that do not require high temperatures. From the nutritional point of view, this method is preferred since there is minimum nutrient loss. The specification for the steam-jacketed kettle should be based on the size needed; type of jacketing; type of stands; pressure of the steam; and type of drawoffs, covers, and other desired accessories.

Relatively small steam-jacketed kettles are commonly referred to as "trunnions." Mixers, blades, scrapers, paddles, whips, or beaters are available as attachments for steam-jacketed kettles. Multiple baskets for preparing two or three different products at one time are also available as attachments to the steam-jacketed kettle.

The source of steam should be checked before purchasing a steam-jacketed kettle. If the foodservice operation is located at a place where there is a steam supply, steam should be used from that source. If not, a special generator for heat will need to be purchased; this adds to the cost of the steam-jacketed kettle. Larger steam-jacketed kettles are very useful in preparing large quantities of soups or sauces.

Adequate devices for tilting and controlling breaks will be required. The capacity of the steam-jacketed kettle required for a foodservice operation may be calculated as follows:

$$\frac{\text{Capacity of kettle}}{\text{(in gal. or liters)}} = \frac{\text{total no. of servings} \times \text{portion size} \times \text{\% headspace}}{\text{128 oz (1 gal.) or 1000 ml (1 liter)}} \times \text{no. of batches}$$

The headspace allowed is normally 15%, which is needed to prevent overflow, spillage, and/or spattering.

Steam-jacketed kettles are very useful, since they heat up in a very short period of time and may be used for cooking or reheating foods rapidly. Also, they can be used for making hot preparations, such as tea and coffee, or cold preparations, such as iced tea, It is also advisable to have an adjustable water faucet over the steam-jacketed kettle and a drainage line close to the bottom of the kettle.

Steamers

Steamers are very useful in foodservice operations because of their efficiency, cleanbility, and for the quality of food they produce. There are several advantages and a few disadvantages of steamers from the foodservice point of view.

Advantages

1. Foods are cooked rapidly, so that large quantities of foods may be prepared in a relatively short period of time.
2. Nutrients are retained to a high degree.
3. Reduced labor is needed, since once the products are placed in the steamer, they do not have to be watched.
4. The quality of food is very uniform when similar settings are used.
5. Foods, particularly vegetables can be cooked directly from the frozen stage.
6. Rice and pasta products may be prepared easily.
7. Special desserts such as custards can be easily made.
8. Foods may be cooked in the same pan they are to be served in.
9. Fragile vegetables that require careful handling, such as asparagus, broccoli, and brussels sprouts, may be cooked successfully.
10. Steamed vegetables have an attractive colour, texture, and crispness.

Disadvantages

1. The type of foods that are suitable for steam cooking are limited.
2. They do not provide for the formation of crusts on foods.

3. Foods cannot be observed while cooking.
4. They require adjustment for getting the exact desired quality of foods.

The points to be considered in buying steamers include the source of steam, pressure of the steam, electrical requirements, number of racks, type of door, and overall dimensions of the equipment.

Blenders and mixers

Blenders and mixers are needed by all types of foodservice operations. Many types of commercial equipment are available. The horsepower of the motor is one of the most important considerations in purchasing this type of equipment. An adequate-size blender should be selected, since there will be a considerable saving in labor and other costs.

Investment in one large blender may be more desirable than a smaller size blender where more batches will have to be run. There are a variety of attachments that may be purchased with mixers such as a flat beater, wire whip, dough arm, pastry knife, wing whip, blades, and scrapers. These attachments are used for a variety of preparations and are indispensable for a foodservice. Long-term usage should be considered in selecting blenders or mixers. If properly selected, they will prove to be one of tile best investments for any foodservice operation.

Dishwashers

Dishwashers are among the most expensive and useful pieces of equipment in any type of foodservice operation. There are many types of dishwashers available on the market with a variety of functions. The most common types of dishwashers are:

- — *Immersion dishwashers,* in which racks of dishes are immersed for cleaning.
- — *Single-tank, stationary-type dishwashers,* in which dishes are placed on racks and dishes are washed with Jets of water within a single tank.
- — *Conveyor-rack dishwashers,* in which a conveyor carries the racks of dishes through the dishwasher.
- — *Flight-type dishwashers,* in which the conveyor is one continuous rack and the dishes are placed on pegs or bars.
- — *Carousel-type dishwashers,* in which there is a closed circuit conveyor where dishes are loaded and unloaded.

The function of dishwashers for washing, rinsing, drying, and overall cleaning should be understood before making any purchase decision. The literature from various manufacturers should be read and comparatively evaluated. The design of the dishwashers should be such that it fits in the overall layout of the foodservice operation.

The capacity of the dishwashers will depend on the number of dishes to be cleaned. Specifications are provided by the manufacturers on different types of dishwashers.

When making the selection, the cost of installation and maintenance should be taken into consideration. There are several other pieces of equipment that are used in foodservice operations such as freezers, coffee makers, waste disposers, trash compactors, meat slicers, and different types of service equipment.

One important aspect after the selection of the equipment is to use exact specifications, since inadequate specifications may lead to very expensive losses. They should be clear, concise, complete, and should include every possible explanation.

Selections should primarily be based on the suitability of the particular model for use within a particular foodservice operation. Some manufacturers provide templates, or small models, of the equipment that are very helpful in designing the layout. Warranties and certification by agencies such as the Underwriters Laboratories (UL), the National Sanitation Foundation (NSF), and the American Gas Association (AGA) should be checked. Plates installed on equipment contain most of this information.

3

Food Purchasing

Food purchasing is described as an art, since it requires talent and sophistication in judging the right combinations of color, shape, size, and consistency of food; as a science, since it involves knowledge of objective measurements of quality; and as part of management, since it requires skill in the overall utilization of resources. Since food purchasing requires a variety of skills and experience, these tasks are usually handled by persons who have had overall management or food-purchasing experience.

A critical step, once the menu is finalized, is to decide how many servings of each item on the menu for a particular meal are needed. The quantity of each ingredient to be ordered depends on this "number of servings," for which accurate "forecasting" is essential-this again requires skill and experience.

Among the several methods of forecasting which range in their complexity and accuracy, the simplest is based on the averages or means derived from data on number of servings. This function is so important that it is often said that a good manager is one who is good in forecasting. In the institutional type of foodservice where there are set menus, it is usually easier to forecast than in a commercial operation. A restaurant can almost never predict when there may be unexpected large crowds.

For example, for a restaurant located on a highway, it is virtually impossible to predict when a bus load of consumers may stop by, Forecasting becomes even more difficult when there are a large number of choices on the menu. A manager should realize the problems associated with over or underproduction of food. Overproduction may result in waste and/or spoilage, whereas underproduction may result in dissatisfied consumers. Both result in serious economic consequences.

Once the number of servings for each item is determined, the next step is to prepare a complete list of items to be purchased. A number of sources of information are necessary for this purpose; forms make the task easier. It is also important to know the meaning and the differences between certain technical terms used in purchasing.

Food as purchased (AP) refers to food as it is purchased without any peeling, coring, or cutting. On the other hand, edible portion (EP) refers to food as it will be finally available in edible form after processing. Thus EP represents the actual usable portion of the AP foods. For purchasing food it is, therefore, necessary to know the relative percentages of AP and EP. EP of the food should be calculated prior to placing a food order. Tested and standardized recipes would normally indicate the amount to be used in preparing a fixed number of servings. Waste and shrinkage losses may also be included in the recipe. If not, calculations are needed before determining the amount of each ingredient to purchase. The final yield may be calculated by:

$$\text{Percentage of yield} = \frac{\text{wt after cooking}}{\text{wt before cooking}} \times 100$$

For example, it 65 lb of cooked ground beef can be prepared from 90 lb of raw beef, the percentage yield for the ground beef in this type of preparation will be 65 divided by 90 and multiplied by 100, which will be 72.2%. Thus, 27.8% more ground beef in raw form is needed to get the desired cooked ground-beef servings. This is also referred to as "shrinkage," a fact that has to be considered in ordering food.

Yield percentages are dependent on various factors, such as temperatures used for cooking, types of ovens, and time, which will vary with the type of the foodservice operation. Serious shortages in prepared food will result if this factor is not considered when planning purchasing and production.

Sufficient margins should be provided in order to compensate for these losses. The fat content of meats will also affect the percentage of yield. It becomes convenient if the range of the yield percentages is also included on the recipe, so that the final EP can be calculated.

This can be derived as follows:

EP = AP – shrinkage (or prepreparation) losses

$$\text{Percentage shrinkage or prepreparation losses} = \frac{\text{losses due to shrinkage or prepreparation (wt)}}{\text{AP (wt)}} \times 100$$

$$= \frac{\text{AP (wt)} - \text{EP (wt)}}{\text{AP (wt)}}$$

Although there are several procedures used for determining the amount of food to be purchased, a recommended standard procedure is outlined in the following steps:

— *Step 1.* From the recipe, determine the factor to be used in calculating the desired number of servings. For example, if the recipe is for 100 servings and the desired number of servings is 300, the factor will be 300 divided by 100, which is 3. If only 50 servings are desired, the factor will be 50 divided by 100, i.e., 0.5. This factor is important in further calculations.

— *Step 2.* Multiply all the ingredients in the recipe by the factor derived in Step 1. For example, the recipe for 100 servings requires 30 lb of chicken; the amount to be purchased for 300 servings will be 3 X 30 = 90 lb (EP) of chicken. Calculate the AP amount of chicken by dividing the EP by the percent yield or the amount of EP provided by 1 lb, or a standard unit of the commodity. Such calculations should be done for all the ingredients in the recipe.

— *Step 3.* Convert the AP value to the nearest possible wholesale purchase unit (such as carton, cases, boxes, lugs, baskets, crates, flats, dozens, bushels, or sacks). The quantity selected should be such that the remainder of the commodity is easily utilizable and is not wasted. Sometimes, ordering in larger units may be economical and desirable. Items included in the menu for the following day or within that week should be taken into consideration. On the other hand, when items are strictly for one-time use only, the nearest possible unit size should be used or alternate uses for the remainder of the commodity should be planned in advance.

— *Step 4.* Once the amounts are determined for one menu item, the same procedure should be followed for other items on the menu, and daily totals for each item should be calculated.

— *Step 5.* Totals for the week, month, or any fixed period of time may be calculated and used for ordering. This duration should be decided by the management, based on the purchasing methods selected by a facility.

Management should decide on the basis of previous experience, how frequently foods and supplies should be purchased. Too-frequent food purchasing may add to the total cost, whereas a long delay in purchasing may result in shortages and other problems. An optimum frequency of buying should be established for each operation. Some of the factors that should be considered in deciding frequency of purchasing are:

Inventory on hand. A complete and continuous turnover of inventory is highly desirable, based on the type of the facility. Some facilities desire to maintain a week's inventory, while others may like to have a month's supply on hand. The volume of business also dictates the inventory required to be on hand. At times, it is tempting to purchase commodities when discounts are offered by purveyors. This is an important decision and should be made after considering all factors, since tying up money in inventory may reduce the amount of much-needed cash flow.

Storage capacity. The size and capacity of the dry, refrigerated, and frozen storage area primarily dictate the quantities of the items to be purchased. It may be desirable to rotate items frequently in order to provide adequate storage for all items. With limited storage capabilities, frequent buying may be essential. Some vendors will store purchases of commodities until needed by the buyers.

Seasonal fluctuations. Since agricultural commodities and perishable items are used in foodservices, seasonal availability is an important aspect to be considered in food Purchasing. It may be economical to buy certain items when there is an abundant supply. Again, storage of such items should be considered before making any decisions.

Type of market and proximity. The type of market and its location with respect to the foodservice are important considerations. For foodservices close to a larger market, such as a seaport or livestock market, larger inventories may not be necessary. For foodservices that only have access to smaller markets, such as a farmers' markets, only smaller inventories may be possible.

Buying methods

Once the foodservice manager has decided on the quantities of the items needed, it is essential to select the most appropriate method of purchasing. The method followed by one facility may not be applicable to another. Buying methods should be incorporated into the policy of the facility, based on the goals and objectives of the foodservice operation.

Before buying methods are established, it is essential to know the "market." There are various types of markets and the term "market" is much broader than the context in which it is normally used.

A market can be defined as a place or a process by which commodities are legally exchanged from one owner to another. Traditionally, mark carry the impression of a place, or a physical facility, where transactions take place. However, from a business point of view, a telephone call or exchanges made on computers may also be defined as markets. The essential aspect of a market is that there should be a transfer of ownership.

Markets are often classified as primary, secondary or tertiary, basic on their level of operation.

Primary markets are those which are large central markets of a particular commodity. Normally, these markets are specific to a commodity, such as fish, cattle, or grain. Transactions on large scale take place in primary markets, which are generally national or regional centers for a particular commodity. Since these are the largest markets for a commodity, prices are set and any fluctuations will affect other markets. All other markets are dependent on primary markets for prices as well as for the availability of specific commodities.

Secondary markets are relatively smaller and are located geographically at various centers to facilitate easy distribution of a commodity. These markets may act as centers of distribution for a variety of products. They receive products from one or more of the primary markets and distribute them to the local, or tertiary, markets. Tertiary markets are local markets that deal in a variety of products at a local level.

This general classification of markets may have some degree of overlap and in practical situations, it Sometimes becomes difficult to differentiate one type from another. Markets may also be classified on the basis of the kind of commodity-wholesale or retail markets and manufacturer, agent, or broker-served market.

In the foodservice industry, the recent trend is to buy foods from agents or brokers who deal in a variety of commodities to an extent that one agent may carry the entire needs of a foodservice operation from foods to napkins, soaps, and silverware.

The functions of a market include (1) the exchange, of commodities; (2) the physical transfer of the commodities; (3) the supply of information pertaining to all aspects of the commodities; (4) the supply of information on rules and laws pertaining to the exchange of the commodities; and (5) facilitation of transactions essential for the exchange, such as the financial procedures involved in the transactions.

One of several buying methods may be selected based on the needs of a foodservice operation-accessibility to the market, type of market, and mode of delivery. The selection is primarily based on the type of operation and the management policies.

Some foodservice managers prefer placing by phone, without comparing any prices from different purveyors, others are more specific and formal in placing orders. There may be purchasing method several advantages and disadvantages in selecting any and, therefore, these should be considered before selecting any method. A good buyer in a foodservice operation should continuously evaluate the prevailing methods and should be prepared to change from time to time, in order to avail himself of the optimum market conditions.

Informal buying

This type of purchasing is usually based on informal deals that often involve oral negotiations. The transactions are usually completed on on the phone. This type of buying is more suitable for small operations, since it does not involve paperwork and is much faster than other methods. For the most part, orders are placed orally, and, therefore, buyers may take advantage of price fluctuations and other market conditions on an informal basis.

On the other hand, these fluctuations may result in higher costs, since there is no prior agreement about purchasing. The primary advantage of this method of buying is that it saves a considerable amount of time and is very convenient.

Quick comparison of prices from a limited number of purveyors is also possible. The buyer selects the vendor and places orders for the quantity of the specific item(s) that need to be purchased. In addition to the use of the phone, contacts may be made by visits to the market by the buyer, or by salespersons calling on the buyer. There are several variations of informal buying, some of which are described below.

Cash-buying method

This is the simplest type of informal buying and is preferred for the smaller type of operation, such as family restaurants or small nursing homes. Food and other commodities may be purchased at local supermarkets, farmers' markets, auctions, or other local places. Since vendors are mostly local, it is easier to find bargains, both immediate and forthcoming. At places where regular farmers' markets are easily accessible, foods may be bought at relatively lower prices and the quality of food may be better, since most of the items are fresh. These fresh foods, such as hand-picked strawberries, vine-ripened melons, garden-fresh sweetpeas, fresh corn, and so on, make very attractive menu items. Supermarkets have the advantage that almost everything is available under one roof. Quantities needed may be picked up whenever desired, particularly if the foodservice operation is located close to a supermarket. Buying food at auctions may also prove to be very profitable, although large quantities have to he purchased and one must be familiar with the methods used in auctions. However, the importance of experience and sound planning cannot be overlooked, even if this method is very simplistic.

The advantages of the cash-buying method are (1) it reduces the amount of money tied up in large inventories; (2) it reduces waste to an extent, since buying can be done in the exact amounts needed; (3) it eliminates the middleperson and his commission, and therefore is usually more economical; (4) it makes portion control easier, since items are bought in smaller quantities as opposed to bulk; (5) it facilitates the analysis of food cost and other bookkeeping, since daily receipts are available; (6) it reduces chances of going into large debts, since small cash amounts are involved and there can be periodic checks on the amount spent; and (7) it is easier to check the quality before buying and decisions may be made on-the-spot.

There are also several disadvantages in using the cash-buying method, some of which are (1) some items and/or brands may not be available on a regular basis; (2) there may be a lot of fluctuation in prices; (3) considerable time is involved in buying, depending on the frequency of purchases; (4) special transportation and delivery methods may be needed; (5) menu planning is difficult, since there is a lot of unpredictability; (6) food production may be delayed due to such unforeseen problems as snow-storms, and the unavailability of personnel or transportation; and (7) it is not practical for large-size foodservice operations.

Quotation method

In this method the buyer prepares a list of items that are needed, their quantities, and their specifications. Before placing orders, the buyer requests selected vendors to quote prices for the items needed, giving their specifications and the quantities needed. These quotations are normally requested from three or four vendors. When all quotations are in, prices are compared and the most suitable price for the required quality is selected. After all decisions are made, orders are placed to the selected vendors for the various food commodities. As an example, the prices quoted by the vendors are recorded right next to each other for comparative assessment. The price selected is usually circled, preferably in red, so that it is easy to order the product from that particular vendor. A list of specifications set by an operation may be provided to all possible vendors and reference may be made to those specifications while placing orders. This saves time and avoids any confusion or misunderstanding when the specifications are quoted over the phone.

The advantages of this method are (1) it provides for comparison of prices on an informal basis; (2) the buyer is assured of the best possible price, regardless of the fluctuations in prices; (3) it informs the purveyor that the purchasing is not irrespective of the price and thus reduces the chances of any overcharging by the vendors; and (4) competitive prices and better quality may be secured since the selection is based on competition.

The disadvantages of this method include the following: (1) it is time consuming and requires relatively elaborate record keeping; (2) it may create problems if the specifications are not very clear; and (3) there is no written record of the quoted prices, since these are primarily verbal transactions.

Blank-check method

As the name implies, in this method selected vendors are authorized a "blank-check" privilege, that is, to deliver specific items at specific times and to bill the buyer without quoting any prices beforehand. This is usually done for limited commodities, particularly those that are in short supply or for which there is no strong competition. Also this method may be used where there are price regulations and when there is an insignificant difference in prices on a long-term basis for the commodity among various vendors. This kind of privilege buying is restricted to reputable vendors who have established business with a foodservice operation. It is also advisable to give price ranges, or maximum prices to be charged, to the vendors in order to eliminate overcharging or any misunder-standing.

The advantages of this method are (1) it is convenient, as it avoids price comparison and record keeping; (2) it is easy to deal and communicate with one vendor; (3) for certain commodities, like bread and dairy products, It may be, advisable to have this method for uninterrupted supply; and (4) it saves a considerable amount of time.

The disadvantages of this method are the following: (1) since there is one vendor involved for specific commodities, there is no control over the prices charged; (2) this method is applicable only to limited reputable vendors; (3) there is no competition involved and so the quality for the price paid may not be assured; and (4) if proper records are not maintained, it becomes difficult to assess the amount spent at a particular time on that commodity.

Cost-plus method

This method of informal buying is also known as the "fixed mark-up" method. A mark-up factor is charged above the cost of the item, particularly for those items with very unstable market prices. This type of arrangement provides safety for both buyers and vendors. Buyers are assured that they are not overcharged because of a rise in the market prices and the vendors are assured of a fixed amount of profit. The cost-plus method is very useful for commodities that are imported or for those that are scarce and subject to seasonal fluctuations. When the prices are inflated for these items, the buyer is assured of a mark-up factor that has been established earlier. This factor may range from 10 to 30% over cost. If carefully utilized, an operation may benefit from this method of purchasing. The buyer may decide on purchases based on market trends for that commodity. Normally, the interest of the vendors lies in the large volume of business that is assured by such an arrangement. Over the long run, a buyer may find this method to be extremely useful, particularly for certain food items that are included in the cycle menus. This method is also useful for restaurants that have their own specialties such as seafoods and steaks.

The advantages of this method are (1) the buyer is assured of the commodity at a reasonable cost regardless of price fluctuations; (2) delivery of special items is assured without any interruption; and (3) it is very applicable for items that are special and that are included on a long-term basis in a menu or menu cycle.

The disadvantages of this method are: (1) the mark-up factor needs careful consideration based on a study of market trends; otherwise a buyer may end up paying more for the products, and (2) if there is no competition involved, the mark-up factor may be much higher.

Formal buying

Formal buying is also referred to as "bid buying" or "competitive buying." Most of the procedures involved in this type of buying are formal and, therefore, conducted in writing. Written sets of specifications are distributed to vendors. Formal invitations or requests for bids are circulated among all possible vendors by various means. Since bids are requested in writing, this procedure is complicated and very time consuming, as compared to the informal method of purchasing.

Formal buying is usually only applicable to larger operations and when larger quantities of products are purchased. Often additional staff, based on the size of the foodservice operation, becomes necessary to handle some of the formalities and paper work required in this method. Records of all transactions have to be maintained, since any claims and legal actions have to be supported by documents.

The main advantages of this method are that it provides for competition and that it promotes fair purchasing policies. This method becomes necessary when a large amount of money is involved in purchasing or when foodservices are operated for a state or federal agency. As in the case of informal buying, there are several methods of formal buying.

Competitive-bid method

This is the most common method used for purchasing by larger foodservice operations, institutional foodservices, armed forces foodservices, and government agencies. In fact, this is the mandatory method required by many agencies. The vendors are Invited to submit bids based on written specifications of the commodities to be purchased. These requests are published in newspapers, related publications, and/or mailed to a list of vendors. Regulations require that equal opportunity be provided to all interested vendors.

Many places maintain a list of approved vendors and the policy for approval is outlined in all fairness to the interested vendors. The bids may be sealed or unsealed and are to be submitted by the set deadline. The bids are opened-possibly in public-at a specified time. The bids should include details regarding general conditions, delivery methods, billing, and discounts.

Bids may also be reviewed by a committee before they are finalized. Also, some bids call for samples of the products that have been prepared and tested in test kitchens, which are special sites used for preparing and testing food products. Objective as well as sensory evaluations are conducted at these kitchens. These kitchens are equipped with all the materials required for food production and evaluation. In large operations, the testing is conducted on a continuous basis, with skilled personnel and dietitians in charge. The identity of the bidder is not disclosed during the testing and evaluation. Based on the results obtained, final bids are accepted, which need not be the lowest priced ones, since quality and other criteria are used in the final decisions.

After bids are selected, the successful bidder is announced, and the price quoted on the bid is made public. This method ensures fair handling and awards of bids. Purchase orders are then completed and sent to the successful bidder. Generally, the lowest bidder is selected, unless the product does not meet the designated specifications or proves to be of inferior quality.

Negotiated-buying method

This method may be included under the informal as well as the formal method, since both types of buying are involved. Informal negotiations are conducted prior to the formal written bid or purchase order. It is used when time limits the formal requests for bids. This method may also be used for the purchase of products whose prices are not subjected to fluctuations and for which there is a narrow margin in the difference in prices.

Buyers may initiate negotiations with several vendors and finally select one vendor. This allows for competitive bidding and competition among the vendors contacted. As in the case of most formal methods, prices are set for a long period of time and this helps the management of the foodservice operations by setting selling prices and keeping menu price fluctuations to a minimum. It also helps the management by eliminating the need for frequent quotations, price selection, frequent food testing, unpredictability of prices, and a lot of paper work. Since a long-term commitment is involved, purveyors agree to enter negotiations only with long-standing, reputable organizations and/or when large quantity purchasing is involved.

Standing-order method

In this method, the purveyor continuously sends merchandise at a fixed predetermined interval of time. The purchase may involve a fixed quantity every time or may involve replenishing the stock from time to time. Milk and bakery product purchases are normally made by this method, which is often used for specific items only. Often the delivery person will replenish the stock, and this saves a considerable amount of time for the receiving person.

Formal agreements are made for this type of delivery in advance and reviewed from time to time. One of the disadvantages of this system is that there is dependence on one vendor and delays may be caused by unexpected problems in delivery. However, it works out well for those items that are purchased daily or several times during a week.

Future-contract method

This method is very similar to those discussed earlier in this type of buying. The future deliveries of the products are assured at a fixed price by entering into a future contract. Although the quantity to be purchased is not set, the prices to be charged are fixed at the time of the contract.

As and when needed, the particular commodity is ordered and bought at the set prices. This, again, assures the delivery of product at a reasonable price without fluctuations in the amount charged to the foodservice operation. This method should be used only after careful consideration and evaluation of the supply and fluctuations in prices of a commodity.

Buy-and-hold method

This method is used under certain conditions, when larger quantities of the product are available on the market at bargain prices. The buyer pays the price of the stock and the vendor is responsible for its storage, delivery, insurance, and losses due to spoilage. This method provides for the purchase of commodities at the most opportune time, as well as for their storage without any obligations. However, one fact that should be considered is the amount of money that may get tied up by the purchase of the commodity.

Specifications

Specifications may be defined as the description of a particular commodity in terms of its size, quality, or condition. Specification, which are very important in purchasing any product, especially foods, represent the technical language in which the buyer communicates with the seller as to what is actually needed. Since there are numerous products and different types and varieties within a product, it is essential to use distinct and specific terminology. An effective communication is completed when it is understood and acted on by the receiver. Thus, effective specifications are those that are complete and full in all respects.

Specifications, commonly referred to as "Specs," are also pieces of information that should be readily understood by most foodservice personnel. They have to be written and selected very carefully, since they represent the quality of food served by any operation. Also, they have an impact on the food costs and consequently the profits associated with the sale of the food.

Specifications also serve as a means of identification of the products and their verification upon receiving. They also eliminate any misunderstanding or friction all along the food flow and in the management process. Since they are very specific, it is highly desirable to record them in writing. Also, they should be accessible and placed at convenient locations for ready reference. It is imperative to plan and select the specifications very carefully and to make them as statements of management policy. They should be planned for the operations and in fact are custom-made for that type of operation.

To blindly follow the specifications of another foodservice operation often leads to expensive problems. Some of the factors necessary in writing specifications are that (1) they should be clear, concise, complete, and simple descriptions; (2) they should be based on management policy and should be viewed as requirements; (3) they should be based on tests and objective measurements that are recognized and are relatively easy to conduct; (4) they should be accurate and specific with no room for misinterpretation; (5) they must comply with the standards set by local, state, and/or federal regulatory agencies; (6) they must be used and revised to increase their usefulness; and (7) they must be based on consideration of technical advancements and improvements.

In addition to the above-mentioned general attributes, the specifications should include the following information wherever applicable:

1. The common, trade, or the brand name of the product
2. The amount to be purchased in the most commonly used units such as case, crate, pound, carton, or lug
3. The recognized trade, federal, or local grade
4. The name and size of the basic container
5. The count and size of the items or units within the basic container, such as 12/2's, 6/#10 cans, 12/3 lb packages, or number of dozens
6. The ranges in weight, thickness, or size, wherever applicable, such as 8 to 10 lb, 1/4 to 1/2 in. thick

7. The minimum and maximum trims, or fat content/ percentages/ ratios, wherever applicable
8. The degree of maturity or stage of ripening
9. The type of processing required, such as freeze-dried, cooked, or peeled
10. The type of packaging desired
11. Any additional information pertaining to nutrients or any modifications to the common specifications and additional clarifications to describe the exact item desired.

The specifications should describe the item desired to the fullest possible extent. Since buying is a very specialized function, the person in charge of it should be well aware of the various aspects of the foodservice System and should also possess the following necessary skills and experience:

1. An awareness of the markets and of market procedures
2. A knowledge of the items to be purchased and their use in foodservices
3. The capability of forecasting needs and responding to the fluctuating market situations
4. An understanding of the various systems within the foodservice operation as well as their interrelationship
5. The capability to understand and set specifications, understand test data, and experience in the proper use of such specifications
6. A comprehension of the laws and regulations governing all aspects of purchasing
7. A knowledge of different food grades and food qualities

8. The capability of judging quality by objective or subjective evaluations
9. A decision-making capability
10. A knowledge of food processing, food labeling, nutritional information and other related I information.

Regulatory agencies

There are several regulatory agencies whose primary responsibility is to assure food quality. They set standards and regulations that are designed to provide wholesome food and safe food processing using desirable practices. These regulations are very helpful to a food buyer in setting the specifications and ensuring that the products are safe and of desired quality. Federal agencies establish standards on a national basis and also provide regulatory control for these standards. Also, they set regulations for foods intended for interstate commerce. Several regulations have been established by these agencies that are very, instrumental in controlling food quality, food sanitation, and overall food marketing.

U.S. Department of Agriculture (USDA)

The Agricultural Marketing Services Act of 1953, implemented by the USDA, is probably the most important law to have a direct impact on food purchasing. It provides for grading and inspection of agricultural commodities. Since there are numerous agricultural commodities, they are categorized for inspection purposes and are handled by different departments. For most of the commodities, grading is voluntary. However, inspection is mandatory for meats, poultry, and other processed foods distributed through interstate commerce.

Inspection agencies are located at several points, particularly at the shipping centers, markets, ports, or other marketing terminals. A stamp of approval is affixed on all approved commodities that comply with the set standards. Standards are set by this agency after careful consideration and after consultation with the industry and experts for the commodity. The stamp is placed on the product (as in the case of meat), container, tape, invoice or other easily identifiable place. The presence of an approval stamp is indicative of the fact that the product meets the federal standard(s) set by the agency and/or by the buyer. Thus, the products can be verified by the agency for the quality of products. This service is referred to as the "Acceptance" service.

Individual specifications, which meet and excel the federal standards, may be set by any operation and an agent from the agency will certify when those specifications are met. An inspection certificate may also be requested. Fees for this service may be paid by the buyer or the seller. This is a very useful service for the buyer, since the desired quality is assured. Specific standards may be set by the organization to meet its requirements as well as when the regulations are too general.

The Agricultural Marketing Service also helps in stabilizing prices, based on the supply, demand, and fluctuations in the prices of the particular commodity. This is primarily done in three ways: (1) by grading commodities less stringently when the commodity is in short supply, and by tightening grading during the peak supply period; (2) by paying subsidies to the farmers for not planting; and (3) by purchasing surplus commodities, which are then distributed free or at a nominal cost to schools, the military, and other organizations. One or more of the above-mentioned methods may be used to stabilize the prices of the commodities. Many school foodservices take advantage of the commodities offered through this service, thereby reducing the costs incurred in foods.

The Wholesome Meat Act of 1967, which is an amended form of the Meat Inspection Act of 1906, requires inspection, at least as stringent as federal inspection of all meats, whether it moves within or between states. It also provides for technical and financial assistance for meat-inspection programs. The Wholesome Poultry Products Act of 1968, as in the case of meats, requires inspection of all poultry and provides for assistance to the state to improve inspection procedures. Tests are also conducted to check any contamination of poultry products. A similar act was passed for mandatory inspection of egg-processing plants and requires a pasteurization process for the freezing and drying of liquid eggs. This act is known as the Egg Products Inspection Act of 1970.

Food and Drug Administration (FDA)

The FDA, as part of the Department of Health and Human Services, has regulations which pertain to various practices in the food industry. One of the pioneer laws enacted by this agency is the well-known Food, Drug, and Cosmetic Act of 1906, which was later revised to the Food, Drug, and Cosmetic Act of 1938. It was designed to provide "safe and wholesome," honestly labeled, and properly packaged products. Further revisions were made to this act, the significant ones being the revision in 1958 (requiring "just cause" for the use of additives) and the revision in 1960 (concerning color additives). The most important amendment was in 1958, commonly referred to as the "Delaney Clause," which states that "producers may not use any additives found to induce cancer in man or animals." This clause has been the cause of controversy from time to time and is still debatable.

These acts have a profound influence on the market, and a foodservice manager should be aware of them and any changes in them. Introduction of new analytical methods and technological advancements may require future changes in these laws.

Another important regulation under this act deals with the labeling of food products. The Food, Drug, and Cosmetic Act states that the labels of packaged items must include:

1. The common name or names of the food item
2. The name and address of the manufacturer, packer, or distributor
3. The net contents of the package, either by count, fluid, or avoirdupois measure
4. The use of language that is easily understood with no foreign language that might circumvent label requirements
5. The specific, not collective names for ingredients, unless the product is commonly known
6. Labels that are sufficiently prominent and easily understood
7. A list, in order of the greatest to least proportion, of the names of all the ingredients used
8. The exact definition of the dietary properties if claims are made for any dietary value
9. The term "artificial," if artificial coloring or flavoring is used or the term "chemical preservative," if a chemical preservative is used for more information, the actual regulations should be consulted.

The Food, Drug and Cosmetic Act also defines "adulteration and misbranding" and in so doing provides important standards for processed foods. Inspectors can ascertain the quality of processed foods by (1) inspecting food samples sent to their laboratories, resulting in the certification of particular samples; (2) inspecting random samples withdrawn from lots, in which case the entire lot is certified; (3) "continuous" inspection in the food plant, thereby certifying on a continuous basis; and (4) intermittent inspection, where only a grade certificate is issued.

Three important standards are checked by food inspectors as follows: (1) standards of quality, (2) standards of identity, and (3) standards of fill. Detailed descriptions of these standards are given below.

Standards of quality

These standards refer to the quality of the food products, which may be measured by objective as well as subjective methods. There are various instrumental, chemical, and other methods that may be used for assessing the quality of foods. Since attributes vary from one food to another, grades are based on different factors. Also, a grading system varies from one food to another. Some of the attributes considered in grading include color, texture, tenderness, and freedom from defects. Grades for processed food items are different from those for fresh ones.

For most processed foods, a scale ranging from 1 to 100 is used, with a product scoring 90 and above being designated as A, 80 to 89 as B, 70 to 79 as C, and below 70 as below standard. This grading system may vary from product to product. It should be noted that the "below standard" does not mean "unwholesome." Reasons for such grading are normally given and it may be economical at times to use these products, especially when their appearance in the finished food product is not very important. Broken foods which may be perfectly wholesome are graded as "below standard," and these may be used in products where their appearance is not significant. Grades also depend on the type of fruit or vegetable. Each food product is graded based on different factors, such as marbling in meats, bacterial counts for milk, and color of apples.

Providing quality grade is entirely voluntary, but most food processors prefer grading in order to justify the quality of their products. A distinction should be made between the grading for quality and the inspection for the wholesomeness of the products, which are entirely different qualities.

Standards of identity

These are standards that have been set to describe or distinguish a product. They are the means of identification of a product and for differentiating it from other products. These standards prevent misrepresentation and misbranding of food products. Exact descriptions of the products and their contents are required by these standards. The USDA sets standards of identity for meat, poultry, and egg products, while the FDA sets standards for other foods.

Certain products may have several common names and therefore these standards identify the products by one recognizable name. For example, fruit cocktail may have a different meaning to different processors and the contents may vary widely. These standards specifically define the contents in order for a product to be labeled and identified as fruit cocktail. The contents and ingredients are also required to be labeled.

The word "artificial" is used when additives fitting into this category are used. Identity names precisely describe the product even if it has a common name. Thus salad dressings, ice creams, preserves, jams, and jellies are all identified and should meet specific standards in order to meet the requirements. A product is designated as "misbranded" if identity names are used without meeting the requirements of the standards.

Standards of fill

These standards refer to the quantity that is required in packaged foods or how "full" a container must be in order to avoid any deceptive filling practices. As in the case of the standards for quality, those containers that do not meet the standards of fill are labeled as "below standards of fill."

The use of federal grades for quality are voluntary, whereas the use of standards of fill are mandatory. Criminal action, conviction, fines and other penalties are imposed on food manufacturers when these standards are violated. Offenders may be ordered to go out of business, pay fines, and/or go to jail. Different weights and volumes are specified for different containers. The approved label ensures that the container is legally full to the quantity stated on the label.

In addition to these standards, the FDA has other regulations that deal with the food processing and nutritional labeling of products. The FDA has also introduced a set of regulations grouped under Good Manufacturing Practices (GMPs).

U.S. Department of Commerce (USDC)

A voluntary grading system is maintained by the USDC, mainly for fish and fish products. The grades assure that there is in-plant inspection during processing. For seafood, the inspection is conducted by the National Marine Fisheries Service (NMFS).

Since this grading is voluntary, a product that is not graded does not mean that it is unfit for consumption or is unwholesome. The FDA and United States Public Health Service (USPHS) are indirectly involved with the inspection of certain types of fish and shellfish. Various grades and technical terms are used for grading and defining seafood products.

Legal aspects

A buyer should be aware of the various laws regulating the purchase and sale of goods. In order to avoid misunderstanding and possible financial loss, it is important for a buyer to become familiar with all the existing prevalent laws that may pertain to his operation. In specific cases, legal advice may be necessary.

Laws of contracts

These deal with the legal aspects of any contract. Legally an agreement, whether oral or written, becomes a contract when parties accept identical terms and conditions, as long as no laws are broken and parties are competent enough to enter into contracts. Thus, a food purchase order is technically a contract that outlines the items desired, their specifications, price, delivery, insurance, and other related matters. The contract, therefore, is an understanding among parties under what conditions items will be purchased or sold, after all prerequisites of a contract are fulfilled.

The following basic conditions need to be fulfilled before any contract can become valid:

1. Parties entering into the contract must be aware of the terms and be in mutual agreement on all of them
2. Payments should take place
3. The objects involved in the contract must be legal
4. Parties must be capable of fulfilling all terms of the contract

Completeness of the contract is essential in purchasing with all details pertaining to the products, price, quantity, quality, time and the duration of the contract worked out it advance. Clarification and understanding of the contract or the purchase order are important from the legal point of view, as well as for smooth transactions to take place. A well-written contract avoids a lot of problems and, therefore, should be considered as implementing management policy. Time is a very important factor in foodservices. Orders have to be delivered within set times and thus contracts should clearly spell delivery dates. In many orders the phrase "time is of the essence" is included in contracts to emphasize the importance of time.

Laws of title to goods

These laws establish certain conditions pertaining to the title that occur after the transfer of ownership of goods. Legally, the title is transferred from the buyer to the seller on completion of the transaction. However, there is often a third party or a carrier of the goods involved in the transfer, which makes it critical to know the point at which the transfer of title will take place. There can possibly be three points at which the transfer can take place:

When the goods are delivered to the carrier for transportation to the buyer. Once the goods are delivered, the seller does not have the and it becomes the responsibility of the buyer to check on the insurance and other charges. The buyer in this case should assume the carrier's responsibility. This is referred to as FOB (Free on Board), where the buyer takes total responsibility of the goods once they are handed over to the carrier.

When the goods are delivered by the seller. In this case, the title does not transfer until the goods are delivered to the buyer. In other words, the seller assumes the responsibility of delivering goods to the buyer. The seller may use the services of individual carriers, but it will be the seller's responsibility to deliver the goods as ordered to the buyer. The buyer has the right to refuse shipment if the goods are not properly delivered or if they do not meet the requirements set forth in the order. This is also referred to as FAS (Free Along Ship). Thus, in this case the seller has the responsibility of the goods while they are being transported to the buyer.

When the seller assumes the responsibility of the products until they are on the buyer's dock. This is referred to as CIF (Cash, Insurance, Freight). The seller is responsible until the goods are delivered and are on the premises of the buyer's facilities. Thus, it is very important to understand where the transfer of title takes place, whether it is at the shipping point or the receiving point. Also, there are several types of contracts and the buyer should be aware of the nature of the contracts.

Laws of warranty deal with the type of warranties provided by the seller. There are primarily three types of warranties: (1) warranties of title that guarantee that the item is what was ordered; (2) expressed warranties, which refer to the statements of promises or facts pertaining to the descriptions, supplies, or models provided by the seller; and (3) implied warranties that refer to the understood guarantee that the product will be of fair quality and will serve the implied purpose.

Warranties have time limitations, although some may cover the life of the item, and this fact should be taken into consideration before placing any order. A buyer should read and understand the warranty, and seek legal advice if necessary, before signing the contract. Many warranties have so many restrictions or clauses or conditions that they may be of little value. So a careful assessment of the warranties is essential.

Laws of agency specify that the approved buyer is an agent or the representative of the company. The authorized agent, as established by this law, will be legally responsible for signing contracts on behalf of the company. This law applies to the buyer as well as to the seller. Thus, a clerk in the purchasing division may sign on behalf of the operation if authorized, and a sales representative may sign on behalf of the seller.

Ethical consideration

In foodservice operations, large amounts of food and other items are involved in purchasing and there are often large quantities of products in storage. In order to avoid severe losses, management has the responsibility to ensure ethical practices at all levels. This is extended to include all employees as well as the purveyors and their agents. A continuous minor amount of loss may erode the profits of an operation very rapidly. Loss of a pound from a 100-lb container may seem negligible, but this, if carried out over a period of time, will prove to be very expensive for the operation. Listed below are some of the points that the management should consider and implement in order to promote ethical standards:

1. Management should put an emphasis on honesty and make it a policy. It should be clearly demonstrated to the purchasing and receiving department that honesty is the best Policy and that management is willing to go as far as possible to see that it is implemented.

2. Management should set an example and be very sincere in all its dealings. A manager who walks away with a loaf of bread every day leaves a very poor impression and it affects the overall morale of the employees.

3. Employees dealing with purchasing and receiving should be assigned specific responsibilities. Specific persons should be designated to deal with purveyors. No other persons should be allowed to interfere with the purchasing and the receiving functions.

4. Management should make a policy of not accepting any gifts or favors from the purveyors directly or indirectly. These offers should be politely declined, and

the purveyors should be discouraged from making such offers. Any gifts, private offers, club memberships, charge cards for personnel use, and other such offers to any employee or manager should be discouraged.

5. Since many problems are associated with the extent of job satisfaction, management should see that the employees are satisfied to the maximum possible extent.

6. Management should see that the specifications are clear and complete and well understood by persons in charge of purchasing and receiving. Frequent revisions and updating of specifications should be conducted. Any loopholes should be checked and corrected.

7. Management should check the credentials and the authority of the dealers or their salespersons. Before entering into any contracts with the purveyors, it is advisable to check their reputation and, if possible, visit their facilities to understand their operations. A manager can learn a lot about the purveyor by talking to involved personnel and/or visiting their premises.

8. Management should provide all the facilities and equipment needed for the functioning of purchasing and receiving. There should be adequate physical facilities for carrying out these functions. Also, the procedures for testing should be clearly defined and placed at a convenient location for easy reference.

9. Specific times, preferably during the working hours, should be set for visits by salespersons. Representatives of as many purveyors as possible should be encouraged to visit. This will demonstrate the fairness of the management and promote the spirit of competitiveness.

10. Management should check prices, discounts, and other deals very carefully and should not play one purveyor against the other. Equal opportunity and fair dealings should be the policy of the management.
11. Management should be vigilant at all times and conduct spot checks as frequently as possible. Management should be willing to demonstrate the best possible methods.
12. Management should promptly investigate any complaints either from the purchasing department or the purveyors. The results of such investigation should be made known to all concerned parties as soon as possible. The very fact that an operation is willing to investigate creates positive ethical standards.
13. Management should take prompt action against any offenders and take measures to avoid its recurrence.
14. Management should reward those that are honest and sincere. This action will boost the morale of such outstanding employees and encourage others to follow suit.
15. Management should provide security for the personnel.

Purchasing of specific commodities

Fresh fruits and vegetables

The perishability of fresh fruits and vegetables makes these commodities very unpredictable, not only from the purchasing point of view but also from the grading and setting up of the specifications. Various factors need to be considered before buying fresh fruits and vegetables. Since there are numerous variations among types of fruits and vegetables, it is impossible to have set standards of specification. Therefore the grading system, the terminology in use, and other specifications are different for individual types of fruits and vegetables.

Grade

There are different sets of U.S. grade standards that are specific for each fruit/vegetable. The quality varies within each set of these grades. These grades may be listed by numbers such as No. 1, No. 2, or by such terms as U.S. Extra Fancy and U.S. Fancy. Since perishable items are involved and quality is subject to deterioration while being transported, it is essential that it be specified that the grade desired is at the time of the delivery, rather than at the time of shipping. U.S. grades are very handy tools and reference sources for buyers, since they avoid the use of lengthy specifications and eliminate any misunderstandings. Any special requirements of a foodservice operation can always be added to the specified grade(s).

Quality

Additional factors of quality that are not specified in the food grades should be included In food orders. The grades may be supplemented by explanation of what is desired and many times it helps if their intended use is also given. Examples of such explanations are: lettuce for salads, tomato for relishes, and parsley for garnishing. Also, it is important to specify and insist on freshness. Wilted, stale, blemished, dry, or cut fruits and vegetables are undesirable. Although it varies for the type of fruit or vegetable, the desirable characteristics include: bright, attractive colors, good shape and appearance, good proportion of weight and size, and absence of any mechanical damage or signs of decay. Lack of freshness may also be a sign of poor handling and transportation. This may result in a shortened storage capability and useful life of the fruits or vegetables, even though they may be suitable for immediate use.

Seasonal availability should be taken into consideration when ordering fresh produce, since their storage capability is also dependent on seasonal variations. Most fruits and vegetables may have undesirable attributes during the beginning and the end of the growing season. These attributes may include sourness, lack of juiciness, lack of flavor, lack of texture, unripeness, or overripeness.

Variety

Variety and type of fruits and vegetables are important, since they specify a particular item among several available kinds. For example, Golden Delicious or McIntosh specify the exact type of apples desired without any misunderstanding. Variety and type are also helpful In selecting the best fruits and vegetables for the purpose. Another good example is the Russet or Katahdin potatoes, which are different in appearance, specific gravity, and cooking qualities.

Size

Size is one of the most important aspects of specification, particularly for fruits. The optimum size desired for the purpose should be selected, since the cost of many commodities depends on their size. Normally, smaller sizes are preferable when appearance is not significant, whereas larger sizes are recommended when whole or large portions of fruits and vegetables are used. Also, larger sizes are preferred for carvings and artistic displays and presentations. Sizes also determine the count that is packaged in a container.

For example, apple sizes may vary from 56 to 252 per western apple box. Similarly, many fruits are sized by count per box or by diameter. The diameter is measured not around the girth, but transversely from stem end to blossom end. Some vegetables, especially greens, may be shipped in large bunches and may be specified in dozens of bunches per container. Terms used for specification should be carefully used from the prevalent terminology. Care should be taken to avoid terms that are not included in the standards for that product.

Packaging

Numerous types of packaging are available for fruits and vegetables. Buyers should be very specific as to the type of packaging or the container desired. An item may be available in more than one kind of package such as bushel baskets, boxes, lugs, sacks, crates, cardboard containers, and so on. The specification should be clear as to what kind of packaging is desired, such as apples by counts per box, cantaloupes in counts per crate, and broccoli in bunches per baskets.

In some cases, the type of packaging selected indirectly indicates the quantities desired. Special packaging, such as ventilated containers or containers for hydro-cooled vegetables, may also be requested and specified. The packaging selected should be based on the quality and the quantity of the products desired and also on the time and distance involved in transportation. Also, the storage spaces within the facility should be taken into consideration. Smaller packaging may be easier to shelf in some cases, compared to large containers and vice versa.

Other pertinent Information, wherever applicable, should be included to enhance the specifications, such as the brand name or the growing area for the product. Produce from one area may have different attributes than that from other areas. For example, fruits from California may have different attributes for the same type of fruits from Florida. Some of the aspects that are pertinent in fresh fruit and vegetable purchasing are discussed in the following examples of selected fruits and vegetables. Detailed specifications should be consulted for actual purchasing situations.

Apples. There are several thousand varieties of apples that are suitable for many different purposes. Apples should be selected on the basis of (1) use, (2) variety, (3) grade, (4) maturity, (5) size, and (6) color. Some apples are better suited for use raw, while others are good for baking. The selection should be based on their intended use. The varietal characteristics should be considered and varieties should be selected based on the most desirable attributes. For example, an apple intended for raw use should be juicy, crisp, sweet, and firm, whereas a good baking apple should have a tough skin to hold its shape after baking; and should be moist, soft, and have high-to-moderate acidity. Some varieties have more than one attribute, making them useful for several purposes; those versatile varieties should be considered good buys. The grades of apples are heavily dependent on their color, as well as other attributes. U.S. Fancy grade apples are more colorful as compared to others. Cost should also be considered in selecting the proper grade for the purpose. Apples should preferably be firm and have good color, properties which are indicative of their maturity. Maturity may be ascertained by such objective measurements as pressure testing or by the use of refractometer. Big apples should be checked for their texture and any signs of spoilage. The size of the apple is based on number of apples in a box or by their diameter. Thus a box of 48's will contain 48 apples per box; these are very large-sized apples. On the other hand, 216's are very small apples at 216 per box. The color of the apples is dependent on the variety and should be selected on the basis of desirability.

Avocados. Avocados are of different sizes, shape, texture and skin thicknesses. Their color may range from dirty green to black. Their characteristics are dependent on the section of the country where they are grown. Quality avocados have a fresh appearance and a soft texture. They may be purchased unripened but care should be taken to judge their degree of ripeness. The ripeness can be detected by slight pressure on the rind or by a fork—the fruit is ripe when it yields to slight pressure. Fuerte, Hass, Bacon, and Zutano are the principal California varieties. Lula is a popular Florida variety, which is in common use. Avocados may be used in a variety of forms, and they add color and variety to the menu.

Bananas. Bananas are imported from tropical countries and their varieties vary with their place of origin. The Gros Michel and Cavendish are among the leading banana varieties. There are no standard grades for bananas. Brownish coloration, bruises, and damaged skin are among the signs of deterioration. They are sold in bunches attached to the stem or in cartons. Peeling losses should be considered when ordering bananas. About three medium-sized bananas will weigh 1 lb. When ripened, they will have a bright yellow color with firm flesh. "Full ripe" bananas have no trace of green and should be used immediately. "Hard ripe" bananas have a bright color with no trace of brown; they can be ripened by storing for 3 days. "Turning ripe" bananas have green tips and are astringent in taste and may take up to 6 days to ripen. It may be advisable to buy large quantities of "turning ripe" or "hard ripe" bananas and store them before use. However, care should be taken to avoid overripening. Also, good deals may be made by purchasing "full ripe" bananas for use without storage.

Grapefruit. Grapefruit varies in taste and juiciness. As is true for most of the citrus fruits, heaviness may be indicative of the juciness. Color cannot be relied on as an index of the quality of citrus fruits. The most popular grapefruit varieties are Duncan (containing seeds) and Marsh seedless (few seeds). There are pink-meated grapefruits that are cross-bred types.

Lemons. Lemons may range in color from green to yellow. They are also sold by size, with 75 to 95 being large, 115 to 140 being medium, and 165 to 235 being small. Lemons may be used for a variety of purposes, and the selection should be based on their intended use. The acid content will also vary to a much greater extent, although green lemons may be expected to be more acidic.

Oranges. Oranges can be divided into sweet and sour categories based on their varietal characteristics. Oranges are also sold based on their size (48's, large, to 163's, small). Normally 1 lb of oranges, as purchase, will be equal to 0.7 lb ready-to-serve portions with membrane and 0.56 lb ready-to-serve without membrane. Also, 1 lb of oranges, as purchased, yields 0.5 lb or one cup of juice. These figures may be used for calculating the amounts to order. Signs of spoilage as mentioned for other types of citrus fruits should be checked.

Peaches. Color is an important factor in judging the quality of peaches. A red color, often referred to as "blushing," may not be indicative of the ripeness. The red color should be surrounded by bright yellow color for the fruit to be ripe. Hard peaches indicate that they are not properly ripened. Deep reddish color and softness are indicative of overripeness. Shrivelling of the skin is a sign of deterioration or overripeness. There are primarily two types of peaches: (1) Clingstone and (2) Freestone. As the name indicates, in the Clingstone type, the flesh adheres tightly to the stone of, the pit, while in the Freestone type, the flesh can be easily separated from the pit. The Freestone type of peaches may result in cost savings in labor and may be preferable for salads. Peaches are among those fruits that are subjected to the process of "hydrocooling." In this process, the peaches are passed through a shower of ice water, which may or may not contain fungicides. This process rapidly reduces the pit temperatures by 20^0 to 30^0 and helps in reducing the postharvest changes, thereby delaying the ripening process and decay during transit. Thus, it helps In improving the quality of peaches. The container label will indicate if the product has been subjected to hydrocooling.

Pears. Pears may be purchased on the basis of size, maturity, and grade. The degree of ripeness is indicated by the color representative of the variety. The Bose variety turns yellowish brown, the Bartlett turns yellow with a red blush, and the d'Anjou turns greenish yellow. Ripeness is also indicated by the softening of the blossom end. Pears have different grades and are sold based upon their size.

Tomatoes. Tomatoes are widely used products in foodservice menus and they should be selected after a very careful assessment. The quality of tomatoes may be judged on the basis of (1) color, (2) weight and size, (3) internal characteristics, (4) maturity, and (5) overall appearance. The size and quality of the tomatoes are not related. Vine-ripened" full-size for the variety, unblemished, and characteristic color are the most desirable attributes for tomatoes.

Tomatoes may be picked at several stages, for example:

1. *Immature green* tomatoes are those which do not have any red or yellow color and contain hard seeds. They are of poor quality when ripened and should be used only if needed in the recipe.

2. *Mature green* tomatoes are glossy but do not have red or yellow color. They have hard seeds and they may be suited in preparations where appearance is not important.

3. *Turning ripe* tomatoes have a trace of red or yellow color. This stage is also referred to as the "breaker stage." They are firm and of fairly good quality when ripened.

4. *Pink* tomatoes have more than 50% of the surface area either red or yellowish-pink. They are firm but cannot be stored for long periods nor can they be shipped too far.

5. *Firm, ripe* tomatoes are at the final stages of ripening and are good for immediate use only. They do not ship well nor can they be stored.

Soft, bruised tomatoes with cuts, scars, or cracks should be avoided, since they are of poor quality and may be the source of considerable waste in trimming. Color, firmness, internal characteristics, size and maturity should be considered when ordering tomatoes.

Lettuce. With the popularity of salad bars, lettuce is among the most commonly used vegetables for salads. Since lettuce is used mainly in the unprocessed fresh form, its appearance and freshness are of prime importance. There are different types of lettuce, the most common being (1) Crisphead (Iceberg), (2) Butterhead (Boston, Bibb), (3) Cos (Romaine), and (4) Leaf lettuce. Generally, in selecting lettuce, the desirable attributes are: firm but not hard heads, freedom from burned or rusty-looking leaves, soft leaves, sweet and juicy flavor, and crisp texture. The overall yield of lettuce is approximately 65 to 75%. U.S. grades are given to lettuce and the following terms are used in describing their quality:

1. *Hard* when the head is compact and has the highest degree of solidity within the type

2. *Firm* when the head is compact but may yield to moderate pressure

3. *Fairly firm* when the head is not very firm but is not soft and spongy
4. *Soft* when the head is spongy and can be easily compressed

Lettuce is kept cooled by various methods ranging from packing in ice to vacuum cooling.

Potatoes. There are different kinds and types of potatoes, which may be described as Round White, Round Red, Long White, Round Russet, and Long Russet types. Moisture and starch content are very important considerations in buying potatoes. Moist and slightly waxy potatoes are suitable for boiling, potato salad, hash browns and other similar uses; whereas dry, mealy potatoes are useful for deep-fat frying, baking, or mashing. Potatoes may be purchased on the basis of grade and size. One of the aspects that may be considered in specifications as well as objective measurement is the specific gravity of the potatoes. The higher the specific gravity of the potato, the more mealy it is. If a potato is placed in 1.08 salt solution and it sinks, its specific gravity is greater than 1.08; if it floats, its specific gravity is less than 1.08. The ideal specific gravity of potatoes for use in baking and mashing is considered to be 1.08, for boiling 1.07, and for frying less than 1.07. Potatoes may be shipped in various types of containers ranging from polyethylene bags to boxes. The specifications should include the variety, type, size, grade, and conditions at the time of the delivery. Good, firm, smooth-skinned potatoes having the desired specific gravity should be selected.

Processed fruits and vegetables

There are well-developed standards for processed fruits and vegetables. Minimum quality standards, set by the federal Food, Drug, and Cosmetic Act are the standards of identity, fill, and quality. In addition to these standards, there are grades used to classify processed fruits and vegetables based on their quality.

Those processed foods not meeting the minimum requirements for the standards are graded as substandard. Labeling a product as substandard does not mean It I's unfit for consumption or that it is of inferior nutritional quality. In fact, based on usage, it may even be economical to use such products, particularly where the identity of the fruit or vegetable is not of prime importance. Grades are based on a number of factors used in scoring, which may vary according to the fruit or vegetable. These factors include color, size, consistency, symmetry, finish, maturity, absence of defects, character, flavor, uniformity of size, type of liquor, cut, and wholesomeness.

USDA grade standards

USDA grades are determined by examination by qualified inspectors. The inspections may be conducted by one of these methods:

1. *Lot inspection*, in which the specific lots of processed fruits and vegetables that are located in plant warehouses, commercial storage, railway cars, trucks, or any other conveyance or storage facility are inspected and graded. In this method, the inspectors have no knowledge of the conditions and practices under which the product was packed or processed.
2. *Continuous inspection*, in which the inspection and grading services are conducted in an approved plant, whereby one or more of the inspector(s) are present at all times the plant is in operation. Thus, in-process checking is made and the inspectors are aware of all the conditions under which the product was processed and packaged.

3. *Pack certification*, in which the inspection and grading are conducted by inspector(s) during preparation and processing, although these inspectors are not present at all times the plant is in operation.

There are several factors that are considered in grading processed fruits and vegetables. The following aspects, which may or may not be used in grading, are important to consider when purchasing processed fruits and vegetables:

Fill of container. Unless defined by the Food and Drug regulations, USDA grades recommend generally that cans be filled as full as practicable without impairment of the quality; and the product and the packaging medium occupy not less than 90% of the water capacity of the container.

For objective assessment and for all practical purposes, this percentage of fill is determined by measuring the headspace inside the can. "Headspace" is the space between the top of the container and the packaging medium.

Containers that fail to meet this requirement are designated as "below standard in fill." There are specified maximum gross headspaces for various can sizes, for example, 27/32 m. for No. 10 can and 19/32 in. for No. 2 cans.

Drained weight. Except for a few products, drained weight is riot considered as an attribute in the evaluation of grade, since it is not a factor related to the quality. However, recommended minimum drained weights are included in the specifications.

"Drained weight" refers to the weight of the canned products after the liquid is allowed to drain for 2 min on a standard sieve under specified conditions. The test is done after the canned product has been allowed to equalize for 30 or more days after canning. Drained weights are important, since the actual yield from a canned product can be determined, and this helps in the calculation of portion sizes.

Syrup density. This also is not incorporated in the grades of the canned Product, since syrup, or any other liquid medium, is not a factor of quality. The type and density of syrup or the packaging medium, which is specified on the label, are important from two points of view: (1) The quality of the canned product is dependent on the density of the syrup. The heavier the syrup, the less the chance of the products breaking up, particularly fruits. Therefore, for higher-quality products, heavier syrup should be recommended. (2) From the dietetic point of view, it is important to know the density of the syrup, particularly in the cases of special diets.

The scale used to measure the density of a syrup is Brix, which relates the specific gravity of a solution to an equivalent concentration of pure sucrose. Roughly, for every degree Brix, a fruit has 1% sugar.

Brix table should be used for the accurate determination of Brix and the sugar content. The taste or tartness of fruits or fruit juices may be described in terms of Brix, or Brix-to-acid ratio. The higher the Brix, the greater the sugar concentration in the juice; and the higher the Brix-to-acid ratio, the sweeter and less tart is the juice. Although canned fruits are riot graded on the basis of syrup density, they are certified as meeting the declared syrup designation. The densities of the syrup may be measured by a refractrometer or a Brix hydrometer.

Scoring factors

Grade's are assigned to each type of product based on several scoring factors. These factors are dependent on the type of product and may be different for fruits or vegetables or their combination. Scores are for such factors as color, character, flavor, size, symmetry, absence of defects, maturity, texture, consistency, finish, liquor or clearness of liquor, wholeness, and cut. It should be clearly understood that these scores are based on the factors and are indicative of the products based on these attributes. Lower scores are not indicative of the poor nutritional quality of the products, since that is not what is described by these factors.

For most of the canned fruits and vegetables the grades are based on the following scores:

— *USDA Grade A* must be practically perfect in every respect, allowing a tolerance of from 15 to 18% within the grade which is scored between 85 and 100 points inclusive.

— *USDA Grade B* must be reasonably perfect in every respect, allowing a tolerance of from 16.7 to 20% within the grade which is scored between 75 and 89 points inclusive.

— *USDA Grade C* must be fairly perfect in every respect, allowing a tolerance of from 20 to 25% within the grade which is scored between 60 and 74 points inclusive.

For certain products, there are only two USDA Grades and in those instances the scoring for the grades is as follows:

— *USDA Grade A* must be practically perfect in every respect, allowing a tolerance of from 15 to 18% within the grade which is scored between 85 and 100 points inclusive.

— *USDA Grade B* must be fairly perfect in every respect, allowing a tolerance of from 18 to 22% within the grade which is scored between 70 and 84 points inclusive.

Table 1
Scoring ranges for grades of canned foods

Grades	*For foods where there is a Grade B*	*For foods where there is no Grade B*
A (Fancy)	90 to 100	85 to 100
B (Choice, Extra Standard)	75 to 89	–
C (Standard)	60 to 74	70 to 84
Substandard	0 to 59	0 to 69

Frozen fruits and vegetables

These are graded in practically the same way as the canned fruits and vegetables with minor exceptions. They are packed in a variety of packages and are available in different weights. Frozen fruits may be packaged in sugar or syrup. It is important to know the media in which they are packaged. They may also be treated with an antioxidant to avoid browning on the surfaces.

Meat and meat products

In any type of foodservice operation there is probably no single item as expensive as, or as important as, meats and meat products. Meat purchases in foodservice operations may range from 30% of the total food expenditure to 70%. Meat purchasing may range from as much as 20% of all operating expenditures for the institutional foodservice to 40% for the commercial establishment. Thus, meat plays an important role in the menu; and the ultimate profitability of many foodservice operations depends on bow the meat items are purchased, prepared, and served to the consumers. It is indispensable to have a well-planned and controlled method of purchasing, receiving, preparing and serving meat items, in order to be successful in the foodservice industry.

There are, also, very well-defined and clear standards and regulations that help in purchasing wholesome and safe meats and their by products. However, it should be emphasized that meat buying is very complex and requires considerable experience. An understanding of the processing of meats from the slaughter house to the processing plants is vital for being an effective buyer. Also, an understanding of the terminology, grading procedures, inspection, and safety as pertaining to meat products is very important.

Antemortem and postmortem inspection

All animals intended for slaughter are inspected and are passed for normal slaughter, labeled as suspect, or condemned. Condemnation is based on the presence of a communicable disease or a condition that may make the meat unsafe for consumption. Those labeled as suspect are those animals that may be immature, crippled, or have a suspected presence of a disease or a condition that needs further assessment. The disposition in the case of those labeled as suspect is based on their condition and further examination. Eventually, they may be approved for slaughter or condemned. Those approved for normal slaughter undergo the process of postmortem inspection, immediately after slaughter.

Based on the inspection of all body parts, meat may be judged suitable for human consumption and a stamp of approval using a nontoxic dye is affixed. If there is any suspected condition, the meat is retained. For some meats such as pork, cooking conditions, particularly temperatures to which they should be cooked, are specified. The unsuitable meat is marked as condemned.

Aging of meats

Soon after death of the animal, several chemical changes occur In meats. There is a stiffening of the muscles, a condition referred to as "rigor mortis." Meat at this stage is referred to as "green." The quality that is most desirable in meat is tenderness. The main meat structures responsible for tenderness are the connective tissues and the muscle myofibrils. The connective tissues found in muscle are composed of the proteins collagen, elastin, and reticulin. Collagen is a tough fibrous protein, which upon hydrolysis yields hydroxyproline. Specific plant enzymes, such as papain (found in papaya), ficin (found in figs), and bromelin (found in pineapples), will attack tissue collagen and render it soft and tender.

Meat from very young animals, such as calves, will contain a large amount of collagen in proportion to other muscle fibers, so that this meat is relatively more tender. This tissue also undergoes changes due to the inherent enzymes, which make the meat tender during the process of aging. Elastin is a yellow protein which is very elastic and which is practically unaffected by normal heat during cooking. The amount of elastin present, therefore, affects the tenderness of the meat. Reticulin fibers are also similar to elastin and are very tough.

Muscle tissues normally present in meats contain the muscle proteins actin, myosin, and tropomyosin. It is the number and size of the muscle fibers as compared to the connective tissues that is responsible for the tenderness of meats. In other words, large fibers will have less connective tissue than small fibers. Thus, both muscle and connective tissues play an important part in the overall tenderness of meats.

The tenderization of meats may be achieved by the following methods:

1. *Natural aging*. In this method the carcass or individual cuts of meat are rapidly chilled at a temperature of 32°F (0°C) at 85% relative humidity. The muscle glycogen gets converted to lactic acid during this process.

2. *High-temperature aging.* In this method, the carcass or cuts of meats are cooled to an internal temperature of 59^{0}F (15^{0}C). The carcass is then transferred to a room that has a temperature of 68^{0}F (20^{0}C). Air is circulated in this room, and the humidity is maintained at 85 to 90%. The room is provided with ultraviolet light to control microorganisms. The meats are held for approximately 44 hr and then removed to a room with cooler temperatures of 32^{0}F (0^{0}C).

3. *Vacuum aging.* Cut portions of meats are packaged in flexible packages and held in vacuum. Meat will age within the package without any significant loss of moisture. There may be a darkening of meat and a musty odor in meats after undergoing vacuum aging.

4. *Application of enzymes.* Proteolytic enzymes may be directly applied to the meat or given intravascularly before slaughter.
5. *Electrical stimulation and massaging.* These are relatively new methods used for tenderizing and research work is being done on the various aspects of these methods.

There are different types of retail cuts that may be obtained from beef, lamb, or pork carcass. The main cuts of beef are:

Hindquarter	*Forequarter*
1. Round	6. Rib
2. Rump	7. Chuck
3. Sirloin or loin end	8. Plate
4. Short loin	9. Brisket
5. Flank	10. Shank

Meat grades

There are different grading systems for meats. In general, meats are graded on two important aspects:

1. *Quality*. Mainly indicative of palatability.
2. *Yield*. Mainlv indicative of the cutability and major retail cuts.

When writing specifications for meats, either a quality grade or a combination of quality and yield grades are required. The overall grades for meats and their descriptions are:

1. *U.S. prime*. Highest grade; meats have fine texture and firm muscles.
2. *U.S. choice*. High in eating quality; less fat than prime.
3. *U.S. good*. Greater proportion of lean to fat; lacks juiciness but is relatively tender.
4. *U.S. standard*. Thin fat covering; high proportion of lean to fat; tender.
5. *U.S. commercial*. From mature animals; lacks tenderness; relatively more wastage.
6. *U.S. utility*. From animals advanced in age; lacks tenderness and juiciness.
7. *U.S. cutter and U.S. canner*. Useful for processed meat products.

It is required that the beef carcass be "ribbed" at least 10 min before it is graded, thus allowing some of the grade-determining factors the time to become evident.

"Ribbing" is splitting the carcass down the center of the backbone and cutting between the twelfth and the thirteenth rib bone to expose longissimus dorsi muscle. The longissimus dorsi, or rib eye muscle, is the longest muscle extending from the neck to the end of animal body. The quality grading is based on:

1. *Classes of animals.* Some of the classes and grades are given as examples below:

Heifer or steer	— Prime, Choice, Good, Standard, Commercial, Utility, Cutter, Canner
Cou	— Choice, Good, Standard, Commercial, Utility, Cutter, Canner
Bullock	— Prime, Choice, Good, Standard, Utility
Calf or veal	— Prime, Choice, Good, Standard, Utility, Cull
Lamb	— Prime, Choice, Good, Utility, Cull
Mutton	— Choice, Good, Utility, Cull
Pork	— U.S. No. 1, 2, 3, 4, Utility

2. *Maturity.* This is indicated by bone size, shape, and ossification. Maturity grades are given from A to E, with A being the youngest and E being the oldest.
3. *Flesh Color and Texture.* White fat and cherry-colored lean are considered top quality. Also lean flesh will have fine texture and light grayish color.
4. *Marbling.* Streaks of fat running through the lean meat is referred to as "marbling." Good marbling is indicative of well-fed animals and of meats that will be tender, juicy, and flavorful when cooked. Although marbling is desirable to an extent, overabundant marbling imparts an oily taste to the meat. The degrees of marbling for grading are abundant, moderately abundant, slightly abundant, moderate, modest, small, slight, traces, and practically devoid.

The yield grades are based on:

1. The amount of external fat-the thickness of fat over the rib-eye muscle measured perpendicular to the Outside Surface at a point three quarters of the length of the rib eye from its chine bone end
2. The amount of kidney, pelvic and heart fat-calculated as 3% of the carcass weight
3. The area of the rib eye-measurable by a special grid; and the hot carcass weight-calculated by multiplying chilled carcass weight by 1.02

The formula used for the calculation of yield grade is:

Yield grade (1 to 5) = [2.50 + (2.50 × adjusted fat thickness (in.)] + (0.20 × percentage of kidney, pelvic, and heart fat) + [0-0038 × hot carcass weight (lb)] - [0.32 × the area of the rib eye (in.^{2})]

Yield grades 1 to 5 are applicable to all quality grades. The yield grades reflect differences in yields of boneless, closely trimmed retail cuts. Yield grade 1 represents the highest yield of cuts and yield grade 5, the lowest. However, the ones indicated by X in Table 2 are the yield grades most commonly available for the quality grades. It should be noted that U.S. Prime beef does not usually have a yield grade of 1 or 2.

When writing the specifications for meats the following aspects should be included:

1. Class of animal
2. USDA grade and the division of grade
3. USDA yield grade
4. Acceptance weight range
5. Fat limitations
6. Condition upon delivery

7. Temperature and packaging upon delivery
8. Weight
9. IMPS No.

Table 2
Quality and yield grades of beef

U.S. Quality Grades	*Yield Grades* 1	2	3	4	5
Prime			X	X	X
Choice		X	X	X	X
Good		X	X		
Standard	X	X	X		
Commercial		X	X	X	X
Utility		X	X	X	
Cutter		X	X		
Canner		X			

The above specifications may be enhanced by using IMPS numbers. IMPS stands for the Institutional Meat Purchase Specifications, which are the official USDA requirements for the inspection, packing, packaging, and delivering of specific meats and meat products.

IMPS are also used for the certification or "acceptance" of these products by the USDA meat graders. Several publications are available that describe the IMPS specifications. One such very commonly used publication is The Meat Buyers' Guide, published by the National Association of Meat Purveyors (NAMP), which contains meat specifications.

These guides are available for standardized meat cuts and for the portion-controlled meat cuts. They are written to simplify the IMPS and to supplement overall meat grading standards. These guides also have colored pictures of the actual cuts of meats that make it easier to understand the IMPS. IMPS are based on a numbering system that facilitate easy identification of different types of meat products.

IMPS No.	Description
100	Fresh beef
200	Fresh lamb and mutton
300	Fresh veal and calf
400	Fresh pork
500	Cured, smoked, cooked pork products
600	Cured, dried, smoked beef' products
700	Edible by-products
800	Sausage products
1000	Portion-cut end products

As examples, the following numbers and descriptions are given to clarify the IMPS numbering system:

IMPS No.	Meet	IMPS No.	Meat
100	Beef carcass	400	Pork carcass
101	Beef side	500	Cured regular ham
102	Beef forequarter	600	Corned Spencer
137	Special ground beef	613	Cured tongue
155	Beef hindquarter	701	Beef liver
200	Lamb carcass	713	Lamb liver
234	Oven-prepared leg	1100	Beef cubed steaks
300	Veal carcass	1189	Tenderloin steak

Poultry and eggs

Grading of poultry is based on class, quality, quantity, condition, or ally combination of these factors. The U.S. Consumer grades for poultry are listed below.

— *U.S. Grade A.* A lot of ready-to-cook poultry or parts consisting of one or more ready-to-cook carcasses, or parts of the same kind and class, each of which conforms to the requirements for A Quality, may he designated as U.S. Grade A.

— *U.S. Grade B.* A lot of ready-to-cook poultry or parts consisting of one or more ready-to-cook carcasses, or parts of the same kind and class, each of which conforms to the requirements for 13 Quality or better, may be designated as U.S. Grade B.

— *U.S. Grade C.* A lot of ready-to-cook poultry or parts consisting of one or more ready-to-cook carcasses, or parts of the same kind and class, each of which conforms to the requirements for C Quality or better, may be designated as U.S. Grade C.

There are also two procurement grades: U.S. Procurement Grade I and U.S. Procurement Grade II.

There is a voluntary USDA grading and inspection service for poultry. Poultry should be specified by part as follows: breasts, breast with ribs, wishbones, legs, wings, drumsticks, thighs, halves, quarters, and backs. The specifications for poultry should, therefore, include (1) name of the part, (2) quantity, (3) weight, (4) detailed description, (5) required inspection, (6) condition upon delivery, and (7) type of packaging.

The grading of eggs is based upon their size, which is determined by their weight per dozen. Since most of the eggs are packed in 30-dozen, corrugated-fiber cases, it is easier to determine and compare their case weights.

The sizes and weights used to grade eggs are:

Size	Weight (oz) per dozen	Weight (1b) per 30-dozen case
Jumbo	30	56
Extra large	27	50.5
Large	24	45
Medium	21	39.5
Small	18	34
Peewee	15	28

Large and medium eggs are the sizes most frequently used in foodservices. These eggs are suitable for frying, poaching, hard or soft cooking, and for dishes where appearance is of primary importance. If eggs are to be used in mixed salads or for baking, size is not so important. If one uses the large-sized eggs as a base, medium eggs are the better buy if they are 12% or more cheaper than large eggs. If not, there is no savings and the larger size should be selected. Similarly, the small eggs are a better buy if they are 24% or more cheaper than the large eggs. Size should not be confused with grading. A jumbo egg refers to its size and not to its quality. In other words, both quality and size should be considered in purchasing eggs. The quality of eggs depends on their exterior as well as their interior condition. The shell should be sound, clean, and unbroken. Eggs lose carbon dioxide and moisture upon storage. The air cell, which is visible under light, enlarges as the moisture and carbon dioxide are lost. The white becomes thin and watery and the yolk flattens out. As a result of these storage changes, an old egg covers a wide area when broken, compared to that of a fresh egg. The yolk is also weak and may break. A test known as "Haugh Unit Breakout Test" is based on the height of the white at the yolk, which is measured using a micrometer. All of these factors are considered in the grading of eggs, which are designated as consumer grades and procurement grades. The consumer grades are:

— *U.S. Grade AA*. Clean, unbroken, and practical normal shells; the air cell almost regular in shape, no more than 1/8 in. deep; clear and firm white; yolk practically free from defects with outline slightly defined. No less than 85% U.S. Grade AA at point of origin, and no less than 80% U.S. Grade AA at destination. Individual cases to be no less than 75% U.S. Grade AA, and no more than 15% U.S. Grade A and 10% U.S. Grade B at the point of origin, and no less than 70% U.S. Grade AA, but no more than 20% U.S. Grade A and 10% U.S. Grade B at destination.

— *U.S. Grade A*. Clean, unbroken, and practically normal shells; practically regularly air cell, 3/16 in. or less in depth; clear and reasonably firm white; yolk outline fairly well defined and practically free from defects. No less than 85% U.S. Grade A at point of origin, and no less than 80% U.S. Grade A at destination. Individual cases to be no less than 75% U.S. Grade A, and no more than 25% U.S. Grade B at the point of origin, and no less than 70% U.S. Grade A, and no more than 30% U.S. Grade B at destination.

— *U.S. Grade B*: Clean-to-slightly-stained shells, which may be slightly abnormal in shape; air cell may be free or bubbly, but not more than 3/8 in. deep; the white may be clear, but may be slightly weak; yolk may be slightly enlarged, and have a well-defined outline. No less than 85% U.S. Grade B at point of origin, and no less than 80% U.S. Grade B at destination. Individual cases to be no less than 75% U.S. Grade B at the point of origin, and no less than 70% U.S. Grade B at destination. No eggs that are less than Grade B can be included.

There are two procurement grades that are mainly used by large processors and rarely by foodservice operations. Thus, for writing specifications for eggs the aspects to be included are (1) size of the eggs, (2) grade of the eggs, (3) type of packaging, (4) condition upon delivery, (5) inspection requirement, and (6) detail description.

Milk and milk products

There are various USDA grades for milk and milk products which should be considered in purchasing these products. In addition to grading, the processing method is also specified on milk packages.

Milk is pasteurized by heating to at least 1457 and holding at, or above, this temperature continuously for at least 30 min. It can also be pasteurized by the high temperature short-time (HTST) method by heating to a temperature of 161^{0}F and holding at, orlabove, this temperature continuously for 15 see. After heating, milk is immediately cooled to a temperature of 45^{0}F or lower. Milk is also homogenized by passing it through small orifices under pressure in order to break the fat globules uniformly.

Cream formation is thus prevented, and the milk so obtained has a slightly better flavor. It should be noted that nothing is added to homogenized milk. The grades for milk and milk products are different. Many places restrict the sale of milk lower than U.S. Grade A. Thus, grades should be checked before purchasing milk and milk products. Grading is particularly important for such products as butter, margarine, and cheese. State and local authorities have different grading systems, as well as different regulations pertaining to dairy products.

A foodservice manager should be familiar with the following types and descriptions of milk and milk products:

1. *Whole milk.* In many states this consists of milk that contains not less than 3.25% milk fat and not less than 8.25% milk solids-not-fat.
2. *Skim milk.* Milk from which fat has been removed by centrifugation. Ordinarily, skim milk contains 0.1% fat.
3. *Two-percent milk.* Contains 2% milk fat.
4. *Certified milk.* Special milk with a very low bacterial count, used specifically for patients after surgery or for nursing homes.
5. *Low-sodium milk.* Sodium is removed from milk by the process of ion exchange.
6. *Fortified milk.* Milk to which nutrients that are present in milk are added.
7. *Vitamin D milk.* Milk to which vitamin D is specifically added.
8. *Concentrated milk.* Milks that are concentrated to different proportions. These may be fresh, frozen, evaporated, condensed, or dried.
9. *Cream.* Separated from milk. Contains not less than 16 to 18% milk fat.
10. *Half-and-half.* Equal parts of whole milk fat (3.25%) and cream milk fat (18%). This milk product has approximately 10.5% milk fat.
11. *Evaporated milk.* Slightly more than half of the water is removed from milk.
12. *Condensed milk.* Sugar is added to the milk before it is evaporated.
13. *Cultured milk.* Certain desirable bacterial cultures are allowed to grow in pasteurized milk under controlled conditions.

14. *Buttermilk.* Cultured milk, containing chiefly Streptococcus lactis. The milk has a tangy, smooth flavor.

15. *Acidophilus milk.* Cultured milk with Lactobacillus acidophilus. Used for its therapeutic value for patients that have been treated with antibiotics.

16. *Yogurt.* Manufactured from fresh, partially skimmed milk, enriched with added milk solids-not-fat. It has a smooth texture and is available in many flavors.

17. *Chocolate milk.* A chocolate-flavored milk.

18. *Filled milk.* Milk In which milk fats are replaced by other fats, mostly fats of vegetable origin.

19. *Dry whole milk.* Milk from which the water has been removed.

20. *Instant nonfat dry milk.* Prepared by removing fat and water from the milk.

In writing specifications for milk, the type of product, grade, milk fat content desired, and the type of packaging should be included.

Fish and shellfish

Seafoods are among the most desirable items in any type of foodservice operation. Unfortunately, their quality deteriorates very rapidly, so that there is a lot of variation as far as the quality is concerned among the same species of a product. Therefore, care should be taken when purchasing seafood, since there are no standard specifications such as exist for meats.

Grading and inspection of fish products are entirely voluntary and are conducted by the National Marine Fisheries Service program of the U.S. Department of Commerce. This inspection and grading is done in addition to the requirements and inspections conducted by the Food and Drug Administration, which apply to all types of processing plants. There are also local regulations for seafood, particularly by public health authorities.

In addition, there are several seafood processors who voluntarily choose to have continuous federal inspection and grading in their plants. The products manufactured under such inspection have a federal seal which signifies that (1) the product is clean, safe, and wholesome; (2) the product is of a specified quality, identified by the appropriate U.S. Grade designation, as determined by the federal inspector in accordance with the established requirements of the U.S. Grade standards; (3) the product was produced in an acceptable establishment, with proper equipment and in appropriate processing conditions; and (4) the product was processed and packaged using good manufacturing practices. Grading is based on several factors depending on the type of product. General factors used in evaluations are odor, flavor, packing, bones, color, appearance, size, broken pieces, texture, and skin.

The U.S. grades for seafoods and their descriptions are:

— *U.S. Grade A* means top or best quality. The products are uniform in size, practically free of blemishes and defects, in excellent condition, and possess good flavor for the species.

— *U.S. Grade B* means good quality. Products may not be as uniform in size or as free from blemishes or defects as Grade A products. Grade B may be termed a general commercial grade, quite suitable for most purposes.

— *U.S. Grade C* means fairly good quality. Products are just as wholesome as higher grades. They are graded low because of minor factors, such as breakage. Where appearance is not important, these may be good buys.

Normally, U.S. Grade A products are easily available on the market. Those with a lower grade are often marketed without any grading on them. Fish may be bought in any one of the following forms:

1. *Whole fish* are sold Just as they come from the water. They have to be dressed before cooking. This involves scaling, eviscerating, and removal of head, tail, and/or fins. The smaller fish are pan-dressed and heads are not removed.
2. *Drawn fish* have entrails removed, which are the cause of rapid deterioration.
3. *Dressed fish* are completely cleaned fish with head on and ready for stuffing, if desired.
4. *Chunks* are cross sections of large dressed fish, having the cross section of the backbone as the only bone.
5. *Steaks* are cross-section slices from large dressed fish, which are 5/8 to 1 in. thick.
6. *Fillets* are sides of the fish cut away from the backbone. They are practically boneless.
7. *Butterfly fillets* are the two sides of the fish cut lengthwise away from the backbone and held together by the uncut flesh and skin of the belly. These steaks do not have any bone.
8. *Fish sticks* are pieces of fish flesh cut into uniform width and length, usually 3 in. by 1 in.
9. *Fish portions* are larger than fish sticks but uniform in size and weight.
10. *Breaded fish* are available in a number of cooked, frozen, and other pan-ready forms.

In writing specifications for seafoods, the following aspects should be considered: (1) name of the product, (2) species, (3) size and thickness, (4) grade, (5) style (skinless or skin-on), (6) type, (7) form, (8) packaging, (9) conditions upon delivery, and (10) inspection requirements.

Mechanics of buying

The mechanics of buying are concisely described in the following steps and explained with examples.

Step 1. *Start with the menu.* For each food preparation on the menu, prepare a list of items that are needed. A separate form for different types of food products is very useful.

Step 2. *Fill in daily Requirements and calculate totals for each item.* Complete the daily requirement and then total the amounts needed.

Step 3. *Request bids and/or quotations.* Quotations and bids for the total amount of products should be prepared based on the requirements.

Step 4. *Select the vendor for particular Item selected.* Based on the outcome of Step 3 select the vendor for that particular item.

Step 5. *Prepare and send the purchase order.* Using complete specifications as described in the quotation or bid requests, fill in the purchase order.

Step 6. *Collect invoices and/or receiving reports.*

Step 7. *Transfer information to inventory records.*

Step 8. *Use requisition forms for issuing from storage.* Any item used from any of the storage areas should be recorded.

4

Quantity Food Preparation

Food preparation is the most important part of the system since all other parts depend on it. The best-planned menu and the efforts of the most efficient purchasing and receiving units may all be ruined if food preparation is not up to the standard. The production section, or department, represents the largest and most critical part of any foodservice operation. A variety of items are prepared by this department in such units as a (1) butcher shop, (2) entrée unit, (3) appetizer/soups unit, (4) vegetables unit, (5) salads unit, and (6) bake shop. Sometimes several of these units are combined. Each unit contributes its part to a meal and an overall effort is needed from each one of them to produce a quality meal in quantity.

Standardised recipes

Recipes that are tested for quality, quantity, procedures, time, temperature, equipment, and yield are called "standardized recipes." The recipes are standardized to the extent that when the specified conditions are followed in them, the result is always a product which is similar in all respects. Standardized recipes assure quality control and are very effective management tools. Standardization calls for careful assessment, testing, and evaluation of recipes before their final adoption. However, it should be emphasized that a recipe standardized for one operation may not be applicable to another operation. Minor variations of equipment and temperature may make a considerable difference. Therefore, it is essential that testing be conducted on the premises of an operation using the equipment and procedures that will be used for the actual food preparation.

There are several advantages to standardized recipes, some of which are:

1. They give in detail the ingredients, procedures, and equipment to be used. Thus, a change in personnel does not affect the food quality or quantity.
2. They facilitate cost analyses of the recipes.
3. They permit a predictable quality of the food and provide for future testing for improvement.
4. They facilitate food purchasing, since exact quantities of food and ingredients to be used are known.
5. They permit easier portion control, if serving portions and equipment are listed.
6. They help to set selling prices for menu items and also facilitate price changes when the cost of ingredients change.
7. They help in work scheduling, since time and procedures used are standardized. Efficient scheduling results in an even distribution of work and job satisfaction.
8. They eventually contribute to consumer satisfaction since quality of food and serving sizes are uniform.
9. They avoid any confusion and reduce the chances of poor handling and food-preparation failures, which could prove expensive for the operation.

10. They help in training employees in good production and handling procedures.

Standardization procedures

The standardization of recipes needs very careful evaluation and testing. In many foodservice operations, it is undertaken by the management with the help of supervisors and/or dietitians.

Standardization also helps in that the operation will have written recipes rather than a vague list of ingredients in the head of a cook or a chef, who may not always remain with the operation. Every recipe that has been tested needs reevaluation from time to time. Household recipes or small-quantity recipes published in magazines or cookbooks are very unreliable for quantity production.

Standardization involves the careful adjustment and readjustment of ingredients and their proportions to produce the most acceptable quality. This calls for subjective as well as objective evaluation. Taste tests should be conducted several times until quality products are assured. Most often the recipes are enlarged and tested from smaller quantity recipes.

The following steps represent the recipe enlarging and standardization procedures:

— *Step 1.* The initial-and usually small-recipe may come from one of many various sources such as cookbooks, magazines, journals, commercial food companies, family-recipe files, other foodservice operations, test kitchens, and special community advisory groups. The first step is to prepare the recipe in the minimum quantity for which it was intended. The finished product should then be evaluated. The smaller recipe should be evaluated first on the basis of preparation method; ingredient proportion; availability of ingredients; cost, yield, equipment, skill, and abilities of personnel; and its overall suitability for the operation. A careful screening at this point will eliminate expensive large-scale testing at a later stage.

— *Step 2.* The original recipe should then be multiplied and specifically tested. In enlarging the recipe, ratios play an important role. For example, the ratio between sugar and flour or flour and shortening is very important. The physical form of the ingredients should be carefully assessed. Fresh, chopped onions may be responsible for flavor in a smaller recipe, but it may not be feasible to have chopped onions in larger quantities as this may change the taste of the finished product.

Enlargement of recipes

There are two methods that may be followed while enlarging recipes: (1) the trial and error method and (2) the factor method.

Trial and error method

This method is applicable to relatively simple recipes in which the ingredients are limited in number. Based on suitability, the original recipe is multiplied-normally twice the size of the original recipe. The yield and other characteristics are evaluated. If the quality and quantity are acceptable, then the recipe is further multiplied. If not, adjustments are made and the recipe retested. This process is continued until desirable quality and quantities are achieved. Special attention should be given to adjustments in processes, such as cooking temperatures, and speed of the mixers. Differences in the desired yield are representative of the need for adjustment and careful evaluation. This method is time consuming and may be tedious, since several variables are involved and adjustment may be difficult.

Factor method

In this method, a factor is used for calculation and accuracy of the multiplied ingredients. The conversion factor that is used for multiplication is derived as follows:

$$\text{Conversion factor} = \frac{\text{desired yield from enlarged recipe}}{\text{yield from original recipe}}$$

If the desired yield is 60 and the original recipe is for 8, the conversion factor would be 60 ÷ 8 = 7.5. This factor is used for multiplication. First, all ingredients used should be listed with the amounts given in the original recipe. In order to facilitate calculation, all amounts should be converted to equivalent weights-for example, ounces from cups or teaspoonfuls.

This method facilitates the testing procedure and should not be used in final preparation of the recipe without testing. In order to decrease or increase the recipe yield, similar factors should be used.

It should be noted that when recipes are increased, the factor will always be greater than 1.0 and when decreasing the recipe, the factor will always be less than 1.0. The total weight of the enlarged recipe can be checked by comparing it with the total weight of the original recipe. The total weight of the original recipe multiplied by the factor should result in the total weight of the new recipe. If not, the calculations should be carefully rechecked for errors.

— *Step 3.* Prepare the enlarged recipe, carefully checking the procedures, time, temperatures, and other parameters. Soon after preparation have the product evaluated by a taste panel. Several forms may be used for assessment of the recipe by the panelists. The results may be interpreted based on the type of data obtained. It may be used (1) for changing special ingredients and procedures to get a better product; (2) for comparative evaluation with other recipes; and (3) for estimating the popularity, acceptability, or marketability of the food product. Thus, this testing may be used in various ways, and the data obtained may prove to be extremely valuable.

— *Step 4.* Prepare the recipe at least three additional times to ensure reproducibility of the desired results. Do popularity tests, cost estimates, and yield tests each time. It is advisable to conduct consumer taste tests at this point. If possible, let the recipe be prepared and tested by similar units, such as franchise stores with very similar equipment, and assess the results.

— *Step 5.* If positive results are obtained from the above tests and the product quality and quantity are acceptable, the recipe is standardized and is ready for use.

— *Step 6.* Prepare a recipe card outlining very clearly the ingredients, procedures, and other information.

Recipe file

A file of all standardized recipes should be maintained; this should be categorized into entrées, vegetables, soups, desserts, etc. This file should be updated frequently. Also, it is advisable to add costs to each recipe, based on the number of servings.

Principles of meat cookery

In any type of foodservice operation, meats represent the most important menu item. In fact, the success of some of the franchise chains and restaurants is based on the meat items on the menu. Meat is also one of the more expensive items, if not the most expensive item on the menu. Meats also contribute significantly to the nutrient content of meals. Adequate care and selection of the best preparation method are necessary to maintain the flavor, tenderness, color, and palatability of meat dishes. Meat is complete protein and provides most of the essential amino acids needed in human nutrition. It also supplies such micronutrients as iron, phosphorus, potassium, sodium, arid magnesium, as well as B vitamins.

In order to obtain the best possible products, it is necessary to understand the fundamental chemistry of meats. Meats are approximately 75% water. The muscle fibers are in the form of bundles arid from the structural units of lean tissue.

Connective tissues surround the muscle fibers and help to support the muscle structure. There are primarily two types of connective tissue-collagen and elastin-both are important in cooking. Collagen, which is yellowish white in color, gelatinizes in the presence of moisture and heat and becomes softer, thus adding to the tenderness and flavor of the meat. In contrast to collagen, elastin is yellow and is a very tough tissue; it is not affected by heat and cannot be softened easily. Various types of tenderization methods, primarily mechanical, are often needed to break and soften these tissues. The amount and distribution of these connective tissues varies with the age of the animal.

Fat is present in meats at various points, including exterior portions, within the abdominal cavity as rolls of fat, between muscles, and within cells. As with connective tissue, the fat content is also dependent on the age of the animal and the type of diet that was fed to the animal. The distribution of fat within the muscle is used in the grading of meats.

The intermingling of fat and muscle is referred to as "marbling." To a certain extent, an optimum distribution of fat is desirable, since this fat melts upon heating and provides juiciness, tenderness, arid flavor to the cooked meat. On the other hand, excess fat is not desirable, since it melts and adds to the greasiness of the meat. In addition to fat, moisture content is responsible for the juiciness of meat. Thus, it is important that time and temperature be optimum for the retention of the desirable quantities of fat and moisture.

Also, an appropriate method should be selected in order to enhance the flavor, color, tenderness, and juiciness of meat. Above all, it is the quality of cooked meat when it reaches the consumer that is most important. Thus, the service and delivery methods should be such that all the desirable attributes of meats are left intact as much as possible before serving.

Shrinkage is a phenomenon that is observed in meats when they are cooked. Since meat consists mostly of water, the loss of water during cooking causes shrinkage. Although all meats will shrink to some degree upon any type of cooking, it is the extent of shrinkage that is of prime importance. There are a variety of factors that are responsible for shrinkage. The most important are cooking time, cooking temperature, and cooking method.

Tenderization of meat is achieved by the use of enzymes, salt, and vinegar or by using mechanical means. These substances act on the collagen and help to tenderize the meat. Such enzymes as papain from the raw papaya fruit, bromelin from pineapple, or ficin from figs have a tenderizing effect on meats. These enzymes are sometimes injected into the animal just before slaughter.

Commercially available meat tenderizers contain one or more of these enzymes, spices, and such flavor enhancers as monosodium glutamate. In larger portions of meat and where hard connective tissues are present, mechanical means such as pounding, grinding, dicing, chopping, cubing, scoring, or beating help to tenderize meats by physically breaking and/or loosening the hard connective tissues. Whatever means are used, it should be ensured that they are effective, since the quality of the finished product depends on the texture of the meat. Marinating with oils, acids, tomato juice, vinegar, lemon juice, and sour cream also help to tenderize meats.

Cooking methods for meats

There are several methods for cooking meats, each resulting in a different type of flavor. These methods are sometimes classified as dry-heat methods (where no water is added while cooking), and the moist-heat methods (where meats are cooked by steam or hot liquids). In dry-heat methods, since no additional water Is added, surface carmelization or browning occurs, which results in enhanced flavors.

Since surface heating is largely accompanied by moisture and since there is not enough moisture to soften the collagen, meats suited for these methods should either be tender cuts or should be tenderized. In moist-heat methods where liquids are used, meats are exposed to temperatures that are not higher than the boiling point of water, which ensures slow cooking; this contributes to flavor development and tenderization.

The moist-heat process can be hastened by the use of steam or pressure cooking. When meat is cooked in water, care should be taken to ensure that the nutrients are not lost in the gravy or in the juices coming from the cooked products. The method selected should be based on the type arid grade of meat. The most common methods of cooking various types of meats are described below.

Roasting

Roasting is a dry-heat method in which meats are cooked in various types of ovens such as conventional, convection, and microwave ovens. Large roasts are usually cooked by placing the meat with the fat side up in an uncovered pan. Moderate-to-low temperatures and long cooking times are used for roasting in order to develop the flavor. Lower temperatures keep meat shrinkage to a minimum. In foodservice operations, roasting poses scheduling problems unless the operation has more than one shift.

Roasting meats in ovens overnight, while convenient, poses various safety problems, such as those caused by improper handling or power failure. If time and temperature are controlled, the product roasted overnight is of a superior quality with well-developed flavors. The optimum temperature for slow roasting will be a setting of 250^0 to 350^0F. This would require a longer roasting time than one at a higher temperature setting.

Tender meat cuts are preferred for roasting; these would include the less exercised portions of beef and those meats attached to the backbone portion of the carcass. In the case of veal, lamb, and pork, most cuts are suitable for roasting. It is desirable to start with defrosted meat in foodservice operations to ensure the quality of the finished product, although under certain conditions meats may be roasted without thawing.

Internal temperatures are the best indicators of doneness of meats, rather than oven settings or external characteristics. The oven-temperature settings will depend on the type of oven used, in addition to the type and cut of meat, the preparation time available, and the seasonings used. A constant low temperature is desirable, since the resulting product is evenly done and is more uniform in color when served.

The approximate cooking times and temperatures for various cuts of meat are given in Tables 1 and 2.

Table 1
Cooking times for beef

Broiling

Cut	*Approximate thickness*	*Approximate total cooking time* — *Rare (min)*	*Medium (min)*
Rib, top loin, T-bone,	1 in.	15	20
porterhouse,	1½ in.	25	35
tenderloin	2 in.	35	50
Beef sirloin steak	1 in.	20 to 25	30 to 35
	1½ in.	30 to 35	40 to 45
Ground beef patties	1 in. (4 oz)	15	20

Braising and Cooking in Liquid

Cut or thickness (hr)	*Average weight cooking time*	*Approximate total*
Pot roast	4 to 6 1b	3 to 4
Swiss steak	1 to 2½ in.	2 to 3
Short ribs	pieces 2 × 2 × in.	1½ to 2
Corned beef	6 to 8 1b	4 to 6
Beef shank cross-cuts	3/4 to 1 lb	2½ to 3½
Beef for stew	1- to 2-in. cubes	2 to 3

It should be emphasized that roasts will continue to cook even after they are taken out of the oven. Thus, roasts should be removed from the oven at an internal temperature that is slightly lower than desired to allow for the few degrees increase after removing.

Roasts should be sliced 15–20 min after removal from the oven, since this "resting" period permits easier slicing. Roasts have their best flavor right after cooking, so there should not be much time between roasting and serving. Slicing should be done across the grain of the muscle, preferably using a mechanical slicer. For the best quality, the size of the slices should be as thin as possible. Portions of meat should be weighed for standard servings. Refrigeration of cooked roasts prior to slicing results in flavor loss.

Likewise, reheating reduces the juiciness of roasts and increases toughness. Considerable amounts of juice are lost in slicing and with the juice go the flavor components and, more importantly, the nutrients. Care should therefore be taken to utilize as much of the meat juice as possible by adding it back to the meat slices or by adding it to the gravy.

Broiling

This is also a dry-heat method and the source of energy may be direct or radiant heat from gas flames, charcoal briquettes, or individual electric units. Relatively tender and thicker cuts are the most suitable for broiling. Prefabricated or "portion -controlled" meat cuts are useful in broiling and result in uniform serving sizes.

The most tender and expensive cuts are usually prepared by broiling. The thickness of the meat plays an important part in the quality and doneness of the finished product-thinner cuts show excessive shrinkage and thicker cuts result in nonuniform cooking. The grid markings on broiled meats are considered a sign of quality by many foodservice personnel as well as consumers.

In foodservices, broiling is done in special broilers or a salamander. The meats are placed on racks, with the radiant heat approximately 3 in. away from the meat. Turning of the meat ensures cooking on both sides. The temperature, as well as the distance from the heat Source, determines the time of cooking and the degree of doneness. The temperature of the heat source may be as high as 1800⁰F (982⁰C). The preferred temperature range for broiling is between 300⁰ and 350⁰F (149⁰ and 177⁰C). The degree of doneness is achieved at an internal temperature of 140⁰F (60⁰C) for rare, 160⁰F (71⁰C) for medium, and 170⁰F (76⁰C) for well done.

Table 2
Cooking Times for Roast Beef

Cut	*Approx. Weight of single roast (1b)*	*Oven Temperature (⁰F) (⁰F)*	*Interior temperature (⁰F) roast when removed from oven*	*Minutes per pound based on one roast*	*Approximate total cooking time (hr)*
Rib, roast ready # 109	20 to 25	250	130 (rare)	13 to 15	4½ to 5
			140 (medium)	15 to 17	5 to 6
			150 (well)	17 to 19	6 to 6½
Ribeye roll #112 or # 112 A	4 to 6	350	140 (rare)	18 to 20	1½ to 1-2/3
			160 (medium)	20 to 22	1½ to 2
			170 (well)	22 to 24	1-2/3 to 2¼
Full tenderloin #189 or #190	4 to 6	425	140 (rare)		45 to 60 min
Strip loin, boneless #180	10 to 12	325	140 (rare)	10	1½ to 2
Top (inside) round #168	10	300	140 (rare)	18 to 19	3 to 3¼
			150 (medium)	22 to 23	3½ to 4
Top (inside) round #168	15	300	140 (rare)	15	3½ to 4
			150 (medium)	17	4 to 4½

Grilling or griddling

This dry-heat method is primarily used for cooking steaks or hamburgers. The fat in the meat itself is enough for cooking. Fat and water are not added, although different, kinds, of seasonings may be used. Once the meat is browned on one side, it is turned for cooking on the other side. In some griddles or grills, special provision is made for fat drainage- The cooking temperatures vary, depending on the ambient temperatures, but normally they range from 325^0 to 350^0F (163^0 to 177^0C). The time and temperature of cooking are also dependent on the thickness of the meat.

Braising

In this method meats are browned in a small quantity of fat. The pan is covered tightly after browning, and the cooking is continued at a low temperature. Braising may be done in the oven, a stem-jacketed kettle, a tilting fry pan, or over the range. The doneness of the meat depends on the internal temperature required for that particular type of meat and may range from 165^0 to 185^0F (74^0 to 85^0C).

Stewing

Stewing or boiling of meat Is done by cooking meat the, presence of moisture. Vegetables or cereals may be added to meat for stewing and special recipes may be used. The meat may or may not be browned before stewing. The flavor of the stewed meat is enhanced by the juices of the meat in which cooking takes place. Stewing requires cooking at a Simmering temperature until it is tender. Steam-jacketed kettles or large floor-mounted kettles may be used for stewing.

Simmering

This involves the slow cooking of meats in liquid for a long period of time. It is a method that is especially useful for less tender cuts of meats that require longer cooking times for tenderization. The advantage of simmering is that meats can be cooked longer without shrinkage.

Soup preperation

Soups, when appropriately prepared and served, provide an exciting prelude to a pleasant dining experience. The fragrance, color, serving temperature, consistency, and taste have a considerable effect on stimulating the appetite. Many foodservice operations are famous for their soups and appetizers. Soups can be served either at piping hot or refreshingly cold temperatures.

However, slight variations in temperature may prove to have an adverse effect on the quality of a soup. Thus, although it is not hard to prepare soup, this menu item requires extremely well-balanced spices, good cooking judgment, and careful handling. It is not surprising, therefore, that most foodservice operations have their own way of preparing soups. Soups are made from basic stocks that can be prepared in numerous ways.

In many foodservices, a stock pot is left on the range in which the ingredients continuously simmer to produce stock for soups. Thus a stock is a strained and concentrated extract derived by simmering bones, meats, fish, poultry, vegetables, and seasonings in a large quantity of water.

Slow cooking extracts the flavors as well as gelatinous substances to produce a rich, flavorful base. Several flavor variations can be made by changing the ingredients in the stock. However, proper ingredients, adequate preparation, and care are necessary in order to produce a good stock for a uniform quality soup. Normally, bones and pieces of meat left over from other items are used in stocks. With the portion-controlled meat purchasing, it is getting difficult to get all ingredients needed for stock and, therefore, there is an increase in the use of commercially prepared soup bases. There are several types of bases that are available for use in different products.

Vegetable coockery

In cooking vegetables and fruits, special care and attention are needed in order to preserve their color, texture, flavor, and nutrients. The acidity or alkalinity of the liquid in which they are cooked also has an effect on their organoleptic properties. There are also special varieties of vegetables and that are more suitable than others for cooking purposes.

Most vegetables and fruits contain organic acids which add to the acidity of the media in which they are cooked. The color is affected by the pH of the media. Thus, the green color in fruits and vegetables is due to the presence of the green pigment, chlorophyll, which changes color in an acid medium to a dull or olive green.

On the other hand, an alkaline cooking medium may intensify the green color. The presence of slight alkalinity may be desirable to enrich the color, a phenomenon that is observed on blanching of vegetables. However, an alkaline cooking medium may have an undesirable effect on the texture of the vegetables as well as a destructive effect on such vitamins as thiamin and ascorbic acid. The cooking times for vegetables and fruits are also important. In order to retain their natural nutrients, vegetables should be cooked for the minimum time possible.

The red color of vegetables and fruits is commonly due to the presence of the pigment anthocyanin. This pigment is also affected by the pH of the cooking medium. Anthocyanins become bluish-red in acid media and blue-green in alkaline media. Both these colors are undesirable. Thus, care is needed when cooking red cabbage, beets, or similar vegetables. The yellow color of the fruits and vegetables is due to the presence of carotenoid pigments. Corn, carrots, and sweet potatoes contain carotenoids, which are also precursors of vitamin

A. These pigments are fairly stable and are not normally affected by the presence of acid or alkali. The flavonoid pigments provide color to white cabbage, onions, and potatoes. They are not affected by the acid medium but generally turn yellow in the presence of alkaline medium. Care should, therefore, be taken in cooking all vegetables and fruits to reserve their organoleptic and nutritive properties.

Steaming

This is the most common, as well as the most desirable, method for cooking most fruits and vegetables. The texture, color, flavor, and nutrients of fruits and vegetables are better preserved when they are steamed. Steam-jacketed kettles or steamers may be used for quick steaming. Perforated pans that allow the steam to circulate around the food product are desirable for use in steaming.

Boiling

This method is based on cooking of fruits and vegetables in water. The main disadvantage of boiling is a loss of nutrients, particularly if the water left after cooking is not used. Care should be taken to see that these foods are boiled in the minimum amount of water as well as at low temperatures. High boiling temperatures may break up the product. Fruits and vegetables may be dipped in hot water in a steam-jacketed kettle attached with the necessary strainers. Recipes used for boiling fruits may require that the fruits be dipped into syrup or sugar containing water.

Baking

The potato is the most common item among fruits and vegetables to be baked foodservice operations. Other foods may also be baked with equal success. Other commonly baked products include apples, tomatoes, green peppers, onions, eggplant, and squash. The foods most suitable for baking are those that have sufficient moisture in them. Upon heating, this moisture helps to soften the cellulose they contain. Baking may also produce a desirable crust on the outside due to the carmelization of sugars. Baking temperatures vary and may range from 350^0 to 450^0F (177^0 to 232^0C), and will depend upon the type of product.

Sautéing and braising

Vegetables are often cooked by sautéing, as for example, breakfast potatoes. Celery, onions, cabbage, and lettuce are often braised. For braising, the vegetables are sautéed in a small amount of fat and then quick-stirred. Vegetables can also be cooked with thickening agents or sauces until tender.

Broiling

Broiling is not the most common method of cooking fruits and vegetables, since a lot of moisture is lost at high temperatures and the vegetables become charred. Only very tender and moist products broil easily. Bell peppers, tomatoes, and onions are the vegetables most commonly broiled.

Frying

Vegetables can be deep fried or stir fried. Deep frying provides a crisp, desirable texture, as evidenced in french fries. It also results in the caramelization of sugar to provide a desirable crust. Vegetable strips may also be dipped in batters before frying. Many vegetables may be parboiled before deep frying.

Ceral-product coockery

Most cereal products are cooked by steaming or boiling which results in the gelatinization of starch. Rice can be cooked in a steamer with twice the volume of water. Salt, water, and a little oil may also be added. Macaroni products or pasta are dropped into boiling water and stirred until they are soft and tender.

Bakery product and dessert preparation

These products are very important in any type of foodservice operation. Only the main principles involved in the preparation of bakery products and desserts will be discussed. The principal ingredients used in baking include the following:

Flour

Although many types of flour are used in baking, wheat flour either alone or in different blends is the usual choice. The protein in the flour responsible for the baked flavor is "gluten," which absorbs moisture and forms an elastic, strong and spongy mass-the batter or dough. Gluten has the unique property of stretching to a considerable degree, which is facilitated by the process of kneading. The network of gluten bands that is formed by stretching becomes firm on baking. Gluten may be developed to form strong or weak bands. Bread, or hard-wheat, flour forms strong structures, whereas pastry, or soft-wheat, flour forms delicate structures.

Shortening

One of the main requirements of baking is to prevent the sticking of gluten particles, thereby producing the desired tenderness. Hydrogenated fats, oils, butter, and lard are used as shortening in baking.

Sugar

In addition to sweetening the product, sugars also help in tenderizing foods. Different types of sugars are used in baking. Fine sugars are used in making cakes and desserts with a smooth texture, while coarse sugar is used for coating such products as doughnuts or candies.

Leavening agents

These are used to provide texture and volume to baked products. Leavening agents must be added carefully and in the exact proportions for desired results. Air is also incorporated into a product when eggs are whipped to a foam. Air leavens a batter and when heated Swells, causing the products to rise and develop a fine, texture. Steam is also used as an automatic leavening agent for many bakery products.

For some products a chemical leavening agent, such as baking powder, is added. Chemical leavening agents give off carbon dioxide, which is responsible for the leavening action. Heat also contributes to the leavening action. Cream of tartar is used with soda to form a single-acting baking powder. Several types of baking powder are currently available on the market.

Yeast

Yeast is used for creating carbon dioxide gas and alcohol in some of the yeast baked products. Yeast growth is at an optimum level at 78^0 to 90^0F (25.5^0 to 32^0C). Yeast is killed at about 140^0F (60^0C). Yeast is added to water before being stirred with other ingredients.

Eggs

These are used in many bakery products and desserts to enhance the baking qualities as well as to provide flavor, color, volume, tenderness, and nutritional value. Eggs also act as a binding ingredient in batters and doughs. Depending on the type of baked product-yeast bread, muffins, or breads-these ingredients are mixed and blended well using large blenders and mixers. Yeast doughs are allowed to ferment. Kneading and mixing of the dough are done by mechanical mixers. The final conditioning of the bread before baking is called "proofing." This procedure results in a soft, delicate product of increased volume. After proofing, the products are baked at temperatures ranging from 375^0 to 450^{0}F (190^0 to 232^{0}C). For some bakery products, immediate cooling is required. Custards are baked desserts prepared from liquids that are thickened with eggs. Soufflés are lightly baked desserts thickened and leavened by eggs. Meringues are made using egg whites and sugar in the presence of cream of tartar; they are often used for topping pies and desserts. Pies and pastries are baked from various kinds of flour, shortening, salt, and water. The amount of fat, the blending procedure, and the incorporation of shortening into flour result in the formation of a flaky crust.

Salads

Salads can be defined as dishes composed of fruits, vegetables, eggs, and meat and usually topped with salad dressings and/or garnishes, often served cold and placed on an underliner. Salads may thus consist of a base, body, garnishes, and dressings. A base, also referred to as underlining garnish, usually consists of salad -greens and is used to improve the appearance of the salad and to prevent it from having a bare look. Also, the base provides for a very good contrast in color. For example, a green base under a red tomato aspic salad provides a nice contrast. Bases are seldom consumed.

The ingredients that make up the salad such as lettuce, raw vegetables, fruits, gelatins, and eggs are referred to as the body of the salad. Garnishes are mainly added for eye appeal and are composed of a variety of items such as nuts, croutons, meats, fish, cheese, fruits, vegetables, parsley, and other condiments. Dressings may be of different colors and textures. They are primarily added for flavor and to help keep the salad fresh, crisp, and juicy. There are different types of salad dressings; some of the most popular are Thousand Island, French, and Russian.

Recent trends in foodservices are toward more salad use, possibly because salads are becoming popular in nutrition-conscious segments of the population. From the foodservice point of view, salads pose certain problems:

1. Maintaining quality is difficult, since most salads need fresh vegetables.
2. Purchasing salad ingredients needs more than the usual attention, since varietal characteristics and grading changes have to be considered.
3. Salads are labor intensive to prepare, since there are several items, most of which require washing, coring, and cutting. Also, some require careful arrangement on serving plates, which may require even more skill and labor.
4. Salads are difficult to keep for extended periods of time without sacrificing quality.
5. Salads with certain ingredients-eggs, for example pose a safety problem.
6. Salads composed of fresh fruits and vegetables are relatively expensive. Their ingredients may have fluctuating prices.

The advantages of salads are that

1. They are relatively easy to make.
2. They can prove to be cost efficient if properly planned.
3. They can be made at the last minute or placed on salad bars.
4. They provide more flexibility in the use of ingredients.
5. They improve the appearance of other menu items by providing different colors.

6. They add different textures to foods.
7. They contribute to the nutrient value of meals.

Types of salads

The primary types of salads, based upon their use on the menu, are described below.

Appetizer salads

These salads, as their name indicates are served before meals to stimulate the appetite for the main meal. Therefore, they are served in smaller quantities and are often chilled. The dressings and other ingredients are carefully selected so as to whet the appetite. These salads are often premade tossed, chilled, and/or arranged salads. An example of an appetizer salad would be the shrimp cocktail salad served in many restaurants and on special occasions. Sometimes small quantities of tossed salads are used as appetizer salads.

Side-dish salads

These salads are also known as accompaniment salads and may be served as a part of the meal to supplement another main-dish item, normally meats. They should be carefully selected to supplement the flavor, texture, form, color, and overall appearance of the main dish. A contrast in temperature is highly desirable in accompaniment salads. These salads are served in larger portions than the appetizer salad but smaller than the main-dish salads. Normally, vegetables, fruits, and cottage cheese are used for these salads. Accompaniment salads should be less filling than the main dish. Thus, as a general rule, a heavy meal should be accompanied by a light salad and conversely. Such meat items as beef and chicken with gravy should be accompanied by light salads. On the other hand, potato, macaroni, and bean salads, should accompany light items.

Main-dish salads

These salads are designed as the main item of the meal and are served in larger quantities; they are also suitable for lunchtime service. Since this type of salad is the main entrée item on the menu, it needs careful planning. The nutritive value, as well as cost of the salad, should also be considered before placing it on the menu. Meats and fish make good additions to these salads, which can also be served for dinner.

Chef salads, which are sold as specialty items of a foodservice, contain special ingredients or dressings. Sardines, roast beef, and cooked chicken may be added to make these salads hearty. Type A salads are made with ingredients that meet the minimum nutrition requirements of Type A school lunches. Unique items and their combinations, such as pineapple, avocados, raisins, dates, tuna fish, crabmeat, olives, and mint add to the popularity and appeal of these salads. Their arrangement in attractive serving plates also adds to the attraction of these salads.

For example, a glass bowl with julienne strips of carrot, cheese, and meats evenly spread on tossed salad with sardines, olives, boiled eggs, and cherries makes a very attractive main-dish salad. Dressings are important in providing flavor to these salads. Various types of dressings should be available for enhancing flavor to the salads. Such cooked items as beans, rice, macaroni, and potatoes, can be used in these salads.

Salad-bar salads

These salads are prepared by the consumers based on the ingredients offered. There are numerous types of vegetables and fruits that can be used in salad bars. Normally lettuce and other greens are cut and placed as the body of the salad. Various types of salad dressings are available for the consumers to select. Garnishes are also provided. Salad-bar selections can Include onions, tomatoes, olives, croutons, nuts, seeds, meats, fish, eggs, pickles, garbanzo beans, and dried meats. Customers enjoy the freedom of choice in designing their own salads, which contributes to their popularity. There is a growing demand for salad bars, which are popular in restaurants as well-as some franchise chains. Cold plates and serving utensils are provided for each salad item.

Dessert salads

Salads can also be used as desserts, and as such they may range in sweetness and caloric content. Light gelatin salads with molded fruits In them are often preferred for their low-caloric content, particularly when heavy items are included as entrées. Fruit salads and mixes are also used; sometimes fresh fruits are used In these salads. Toppings normally Include cream, cherries, nuts, or other fruits. Dessert salads may also be used as snacks. Sweet garnishings or dressings go well with these salads. Syrups or caramelized liquid sugars can be mixed with the fruits used in dessert salads.

Salad green

Salad greens are used as the, base in most salads, as well as underliners. The technological advancements made in vacuum cooking, dehydrofreezing, rapid transportation, growing methods, and new varieties have made it possible to use most types of salad greens. Texture, color, as well as flavor, are provided by salad greens. Their freshness is essential to provide the overall characteristics of salads.

It is essential to prevent excessive moisture loss from salad greens in order to keep them from drying. Wet cloth or paper is often used to keep the prepared salad greens moist. Although lettuce is the most commonly used salad green, there are a number of other greens available as described below.

Iceberg lettuce

Also called head lettuce, this is the most often used lettuce in salads. It has a round, firm head with tightly packed bright-green to very pale leaves, which are curly and overlap slightly. It makes a crisp and chunky salad item shredded, cubed, sliced, or quartered. Its juiciness and sweetness adds to the flavor of a salad. It is often used as a base ingredient in mixed salads or salad bars.

Also, variety can be introduced by serving it In different shape's In addition to tearing leaves into bite-sized pieces. It call be used as lettuce cups, since leaves when gently separated from the head make versatile cups or underliners for salads.

Lettuce wedges can be used with special dressings, such as Thousand Island or parslied vinaigrette dressing. It can also be cut up into then slices or rafts and used as the base for salads or oil sandwiches. Chunks or shredded lettuce may be used in tossed salads or other types of salads.

Romaine

This type of lettuce, also known as cos lettuce, has large, elongated, firm, upright leaves, which are arranged in a cylindrical head. The leaves, which have a distinctive nutty flavor that is sharper than iceberg lettuce, are crispy, succulent, and slightly pungent. It combines well with other vegetables such as tomatoes and avocados, and the flavor is enhanced by special dressings.

Bibb lettuce

Bibb lettuce has deep, rich, green and yellow leaves that are soft and velvety. The leaves are arranged like small rosettes which are whitish green toward the core. It has a distinct delicate, buttery flavor and contributes a sweet, tender, and chewy texture to any salad made with it.

Leaf lettuce

This lettuce has leaves loosely branching off from its stalk. There are numerous varieties, each of which has a different color and leaf shape. The leaves, which are clustered or pressed together, do not form heads. Large, leafy bunches have flat or curly leaves that are very fragile and tender. Leaf lettuce provides a delicate sweet flavor and crisp texture in tossed salads as well as in undergarnishes for molded or cooked salads.

Big boston lettuce

This type of lettuce has a round soft head with medium-sized light-green outer leaves and light-yellow inner leaves. The leaves are tender and velvety. It is very perishable and is not as sweet and tender as other butterhead varieties.

Curly endive

This lettuce has a crown of narrow ragged-edge leaves that curl at the ends and have large ribs. Its outer leaves are darkish green in color and are bitter compared to the inner leaves, which are sharp and tangy. The head is yellowish white with a milder taste compared to its outer leaves. It has a slight prickly texture and bitter flavor, which blends very well with some of the more bland salad greens.

Escarole

This is a variety of endive with broader leaves that do not curl at the tips. The leaves are deep green at the edges and pale yellow at the heart.

Spinach

Spinach, with its tender, round, and crisp leaves, contributes a specific taste to salads. Its deep-green leaves provide an attractive color contrast. It can be used alone or in tossed salads, where it blends well with a wide variety of dressings.

Watercress

This is a small, dark-green plant with long stems and thick round leaves that have a pungent flavor. The flavor is very distinctive and peppery. It can be used in tossed salads or as an undergarnish.

Other greens

Mustard, kale, dandelion, collard, and turnip greens can also be used in salads. Some of the vegetables and fruits that can be added to salads are given in the following lists.

Vegetables

Alfalfa sprouts	Garlic
Artichokes	Mushrooms
Asparagus	Olives
Bean sprouts	Onions
Beans, green	Parsley
Beans, lima	Parsnips
Beets	Peas
Broccoli	Peppers
Brussels sprouts	Potatoes
Cabbage	Radishes
Carrots	Shallots
Cauliflower	Squash
Celery	Sunflower seeds
Corn	Tomatoes
Cucumbers	Turnips
Garbanzo beans	Water chestnuts

Fruits

Apples	Kumquats	Persimmons
Apricots	Lemons	Pineapples
Avocados	Limes	Prunes
Bananas	Melons, cantaloupe	Pomegranates
Cherries	Melons, honeydew	Raisins
Cranberries	Nectarines	Raspberries
Dates	Nuts	Strawberries
Figs	Oranges	Tangerines
Grapefruit	Peaches	Watermelon
Grapes.	Pears	

Basic principles of salad preparation

Although most salads should be assembled as close to serving time as possible, salad greens can be prepared several hours ahead. The quality of the salad greens can be lost very quickly, since they are highly perishable items. Exposure to air, water, heat, and improper handling can cause them to deteriorate. Even heat from human hands has an adverse effect on their quality. Also, the acidity of certain fruits added as garnish may have undesirable effects.

Stainless steel equipment is needed for cutting, storing, and handling of salads. Also, strong vegetables—onions, for example—should be kept and handled separately in order to prevent the intermingling of odors. Salad preparation requires a lot of creativity, since contrasts in color, texture, form, and flavor are needed. In addition, salads can be made by using a number of ingredients that provide for the creation of a unique salad specialty or an original food creation. A combination of eye appeal, arrangement, flavor, texture, consistency, dressings, and variety can provide attractive salad dishes. Many types of salads can be included on a menu and can be served In several ways-as appetizers, main dishes, desserts, or meal accompaniments. Leftover vegetable salads can be reused in soups and/or vegetables. Such fruits as apples, bananas and peaches when used as garnishes darken on exposure to air due to oxidation. Care should therefore be taken to see that they are pared as close to serving time as possible and that they are dipped in a slightly acidic solution, such as lemon juice, to avoid discoloration.

Care should be taken that salads are prepared away from the heated areas in the kitchen, since the heat may cause the wilting of fragile leaves. All serving equipment should be property cleaned, since traces of dressings and oils impart a rancid odor on deterioration. Once the salads are prepared, they should either be refrigerated or kept moist in order to preserve their crispness. Salad dressings should be added as close to serving time as possible, since dressing may result in wilting of the lettuce. Also, the dressing may break and look unattractive placed either too heavily or too soon in advance of serving time.

Call should be taken in handling salads containing highly perishable items, particularly when cooked and raw ingredients are in contact with each other, as in the case of tuna salad, egg salad, potato salad, and roast beef salad. All wilted, discolored, or spoiled leaves should be removed prior to cutting the salad greens. In most varieties, coring can be done by cutting around the core edge with a paring knife. It is preferable to rinse greens in cold running water that has a temperature between 40^0 and 70^0F (4.5^0 and 21^0C). Leaves should be thoroughly washed to remove any dirt or other particles. Where heads are to be used intact, water should be allowed to run gently into the core and all leaves washed thoroughly with running water. After washing, the greens should be placed on a colander for water drainage.

Commercially available antioxidants may be used by dissolving the specified quantity in water to preserve the crispness and to enhance the appearance. It is advisable not to leave the greens in water for an extended period of time in order to preserve their nutrient quality. Excessive moisture also speeds up the spoilage process.

Salad arrangement

The arrangement of salad plays art important role in its alit-activeness. Art ample amount of greens with good height is very appealing. Large chunks or pieces of lettuce will help in increasing the height and the size of a salad. Garnishes and seasonings add to the attractiveness of the salad, while the color of the dressing adds to then-richness. The arrangement should be such that the main ingredients or principal contents of the salads are not masked. It should also be remembered that the crispness of a salad is lost if salad greens are cut into very small pieces. Herbs and spices may be added to enrich the flavor of the salads.

Attractive garnishes can be made front certain raw vegetables. Some of these are radish roses, green pepper rings, carrot curls, cucumber slices, mini corns, mini sprigs, and parsley toppings. These garnishes, which are simple to make after a certain amount of practice can be preprepared and stored. Other garnishes can be obtained from such leftovers as croutons, toasted slivered almonds, colored coconut, sliced hard-boiled eggs, and sliced pieces of pomegranate. Thus, a contrast in color and flavor can be easily provided by selecting creatively from numerous foods and ingredients which can be used in making salads.

Gelatin salads

Many attractive dessert salads are made by using a gelatin base. Gelatin, which is a tasteless and odorless protein, is usually extracted from bones, hides, skins, connective tissues, and other cartilagenous substances. It acts as a thickener for cold liquids and is practically unaffected by the acids or alkalis used in foods.

It should be noted that because of certain enzymes in raw pineapple, figs, and papaya, these fruits cannot be used in the raw state in gelatin salads. These enzymes do not allow the gelatin to gel since they break down the proteinaceous gelatin structure.

Although it is very easy to form gels with gelatin, it requires careful control of the tittle, temperature, and ingredients. The addition of sugars and milk increases the firmness of gels, whereas the addition of acids or certain solids weakens the gel structure. Large quantities of expensive materials can often be lost if gels are not formed because of careless preparation.

There are various types of flavored and unflavored gelatins available on the market. In general, plain gelatins must be hydrated or softened in cold water before they are added to hot liquids. Gelatins must be properly softened and dissolved to assure a uniform gel structure. This is a very crucial step where many new workers or students will need a lot of practice in order to reduce the chances of failure.

Gelatin structures once formed are tough enough to resist breakage in normal blending operations. In hot weather, it may be desirable to increase the proportion of gelatin in salads. When gelatin is completely dissolved in the final liquid, it should be chilled carefully. The gelatin should be cooked to a consistency similar to that of a heavy syrup and then used for addition of fruits or for other decorative purposes. It should be syrupy enough to hold any suspended fruits or ingredients.

Decorative gelatin molds can be made by pouring syrupy gelatin over prearranged foods on the bottom of the mold. Several layers can be formed in this manner. Interesting salads may be made by creatively using various types of mold to provide interesting shapes and layered ingredients.

Endless combinations of gelatins and other foods can be made to produce interesting salads. A multidimensional effect can be produced by using "swimmers" and "sinkers." Sinkers include such items as oranges, canned fruits, and grapes. Swimmers include fresh fruits, bananas, and nuts. Gelatins can also be made into cubes, flakes, foams, multilayers, aspics, mousses, creams, charlottes, and chiffons, etc.

Gelatin salads once prepared should be allowed to set for approximately 24 hr for best results. The firmness in the structure develops upon chilled storage. It should be noted that the use of larger quantities of gelatin than required may result in tough gels. Also, the thicker the gel, the more easily it will break.

Molded gels should be carefully removed from their containers. Once well set, they can be readily removed by immersing the mold in hot water for a short time and inverting it. Hot, wet towels may be used instead of immersion in hot water. Gelatin foods should be refrigerated. Care should be taken for salads in which such perishable items as eggs or fish are used. Freezing of the salads will result in a breakdown of the gelatin structure. Gelatin salads should be served as soon as possible. Gelatin salads therefore provide versatility, attractiveness, and the opportunity for creative food design. In some restaurants, huge gelatin salads are used for decorative purposes or as centerpieces on buffet tables.

Salad dressings

Salad dressings are sauces that are specially blended to provide flavorful combinations to complement and season foods to which they are added. They enhance the flavor as well as improve the overall appearance of salads. Most salad dressings are emulsions, primarily of oil and vinegar which are made by combining two Immiscible liquids, with the aid of an emulsifying agent. For example, in mayonnaise, eggs act as an emulsifying agent by coating the fat droplets and making them immiscible to form an emulsion of the oil and vinegar. The preparation of salad dressings requires careful and slow blending of the immiscible liquids. Emulsions can be temporary or permanent. Temporary emulsions break down after a certain amount of time.

Vinegars in emulsions can be replaced by other acid ingredients, such as lemon or fruit Juices. Bland oils-corn oil, cottonseed oil, safflower oil, and soybean oil, for example-are used to make dressings. In order to retard rancidity, antioxidants (BHA, butylated hydroxyanisole; BHT, butylated hydroxytoluene; and EDTA, ethylenediaminetetra-acetic acid) are added. Although there are several types of dressings, most of them can be classified oil the basis of their method of preparation. The four basic types of dressings are described below.

French dressing

These dressings are temporary or unstable emulsions made of fixed proportion of oil and acid, blended together with different types of seasonings such as paprika, mustard, garlic, sugar, and salt. Salt and seasonings when blended from a temporary emulsion with oil and water. Upon storage the emulsions break down but can be easily reformed by blending. The taste of these dressings varies depending on the proportion of oil and acidic ingredients. Several seasonings can be added to provide special flavors.

Mayonnaise

Mayonnaise is the base for a number of dressings and sauces such as Thousand Island dressing, Russian dressing, and tartar sauce. It is prepared by blending oil, water, egg yolks and/or whole eggs. Mayonnaise forms a permanent emulsion that does not break down easily. Egg acts as an emulsifier and helps in the formation of stable emulsions. Sometimes, gelatin or cooked starch is also used as an emulsifying agent, although these are not as effective as eggs. Mayonnaise is not easy to prepare, since proper methods, ingredients, and practice are needed to make a good dressing.

Cooked, or boiled, dressings

These dressings are oil-vinegar emulsions that contain much less oil and that are thickened by starch and egg yolk. A starch paste-made from flour, cornstarch, or other thickeners-is added as a thickening agent to these dressings. Since these thickeners have a tendency to become lumpy, care should be taken to see that they do not coagulate or get scorched while cooking.

Cream dressings

These are dressings to which sour cream, cream cheese, or whipped sweet cream are added. They can then be seasoned with vinegar and other ingredients. Several variations are made possible by adding different types of spices and condiments.

5

The Marketing Environment

Every business has a purpose. Sure, its main purpose is profit, but that is like saying that the purpose of life is survival. A business has to provide a benefit to customers which is seen by them as a perceptible reason for its existence. There has to be a mission for the business which is not its existence and which is not merely oriented to profit.

A mission describes how the business will achieve a profitable outcome. It has to nominate its purpose for being and stipulate the benefits it intends to provide to its customers and staff and, in the broadest sense these days, the contributions it intends to make to the greater good of society.

Before corporate goals are finalized and marketing planning can commence, management has to make a careful scrutiny of the market environment before deciding in which areas of the market it intends the business will operate. There may be many options, but not all options will be viable.

Some markets may be overcrowded, others too difficult to be worthwhile. In addition, management has to assess the financial and human resources at its disposal. It should not attempt to compete in a market against competitors who can out-gun the establishment with money, size and superior experience.

The corporate goals and the corporate philosophies give an operation its purpose, style, image and policies, and they need to be written down in the form of a mission statement.

A mission statement isn't something which gets stuffed in a drawer and forgotten about. It should be a living document which is meant to keep the business on track. It is usually easier for a licensed club to prepare a mission statement because in most cases the club is created mainly for the benefits of its members or the needs of a local community, and such needs are known at the time of inception. For example, the mission statement for a golf club which is in a provincial town may read like this:

> Our aim is to provide membership to the local community which will enhance its quality of life. Such membership will give access to a challenging course. Furthermore, members will have exclusive club rooms providing a choice of either relaxing in a quiet, convivial lounge equipped with satellite TV, or the use of a fully stocked bar and accompanying restaurant. It is also the aim of the club to provide accommodation for a limited number of members' guests or honoured visitors who will be invited at the behest of the Club's board of management.

The message conveyed by this mission statement example provides little doubt about its intentions, and one gets the picture of an ageing membership with very settled, traditional views of life.

The business decisions required in the formulation of the mission statement, or the re-formulation when conditions change, depend on the environmental factors of the market in which it operates. The areas of specialization or emphasis will depend on the needs of the market to be targeted and the knowledge and experience of the operators to satisfy those needs adequately.

The aim of large hotels, for example, is to produce a quality guest experience. A hotel is a product in itself but which has many diversified sub-products forming a product mix. Its products may include accommodation, bars, off-sales, restaurant, laundry and, in many cases, a variety of recreational facilities such as leisure club, golf course, tennis courts, equestrian centre and more. Which of these products should be offered to customers and in what form? Whatever management decides, the reputation or image of the hotel will impact on all its products. A small hotel has to fit as a whole entity into the physical and social ambience of a city or local community. A large four or five-star hotel has to meet the needs of a much larger clientele—domestic and international business people and tourists as well as the local market—but it still has to fit in with the environment of the region.

All of these considerations should be incorporated into a 'mission statement' so that there can be no doubt about what type of operation it is in the minds of its customers, its suppliers, its employees and every other individual or company associated with it in some way. Here is a case situation where an establishment did not make it clear what it was.

The point of the case situation is that the hotel wasn't making its 'residential only' feature obvious from the beginning. The benefit being offered was a good night's sleep in a quiet, undisturbed atmosphere. It is arguable whether an alcohol-free policy could guarantee peace and quiet; however, the hotel was offering a marketable difference from the high-profile places in the same market. The mission statement for an establishment like the example may read like this:

> Our aim is to provide an alcohol-free environment for guests so that there is an alternative for those

> people who prefer to abstain. Around 30 per cent of people seldom or never drink alcohol, and it is our intention to cater for their needs. This should give our establishment a unique advantage and a strong competitive position, surrounded as we are by many licensed hotels with few differences between them other than price and standards of accommodation and service. It is also our aim to be residential only, which will limit costs involved, as opposed to a multi-outlet style of operation. This again will benefit our non-drinking guests by offering them low-cost accommodation.

The hotel's problem is that it has not communicated this mission to its market, resulting in customer confusion, unrealistic expectations in guests and probably missed opportunities.

Environmental factors

Environmental factors are either internal (controllable) or external (uncontrollable). The external, uncontrollable factors (also called macro-environmental factors) are market demographics, economics, competition, changing social needs and lifestyle values, new technology and governmental and legal forces.

The internal, controllable factors (also called micro-environment factors) are the financial capabilities of the establishment, its human resources, its location, its suppliers, its agents or distributors, and its knowledge and ability to produce a product which matches the requirements of the market and an image or position in the market which is competitive.

It can be argued that location is 'uncontrollable' in that moving a property is not possible. However, the choice of location was controllable at the time of inception, and in any case the business can be relocated separately from the building. For example, a fast food outlet located in a business park which is about to close can successfully relocate the business in a building in the heart of the city. Each of the environmental factors is subject to change, and clever management has to be alert to both short-term and long-term changes and make adjustments to the product mix and allocation of human and financial resources to cater for the change. Adjustments to social change, for instance, have become necessary on several occasions in recent years.

The preference for more casual dining, for example, has caused many hotels to change their restaurants to become less formal. The strong interest in health and fitness has led numerous hotels to add leisure centres to the range of sub-products. Growing awareness of the consequences of cigarette smoking has led to the growth in demand for non-smoking areas in restaurants.

A hospitality establishment has to be mindful of its total customer potential and the degree of competition it will meet when attracting custom. A hotel cannot position itself to appeal to everyone. It must decide which segment of the market it intends to try and capture, which requirements of that segment of the market it intends to satisfy and whether it has the resources to do it. The large hotel groups set out to dominate a market with a tried and proven formula which has worked in most other markets.

Demography is the statistical study of human population and distribution. Every hospitality establishment needs to consider its customer potential in terms of numbers, age, gender and income and whether it will draw its custom from local, regional, national or international sources.

For example, a theme restaurant which offers Scottish regional food would have limited potential for success in Glasgow where there are already several competitors offering the same type of fare. There would not be the population numbers to justify another restaurant of the same type. Its only hope would be to invest considerable time and effort into taking the available business away from the existing players. That would be expensive, and its success doubtful for many reasons.

Similarly, there is always a restaurateur who fondly believes that there is room for a really good restaurant which is the pinnacle of gourmet food and immaculate service. In a depressed economy and in an area which is mostly populated by middle to low income earners there are seldom the numbers to justify such a conclusion. There are more financial casualties at the top end of the restaurant market than there are at the far larger lower end where price and value are the major considerations.

In a small town, the community's needs for entertainment, celebrations, dining and various meetings will usually revolve around the local hotel if it is marketed properly. The environment dictates the type of operation management needs to run. A city establishment has a far greater market potential, certainly more diverse, but it has to decide which of the many social and lifestyle markets to target.

Lifestyles change with each generation or every decade. When the children of the 'baby-boomers' of the post-Second World War era grew up and started spending, they had a quite different set of values and sought more conservative experiences than their parents who were 'raised in a bubble of affluence'. They were far more individualistic, avoided the aspirational cultures of their parents and had little style with which marketers could accurately identify.

As it is usually lifestyle and aspirational values which direct much of the marketing effort, the post-war generation posed a problem for the marketers since they were not motivated by former lifestyle values. The result for hospitality marketing has been a splintered market environment requiring careful observation and research.

People's views of the world and the society in which they find themselves are conditioned by the country of their origin and the society which shaped their beliefs and values.

Knowing this, many of the large and successful Asian hotels, for example, have developed their facilities to meet the demands of the Western cultures while still retaining some of the charm and mystery of their own environments. Although hotels are anxious to obtain their business, sometimes less consideration is waiting for Asians visiting establishments in Europe.

The hospitality industry is one which has to be multi-cultural in everything that it does. When preparing their menus, for example, food and beverage managers are affected in their choice of dishes by a wide variety of food and beverage preferences. In its accommodation arrangements managers have to be tolerant of racial differences.

As a consequence, there is a sameness about hotels wherever one travels in the world. A traveller drugged and dropped into a hotel in most large cities wouldn't have a clue where he or she was for quite some time! However, this devolution of the hotel industry now offers opportunities for specialization in the products on offer and thereby attracting specific markets to certain establishments.

When one is in business, one cannot operate in a self-controlled vacuum. As well as appealing to customers there are other groups in the environment to be considered, which can be termed 'publics'. A public is a group of people or organizations which can impact on the business's ability to achieve its objectives. There is the financial public, the banks, insurance companies, credit-checking companies, credit-card services and so on, all of whom can affect the financial standing of one's establishment. There is the media public, and in its many forms the media can singularly influence the public for or against an establishment. There is the public of 'concerned citizens', which are action groups of consumers or single issue political bodies which set themselves up as community 'watch-dogs' and concern themselves with physical and social issues.

Consumerism has been a strong influence on all business in the past twenty years. It has grown in strength to the point where most governments will bow to the pressures of consumer groups, or at least drastically modify their legislation in consideration of their ability to affect voting intentions.

For instance, consumer pressure has led to the hospitality industry being forced to go 'green' by the EC packaging directive which demands more recycling and less waste. There is the industry public, comprising associations and government agencies which are meant to monitor the industry and cause changes or controls supposedly for the benefit of industry members. Most of these publics are handled by various specialists for the larger hotel groups, but for smaller hospitality establishments the job usually falls onto the owners' shoulders. The publics in any environment should never be ignored as they have a habit of impinging on the industry's operations both generally and singly, often for its benefit, but more often to its detriment.

In times of recession, people seek greater value from their expenditure. The numbers travelling and wanting accommodation fall. The size of an operation affects the economies of scale necessary to meet boom, recession and recovery times, and needs to be understood in advance of their happening.

Different markets are often sought under different economic conditions. There are also those who remain committed to delivering the 'top of the range' style of service for those guests who are less affected by economic change. Often it is more hazardous to plan for an improvement in the economic environment.

Governments cause much change in the business environment by altering interest rates, braking or boosting economies through fiscal and monetary measures. The increased indirect taxation by the Major government 1994-95 has led to fragile consumer confidence and reduced discretionary income. In such situations, it is the luxury items, such as eating out and weekend breaks, that are the first to be abstained from.

Local councils, environmental health departments, public works departments, licensing boards, fire departments, regional and national tourist boards, conservation bodies—the list of bureaucracies keeps on growing—are a formidable obstacle for planning in anticipation of stable conditions for growth. Apart from lobbying various levels of government, individual establishments have little control over their economic and political environments, and most establishments have to ride the changing circumstances.

Ecological influences

The impact of human interference on the planet's physical resources is now a major issue in most people's minds. There is growing concern that we might be destroying the Earth's atmosphere, its oceans and much of the natural environment through a whole range of artificial pollutants. Governments are taking heed, and before developments can occur in most Western countries an 'environmental impact statement' is required.

Ecological concern is restricting mining and building projects. It is seldom possible to embark on large tourist developments, for example, without encountering a series of controls and the protests of 'environmentally conscious' groups. Even small businesses have to be concerned with matters like waste disposal and environmental despoliation.

The way we do business has changed rapidly in the past thirty years as a result of new technology, mostly in the area of electronics. Far more is yet to come, and foremost among these will be computer technology, information transfer and video conferencing.

Alvin Toffler's forecasts in his book, *The Third Wave,* concerning the 'electronic cottage', are proving to be imminent. Leading hotels are already catering for the 'new wave' business person with in-house facilities.

Toffler predicted that new computer technology, the modem, videophone, facsimile machine and video conferencing facilities would enable increasing numbers of people to work at home in their 'electronic cottages', significantly reducing the 'dead time' of travel and minimizing the need for large office buildings simply to provide space for people to work.

Ours is already a highly-regulated society, but the spread of new government rules and regulations in all areas continues unabated as people try to create the perfect society through legislation. Health concerns, especially with alcohol, smoking and food, are the ones which directly affect the hospitality industry as governments again endeavour to provide protection through new Acts of Parliament, such as the Food Safety (General Food Hygiene) Regulations 1994.

However, government deregulation can provide market opportunities; for example, 1995 saw the advent of Children's Certificates, which allow children into the bar area of a pub if they are accompanied by an adult. The industry responds to the changes by turning them into customer benefits or by providing facilities which meet their requirements.

People's perceptions of a place are dictated by its location. Even being on the wrong side of a road can change people's perceptions. Is the place going to appeal mainly to business people, tourists, locals, the farming community, domestic and overseas visitors, sports enthusiasts, non-drinkers or families? Whomever the hotel targets, the location must match the market's expectation in physical location, size, presentation and facilities. No-one has a market to themselves, or not for too long. The competitive environment will materially affect the marketing decisions on a continuing basis. The intensity of the competition, and where it is intruding into the hotel's market base, will determine the reaction which may be required to counter it.

Competition can also come from a different quarter when the market environment changes. For instance, in a recession, a large hotel's competition for accommodation can emerge from guest houses, budget lodges and pubs with rooms, when previously its main competition came from hotels similar to itself. Capital and cash flow are vital for survival. The ability to meet the long-term goals of marketing is often under-estimated. For example, there is nothing worse than trying to earn a reputation for a service, a product or a facility when staff, money and supply sources are unreliable. The presentation of the hotel's facilities has to be uniformly impressive, clean, fresh and well maintained.

6

Purchase Motivations

There are huge numbers of people all around the world with the desire and the money to spend on travel, accommodation, entertainment and leisure. They represent a diversity of nations, occupations, incomes and personalities and they have a wide range of reasons for wanting a particular hospitality experience.

For practical purposes, therefore, the total market has to be subdivided into many smaller markets, and by the use of market analysis an establishment can determine which segments best suit one's location, property size and type, expertise and resources. The selection of the most appropriate segments is target marketing, and its purpose is to provide a focus for the whole marketing effort. It is people's preferred lifestyle which determines their behaviour and guides the pattern of their purchases. Not everyone wants to live the same way, and therefore there are lifestyle preferences which can be clustered to form market segments.

Once management knows the thinking of each of these market segments, it is in a position to decide which segments to target, and the strategies that are developed for those segments will be more incisive if management is armed with the reasons for their various behavioural attributes and attitudes. Trying to understand behaviour patterns of a whole market for hospitality has become increasingly difficult in the last five years, and the signs are that it will become more so.

For the hospitality industry only one thing is certain: people will continue to want places to eat, drink and sleep. But how, where and when they will want to do these things is a matter of continuing complexity. It is no longer possible to erect formula hotels on any site in the world and expect them to return dividends on the investment.

Too many investors have burnt their fingers. Kleinwort Benson, in their 1995 annual review of Quoted UK Hotel Companies, estimated that in total there are around 35 000 hotel rooms in the UK, accounting for almost 10 per cent of total hotel room stock, which are obsolete and on the market for sale.

The large chains are substituting many of them with budget lodges, which are being developed predominantly in secondary and tertiary locations. They are among the best performing hotels in the market and are replacing the full feature and limited feature hotels in these locations.

New-built hotels in major and primary locations in the mid and upper levels of the market are a rarity, and likely to remain so, in the short to medium term at least. In London, in particular, there are no material additions to supply planned in the foreseeable future.

The truth of the markets in the 1990s is that the industry needs to provide travellers with the services and the facilities they really need rather than the five-star luxuries they can no longer afford. What has happened? In a nutshell, change is happening at a speed which has made the unthinkable of yesterday the reality of today.

The demographics and lifestyles of most countries are changing quite dramatically. In the UK, for example, the population is increasingly greying, women are having fewer children, and later, there are an increasing number of single-parent homes, higher levels of education achievement and the number of women in employment continues to rise.

This, combined with rising unemployment, recession, the widening gap between the haves and the have-nots, is changing consumer expenditure patterns. We also have changes in attitudes to the ecology of the country which are altering demand for many types of products. Advances in technology are allowing the introduction of new products which are rapidly being accepted by consumers.

Significantly, there seems to be a return by many of the younger generation to adopt core cultural values of fifty or more years ago.

There is a growing disillusionment with current politics and ideologies, less interest by large numbers of the population in extravagant materialism and a cynicism about advertising claims. There is a large gap between the aspirations of people over 40 and the generation under 30. The world is becoming multi-cultural, with most societies having similar attitudes towards the things which comprise a civilized existence.

There is a growing sameness about cities, with the omnipresent Coca Cola and McDonald's signs, for example, emerging in the most surprising places. The development of satellite communications and the intrusiveness of TV have removed many of the mysteries that once surrounded the political, cultural and geographical features of remote areas.

One would have thought that information and education would bring greater understanding between races and nations, but ancient grievances and ethnic intolerance remain. Rather than the world becoming closer, it seems that these differences between races and nations have been exacerbated in some regions.

The removal of the Iron Curtain, and the demise of the political regimes which dominated Eastern Europe and Russia, for example, have created separate states and countries with distinct regional antagonisms which are historical and racial in origin.

In the future there may well be a reversion to a tribal border mentality. The warnings uttered by writers such as Nesbitt, in his book *Megatrends,* and Toffler, in his books, *Future Shock* and *The Third Wave,* cannot be taken lightly as, in the main, they continue to be awesomely accurate.

One of the trends these writers identified is the new computerized information transfer technologies which will create a huge employment pool for homeworkers. The same technology makes it possible for the home to become the main entertainment source.

Shopping can be done from home. Whereas the older generations are not racing towards early adoption of this way of life, the new generations probably will. Already there are ominous signs of them being far less interested in the world around them and possibly a reduced desire to travel. The effects this group will have on travel and tourism have yet to be seen.

These are broad generalizations, of course, but they may explain the slow growth in travel to some countries and the effects it will have for a while on future hospitality demands. Already the styles of eating out being requested are changing and causing the demise of many silver service and fine dining restaurants, as large numbers of people all over the Western world turn to a less formal eating out experience in favour of fast food, brasserie and American diner-style eateries.

Buying influences on behaviour

Before making a purchase, buyers go through a series of decision processes and, in most cases, others are involved in the process. The stages of purchase are the same as those used in selling, and can be remembered by using the acronym A.I.D.A. which stands for:

A. Awareness

I. Interest

D. Desire

A. Action

Before the purchase is finally made there is a nervous period when most, would-be buyers require convincing that they are doing the right thing and they look for reassurance from others. Once their doubts are overcome, they usually proceed to buy. It is interesting to note that there is evidence from work done by several research agencies in the United States which suggests that most advertising is read by purchasers who seek reassurance that they have made the correct decision.

Post-purchase jitters are the reason why after-sales service is so vital. The key to getting customers to come back, or converting a once-only customer into being a regular client, is to concentrate on making sure of satisfaction after the event. This is why every establishment should know the name and address of every customer and maintain regular contact from immediately after the sale and thereafter.

The lenses of distortion

Despite heated denials when the matter is raised, most people buy to please or impress others. Who they are pleasing or impressing may vary. Spouse, parents, boss, close friends and relatives are the most common influencers. Thus the product is perceived by the purchaser through other people's eyes and this distorts what they are seeing, which is why the attributes of many products are overlooked by the buyer.

It explains why some people keep on making the wrong purchases; they are actually being motivated by their desire to impress or please someone else, maybe even a mythical group of peers who exist only in the person's mind. 'Where did you stay?' is a question frequently asked of a returning traveller, followed by 'How was it, any good?' Everyone prefers to give answers that will impress the questioner.

For marketers, just as important as the person actually making the decision are the unseen people who influenced the decision. This is wen known to marketers of weekend breaks, for instance. They market to women because they know that the woman is going to either tell the man what to book, go and book it herself or, certainly in the case of most situations, the man is going to ask the woman's opinion before the books. Who influences the decision where to go for holidays? In the majority of cases it is the wife or girlfriend. When a couple are going out for dinner, who usually gets their way? The family of five is driving along the motorway at lunch-time. Who decides where they will stop to eat? The roles involved in buying motivation are:

— the *initiator,* the one who first suggests or thinks of buying something;

— the *influencer,* the one whose advice or opinion counts most in the decision to buy;

— the *decider,* the one who makes up everybody's mind;

— the *purchaser,* the one who actually makes the purchase;

— the *user or users,* who often have plenty to say about the purchase afterwards.

In hospitality, the person in a group who pays the bill may not be the one you are trying to please, or the one who says whether they are coming back next time. In the corporate scene, the identification of the key people and the roles they play in making a decision is more complicated because there are usually more people involved in both influencing and deliberating over the decision. The secretary phones through the booking, but who was involved in making the choice of establishment? In the case of a new product, a new service, or a product which is new to the prospective customer, there is always hesitancy.

Some people make decisions earlier than others, and they are called early adopters. They are the first to go to a new tourist resort, try out a new bar, or select from the chef's specials. At the opposite end are the laggards, who make sure that everyone else is satisfied before they take the plunge. In between are the early majority and the late majority. The job of a marketer is to identify these processes and assist the purchaser to make an easy decision, remembering that it is word-of-mouth advertising, or simply the 'good word' being passed on by satisfied customers, which is critical to an establishment's acceptance and eventual success.

Purchase behaviour

Most people would like to think that they are masters of their own destiny. The truth is, in most cases people make purchases which are motivated by two major factors:

1. Their aspirations to be a certain type of person who lives a particular way of life.
2. The cultural and social influences which have formed the society in which they live.

The sort of person anyone wants to be is affected by

his or her self-perception, personality, desired lifestyle, social class attitudes, intelligence and physical capacity to achieve. These are inner-directed considerations and are usually the result of the genes that made them and the environment into which they were born. Further modifications of a person's purchase decisions are a result of his or her age-related needs, gender, living mode, race or nationality, financial resources and parental, marital or peer group pressures.

People's identities are created by a combination of their possessions and the things they do because they are outward, visible signs of individuality. Their name, family background, nationality, occupation, home and district, car and household possessions, schooling, professional and trade associations, are all possessive factors that give a person a sense of being and belonging. Their 'beingness' is further substantiated by what they 'do', such as their sporting activities, hobbies, interests, work and socializing. People's identities and self-perceptions are also revealed to us by their personalities.

Performers

These are people who like to be noticed. Often loud and ostentatious, they are talkers, extroverts, gregarious and usually stimulating people to be with. They prefer bright colours, striking fashions, outstanding cars and have lots of friends. They go out a lot and want to be where the action is so that they can be noticed.

Rulers

This group of people are less friendly, cooler and calculating. They like to be in charge of people and situations. They are usually active, hard-working and task-dominated. They seek and mostly obtain positions of power.

Followers

This is a friendly personality group of people who are often shy and like to avoid trouble, facing up to it when they have to and often with considerable determination. They prefer home and a nice comfortable environment without being too noticeable. Essentially cautious and conservative, followers mostly prefer supportive roles in the community.

Thinkers

These are independent, usually preoccupied types of people who work at their own pace. They are systematic, task-orientated people who shun the limelight. They work to regulations because they like to know where they stand in most situations, erring on the side of caution. Utility is more important than looks, so sports cars and the bright lights are not for them.

Social classes

It is probably a combination of personality (mostly set in concrete by the time a person is eight years of age), genes and social/cultural influences which produce the social classes. It is unpopular to talk about social classes, some people preferring to believe that there are only two—the privileged and the disadvantaged. This latter attempt at categorization stems from the belief that class is a consequence of financial opportunity or accident of birth. The evidence of a multifaceted and complex society suggests that people are not forced into a social category, but rather they choose to position themselves in a social category. Only a minority have no choice. This may be an arguable point of view, but a study by Warner and Lunt, and a subsequent study commissioned by the Chicago *Tribune,* established that:

> there is a social class system and substantial differences exist between classes with respect to their buying habits. The classes do not think the same way

> and they respond differently to a seller's marketing programmes. Furthermore, money does not necessarily equate with living standards, with some trades people earning more than the professions but having quite different views on how the money should be spent.

The six social classes are termed upper-upper, lower-upper, upper-middle, lower-middle, upper-lower and lower class. The differences are explained in part by the personality types of each group.

Social classes have their own set of values and beliefs which serve as criteria for normal behaviour and influence their choice of the brand and the quality of their purchases. This is very apparent in hospitality, with the whole gamut of establishments catering for a class and lifestyle customer mix. Those who would deny the existence of class and lifestyle distinctions fly in the face of the evidence before their eyes in every hospitality establishment in the country. Some people react to the social box they are in and occasionally may do things which are 'out of character', but most conform to class and personality type.

7

The Product Mix

The product mix is the range of facilities and the quality level of services that an establishment offers to its customers. Because of the expense involved in building and providing these products, a property has to be reasonably assured that the customers want the extras.

The management of a five-star hotel may perceive the extras as being a necessary part of their product mix to attract custom. A de-luxe property generally believes that having a wide range of products is an important aspect of its quality image and that the upper-upper or lower-upper class attitudes of its targeted customer mix would be mortified if they were not available.

Matching the customer mix with a carefully planned product mix is a series of decisions crucial to a hospitality establishment. It has to be sure which products to have as part of the normal room rate, which ones to offer as extras and which ones not to have at all. It all depends on the customer mix that the property decides to target and the expectations of each customer segment.

Having completed a market analysis and then selected the mix of customer segments for targeting, the facilities provided have to attract the customers wanted. This is customizing the product for the needs and wants of known customers as opposed to creating the products first, then looking for customers later.

Product lines

A product mix has width, depth and consistency. A product line is a group of product items which are similar in their purpose and function. Every major hotel usually has three main product lines: accommodation, restaurant facilities, and bars.

The product width depends on how many additional product lines a hotel offers, such as shops, sports and leisure facilities and hire cars. Some resorts have a wide product line and embrace an extensive range of services. Others keep it simple and inexpensive.

The number of items in each product line determines the establishment's product depth of choice. A hotel with a choice of four restaurants, for instance, as a depth of four items. Consistency relates to the similarity of the product lines to each other in their appeal to the customer mix.

Each product line requires a marketing strategy, especially if the items are chargeable extras and have to pay for themselves. Some lines are subsidiary to the main promotion of the establishment, such as the availability of a swimming pool; just by 'being there' they meet the needs of the customers and are not expected to make a profit contribution. The costs are covered by the room hire sales as part of doing business. The style and size of an establishment generally dictates its product lines, depth and consistency.

The basis of any hospitality business is to provide a place where one can sleep, eat, meet, have sex, drink a beverage, drink alcohol, talk business, exchange gossip, rest, relax, be private, be noticed, play sport, wash oneself, wash clothes, escape, celebrate, entertain, impress, shop, have fun, do nothing, do anything, be waited on, be massaged, have a sauna, dance, listen to music, spend money, feel important, see important people—nearly the whole gamut of human experience can be had in a place of hospitality.

As one hotel manager aptly put it, 'Sometimes you have to be prepared to walk away from business.' Some customers are not worth pursuing because to provide for them is an investment which is unlikely to return a profit. For instance, a large hotel will probably have a swimming pool, an item which most managers consider to be a mandatory item in their leisure product-line.

However, what if the pool is only used by a handful of customers each week? A pool is expensive to build and maintain, and occupies a large area of valuable space which perhaps could be put to better profit-making purposes.

Many product lines are merely the result of management making marketing decisions based on industry habits, pandering to a customer demand that may not exist. The establishment without a pool, for instance, may lose some customers, but pick up a lot more by using the space for something else.

Similarly, having a fitness centre seems like a good idea, but a customer count of those who use it often reveals that only a few of the customers want it. Nevertheless, having these extras may be important for the total image of the property.

Styles of operation

The primary accommodation places are termed hotels, guest houses, bed and breakfasts, budget lodges and resorts. Each term is meant to describe a type of place where one can expect a certain product mix and style of service. There are some grey areas in these classifications, though, with some guest houses providing services competitive with highly ranked hotels, and some hotels verging on offering resort-type facilities.

Applying a star rating is a broad classification used by the industry for positioning a lodging place's product mix, price and level of service. Management believe that they have to live up to a rating label which they have either given themselves or which has been assigned to them by an independent organization which publishes a hotel guide, such as the Automobile Association.

Although customers may use a star rating as an initial guide, ultimately they will base their choice on personal experience and the recommendations of others. A hotel's reputation is earned by quality service, and a star rating may have no relevance to its occupancy rate or numbers of satisfied customers.

The size of an establishment has a bearing on the appeal to the customer only if a large place has the width of product lines, and this is not always the case. Some of the largest merely have a lot of rooms. Some of the smallest, such as boutique hotels, offer more personalized service and comfort.

The 'value engineering' concept of hotel construction (a phrase to describe the concept of arranging a standard product mix which will offer value to any customer anywhere) seems to produce a sameness in hotel design. The attempt to provide a multipurpose operation to suit everyone in the end pleases no one in particular.

This formula approach to marketing is not using targeting to effect and is unlikely to produce a breed of satisfied loyal customers who are going to go away and 'sell' the place to their colleagues and friends. However, a current exception to this viewpoint is the success of the budget lodge formula, where customers are seeking convenience and accessibility in terms of location and price, and the occasion of use does not warrant personalized, 'high-touch' service.

World-class hotels are aimed at the top end of the travel market. After a period of high growth, a large number of these towering structures which have risen almost everywhere in the last twenty years have hit the wall of dwindling customer demand. They remain desperately quiet in many locations due to a global economic down-turn and because the growth segments of the hospitality market are cost-conscious and want less glitz and more value.

The trend of travellers in the 1990s suggests a growing demand from people who want to stay where they feel most comfortable and at a place which best suits their pocket and needs. The simple, cost-saving benefit of building a property around customers instead of expensive facilities seems to have escaped many investors.

The return from a million-pound investment in a marble-lined foyer may be zero in comparison to a less -expensive, smiling, helpful and interested concierge supported by a willing staff. The customers will probably never come back to look at the marble foyer again, but they will come back to experience the dignity and comfort provided by caring service.

The keys to success

Michael Hurst, one of the best educators in the world on hospitality, stipulates that for an establishment to be successful the customer has to be given an experience beyond his or her expectations and become an unpaid sales person for the place.

As he says, 'The majority of custom comes from word-of-mouth recommendation.' He cites the case of a 130-room property that he managed with his partners which opened in a poor location with only two paying customers the first night. He never spent a penny on advertising and yet within the first year it had a 93 per cent occupancy rate. There is always a new property which seems to be brighter, bigger and glitzier than the ones before it, and it will drag in the early adopters who like change and want to be 'where the latest action is'. Long-term survival, however, will always depend on the lasting quality of the guest experience.

While the big places spend their money in a bid to gain the fickle 'switchers', a small guest house close by can be attracting regular custom and making money consistently while watching with curiosity as the bigger places go into an ever increasing debt spiral.

Location and distance

Location and distance will always be the primary determinants of an establishment's success. Not everyone can do a 'Michael Hurst' and recover from being in a back street in the wrong end of town. Proximity to places where customers want to engage in other activities is always best, such as being near an airport, on a major motorway, next to shopping, sporting or conference facilities, close to a business centre, in the heart of a local community or part of an attractive holiday destination. Wherever the property is located, more business will come from the nearest customer sources than the distant ones.

Product assessment

An establishment's facilities need to be constantly reviewed. There are two sets of criteria—economic and strategic. The two work together.

Economic

Any establishment requires a huge investment in money and time. The investors are invariably looking for an early return even though they know that planning through to actualization takes years.

Management seeks to use the property and its products to achieve growth, sales, profit, market share and to make the best use of its capital and human resources. Each product therefore has to be assessed on its ability to make a contribution to management's objectives, and that is dependent on market size—the availability of customers.

Strategic

In the pursuit of economic objectives, management has to consider the competitive intensity and the customers' expectations., It has to plan for maximum retention of customer loyalty, customer attraction and how that will lead to other purchases. All of these considerations are reliant upon product and market homogeneity.

Decisions about products should be made strategically on what the customers want and how the customer mix feels about each one, as well as considering the more pragmatic economic approach.

If product mix is altered to achieve an economic objective, management faces the consequences of a change in the customer mix. For example, a hotel which abandons room service because it is not making money, or allows it to run down so badly that it is a customer turn-off, may be 'penny wise and pound foolish'. It is sometimes better to recover losses on a product which is essential to the needs of a market segment with profit from other products.

The product mix formula

The simplest method for developing a product mix to match the customer mix is to ask the customers. Why sit around guessing what the customer wants? If management has targeted a segment, it should have a good idea why. The decision has presumably been based on that segment's reasons for travel and its expectations of product/service and price. To fill in the gaps of knowledge, a consumer survey of the targeted segment will provide the missing pieces. Armed with knowledge about the groups comprising the targeted customer mix, the product mix becomes a combination of items selected from the following product lines.

Accommodation product lines

Large, medium or small self-contained, fully serviced apartment or suite, separate self-catering accommodation, two- or three-room self-service suite, large, medium or small room with en-suite bathroom, family bed layout, twin double beds, double or single beds.

Catering product lines

Banquet halls, restaurants of varying nature, coffee shops and brasseries, room service.

Beverage and bar product lines

Room service, room mini-bar, cocktail bar, lounge bar, private bar, club bar, public bar, restaurant bars.

Entertainment product lines

Nightclub, band, dancing, live theatre, cabaret, movie hire, arcade games.

Business services product lines

Meeting rooms, conference facilities, computers, fax, secretarial, photocopying, translators, etc.

Personal services product lines

Valet, hairdressing, nail care, grooming, dry cleaning, laundry, ironing, clothes hire, creche, baby minding, playgrounds, nannies, in-house doctor, chemist, nurse.

Leisure facilities product lines

Swimming pool, sauna, massage, fitness centre, aerobics, etc.

Sport facilities product lines

Tennis, golf, squash, skiing, sailing, equestrian, etc.

Leisure-pleasure product lines

Hire cars, limousines, mini-buses, boats, sightseeing tours, theatre, sport, concert booking service.

Signature product lines

Toiletries, towels, bathrobes, slippers, T-shirts, gifts, souvenirs, etc.

When choosing the product mix, bear in mind that each product line comes with a cost for the customer one way or another, either in the total charge-out rate or by separate charges for each product used during the stay. How many will be willing to pay the price?

By using targeting to arrive at an ideal customer mix, the profile of the segment's basic wants and the product mix can be decided with a strong measure of assurance. The customer knows what is the value to him or her. The bottom line is always cost, and the customer value is arrived at by the simple equation:

$$\text{Value} = \frac{\text{costs}}{\text{Benefits}}$$

Product life cycle

Hospitality, even though it is a fundamental aspect of civilized life, is subject to fashions, moods and trends. The four stages of the life cycle are introduction, growth, maturity and decline. At the introduction stage, the property is new, and having gone through the early assessment stages of market analysis and feasibility it is launched and brought to the attention of the targeted customer mix by promotion. If the property and its products are acceptable, it will achieve growth and, hopefully, some degree of prosperity.

At the maturity stage, the property will have reached its maximum growth and stabilize. It should then be returning some profit on the original investment. This may take several years.

The decline stage is generally reached when other places enter the market, the facilities become tired and need refurbishing, the market's needs and wants alter, or changes to the establishment's surrounding location occur. The length of the product's life cycle varies, and some concepts have more durability than others. For example, Claridges in London, Raffles in Singapore, Gleneagles in Scotland, George V in Paris have not changed their basic formats, but there have been subtle adaptations to the needs of the customers over time.

Sometimes it is better for a property to target a new customer mix, or subtly phase one segment out in favour of another. This will probably lead to some changes to the product mix, the dropping of some items in a line or adding new ones. A restaurant which is no longer serving the needs of most segments can be refurbished, restyled and renamed.

A property and its product mix should be constantly under review. When the point is reached for a change to any of its product line items, there are four basic decisions to be made: build; hold; harvest; or divest. If the market demand for a product is increasing and the product can be expanded to cope with the additional business, it makes sense to build or extend the product.

This would depend on assurances from various market, economic and industry indicators that the upward trend will continue. In some cases, when the demand warrants it, management will line extend and add more items to the product line, such as increasing the number of bars, perhaps with differing prices and themes.

Another example would be a hotel line extending its leisure facilities, adding to an existing golf course some tennis and squash courts, etc., thereby providing a full mix of sports alternatives.

Holding, or maintaining, a facility would make sense if, for economic and strategic reasons, nothing is to be gained by making any change. Unfortunately, sometimes management holds on to a product too long, despite dwindling customer numbers, for sentimental reasons or fear of change. Often there is a belief that additional promotion will solve the problem, and then management is throwing good money after bad.

Harvesting makes sense if more profit can be gathered by simply maintaining a facility. For instance, this would apply in the case of a restaurant which fills regularly and where patronage would not suffer if the prices were raised marginally over a period. Where a facility is losing money and has no strategic advantage, it may be time to divest it.

This may apply to a hotel function room, for example, which occupies valuable space in the building. If it is under-utilized for its original purpose, catering for concerts, displays, meetings or functions, the space may be better used for another purpose. Another approach is to franchise out a facility to a supplier; for instance, a number of London hotels have done this with their restaurant outlets.

A drastic change for a declining property to make is to refurbish, rename and reposition the property and target an entirely different customer mix. Sometimes it is better to sell the property and start afresh with a new one. Most properties need redecorating, but not just when the place starts to look tired and worn. Redecorating is required whenever it is necessary to maintain a contemporary sense of style that is compatible with its customer mix.

Drastic change to the property or its product mix can lose customers. Customers develop a feeling of ownership about a property they use a lot, and, like an old friend, they do not like to see it change. The problem for management is that nothing stands still in the hospitality business. To not meet the challenge of external changes is fatal. However, the important detail is to recognize what the changes mean so that change is made for a reason. That reason should always be to meet the existing customers' expectations and attract new customers.

The world is full of property owners who start out with the premise that it is theirs to do what they like with it, and they do, irrespective of the customers' preferences and needs. They overlook the point that the customers think that it is their place and that is the reason why they keep coming back. All that sensible owners have to do is to capitalize on that innate sense of proprietary interest and encourage the customers to involve themselves in the property and they will always have loyal, and mostly forgiving, clients.

A hotel depends on the continuing success of its base products— its room hire, restaurants and bars. If any of these key areas of revenue are not working properly, it affects other products, its market position and profit. This means that management must constantly appraise the performances of its products in search of doing everything better than before while maintaining that sense of excitement and interest.

Product development, either through improvement or modification, is a growth strategy. Its purpose is to retain existing customers and attract new customers. Product development is a continuing concern. Management has to improve sales, if possible, remain competitive and increase or maintain profit levels by improving the products by adding new experiences for the customers.

Product life cycles

Every product has a life cycle which involves

— *Development*, which is where the product is conceived, researched and market analysed, target markets selected, the product is tested, given a feasibility study and made ready for sale, provided that it passes all the test criteria.

— *Introduction*, when the product is exposed to the customers and given promotion to provide awareness and assist in the selling process.

— *Growth* occurs if the product is accepted by the customers, and if it is, sales begin to repay the effort of creating the product.

— *Maturation*, when the product has reached the peak of its sales performance and is providing good profits. It is also when there is considerable competition from other organizations.

— *Decline*, when the product becomes a bit boring and sales begin a steady slide downwards.

— *Death or revitalization*, when the management has to decide whether to let the product die a natural death or revitalize it in some way.

Depending on the product, each of these stages can either be drawn out or startlingly brief. Without growth or innovation, a hotel, restaurant or any hospitality establishment faces the problem of looking like a tired facility, a ghost which haunts every establishment after it has been in business for a while.

Product development can represent a problem for management because change usually has a broad range of effects and unpredictable outcomes. It is a time when disastrous mistakes can occur. Most of them happen as a result of management making changes to increase sales without checking to find out if the changes are what the customers want..

There is no point in changing a winning formula; just keep on improving it. It is not that people do not like change, it is just that they do not like being changed. They hate being told, 'Things are going to be different around here. What we're going to do is.... Therefore before changes are made their outcomes need to be forecasted and assessed. For example, in order to increase bar sales a hotel may decide to extend its public bar, redecorate it and add two additional bar people to cope with the supposed lift in sales, the presumption being that there is sufficient demand to warrant the expenditure. That is fine, but an examination of all the factors affected by change could alter that decision.

The starting point for developing a product or improving it involves consultation with the customers and research. Time and time again, this will reveal some improvement, modification or change that will help to increase sales, build customer numbers, improve market share or reduce costs.

Sometimes the assessment will reveal that the product or facility should be closed down because it has exceeded its useful life. When seeking to improve or change a product there is a host of strategic options to consider, involving promotion, staff, price offers, change in merchandise, product presentation, infrastructure, decor, product quality, efficiency, timing quantity, systems, specialization, productivity, expansion, contraction or diversification.

The reasons why people choose to use any establishment's facilities provide the key to product development. Whereas accommodation and food are the basic reasons, the added value they seek may be convenience, escape, companionship, an unusual experience, a special occasion, a popular activity, entertainment, fun, comfort or sheer indulgence.

Certainly their choice of establishment will be influenced by the friendliness of the staff. There is also class consciousness which influences many people, most preferring to be with their own 'types'. The popularity of a place is a strong draw card for others. There is a sense of security when people are with others like themselves. The key to product development in most cases is to build on a successful product base and a sound position in the market.

When property owners are faced with a 'death or revitalization' option there is always a tendency to blame the location or the building itself, and they either refurbish or sell. If they sell, what often happens is that the new owners buy a lemon and do no better than the previous owners. Something really different and better in the way of customer experiences may turn around the fortunes of the place. It is not easy.

Managing an establishment in the hospitality industry is like directing a live theatre performance. It is a long-running show that should keep on getting better and better. If it is a good show, people will come from miles around to experience and enjoy the actors' performances. This means developing exciting and interesting new products, which in most cases will simply be innovative ways of doing things that most places do.

The secret of Club Mediterranean, a company which has marketed organized holidays around villages built by the company in attractive, beachside locations, was not the concept of cheap holidays so much as having fun-loving organizer managers.

The organizers were carefully chosen for their friendliness, love of fun and the ability to involve people in activities. They were always gracious hosts and the heart and soul of the villages. Club Med has now been going for forty years, and it too has changed over the years to meet the changes in people's needs. The owners use targeting to pick their markets as a result of focus groups and extensive studies of customer behaviour. Their products are then carefully developed to satisfy new markets while never losing sight of the basics of their successful operation.

The best hospitality establishments have a flair for making people feel relaxed, comfortable and welcome. They provide a busy, sometimes even noisy, environment with lots of things happening and many people coming and going flair customers who like that. They also consider those who prefer quietness, privacy and solitude, and make sure there is a special place where people can retreat when they need to be that 'away from the madding crowd'.

Hospitality is about providing customers with a sense of occasion, the feeling of being involved in something special. And, as has been said many times, it's the extras that count, and that means developing the way of doing things which goes beyond the customers' expectations.

Forget new systems as a means of attracting new customers unless the system is perceived by the customers to be of direct benefit to them. Systems are designed for the operation's efficiency. Give customers something to talk about. Let them take away a memory of a wonderful occasion. That requires management to develop products which customize the place. It means shaping the products so that they are special and different for individuals and which avoid the pursuit of sameness.

There is not a right or wrong way to do things, only ways that customers appreciate. Products make statements about people. What you offer tells the customers the sort of place yours is. What they expect and will accept from a place tells everyone the sort of person they are.

Therefore management should set out to capture markets that have a synergy with each other and, with your customer mix in mind, let them grow with you. Explain the reasons for the improvements so that they appreciate what you are doing for them. Unless a hotel has completely 'lost its soul', management should seldom consider abandoning its core base of customers, but should concentrate on building on the existing base.

Management would do better to think of improving rather than changing. It makes sense to do what a place is doing better than to try to do what someone else is doing and not do it as well. Products can be developed independently of each other.

A place can make gradual changes to each product without exciting the natives, perhaps beginning with a new concept themed bar while retaining the old faithful. When the new one gains acceptance renovate the old one, then move on with the planned improvements to the restaurants, and so on.

Synergy is the relationship between the place's mission, positioning and its distinctive competencies. Hart and Troy say that synergy is the key criterion used to evaluate growth options and guide investment and new product development decisions.

It is especially critical in regard to considerations involving diversification because diversification in this area often involves taking on business that may be new and unfamiliar to current management. Financial troubles may result from over-extended resources when a company fails to evaluate growth opportunities in terms of basic synergies.

There are many effective product development strategies to consider which can be added to existing products.

A hotel, for instance, should think about increasing the range and nature of merchandise on offer through shops, bars and reception areas. There may be scope to develop interesting holiday packages, local tours, discount vouchers for shops, ticketing facilities for theatres, sporting events, casinos, etc.

If the restaurants and the food are a feature of an establishment, it may consider offering new eating experiences. In this case, it would be best to use the Michael Hurst approach and experiment with different dishes and, when the customers are vocal in their approval, make the dishes a regular item on the menu.

Opportunities could exist for capitalizing on assets by upgrading some sections of the accommodation into different categories, such as self-catering apartments, family suites, temporary offices, display areas. If there is a swimming pool, perhaps add saunas, massage, swimming lessons, water aerobics, etc.

Many establishments offer a wide range of services. Adding more presents a problem when they would rather remove many of the less profitable ones. The retraction of services and facilities which customers have come to expect is difficult. However, the same outcome analysis can be used, this time to test how many customers would be lost by the change. With all new products, experimentation is important before final commitment. Test marketing saves time and money and avoids the embarrassment of failure.

New concepts take time as a rule before there is market acceptance. This is called the diffusion process. Some people are early adopters and others take time to accept change. The greater the relative advantage of a new concept to the customer the more compatible it will be with his or her status and lifestyle and, as a consequence, the sooner it will be purchased.

One of the barriers to acceptance is complexity. Another barrier is communication. The easier it is to communicate a new idea and the simpler the idea is, the more readily it will be understood. Timing the introduction of a new product is also vital. Changes can be too soon, too late, or ill-timed. Feeling the mood of the customers is the only way to judge timing.

Three other issues can influence product development strategies:

— *Recycling*. Investigate old ideas that can be reintroduced. In fact, most of today's new concepts are yesterday's old concepts in different clothes. The advantage of copying old ideas that will suit today's markets is that they have a track record, a history of success that can be emulated and examples of failures that can be avoided.

— *Fads and fashions*. These are mostly different ways of doing the samething. They are often copied by others and then they become 'what everybody does' and lose their point and value. There is no doubt that to ignore them can be folly, but to slavishly follow them is often economically unsound for establishments building an individual positioning image.

— *Trends*. These are usually decided by economic and technological developments. When times are good, people travel and spend more, and the opposite occurs when the economy tightens. There are usually early indicators of trends.

Hospitality is a person-to-person, customized business, and the volatility of its markets means that situations seldom remain stable. To be successful, management must be thinking all the time about how to make the place better for customers.

8

Service Strategies

The objective of a hospitality business is to provide guests with a place where they feel welcome, appreciated, relaxed and have an enjoyable experience. Service is what an establishment does to and for its guests to achieve this objective. Service is not about smiling and servility. It is a strategy which considers the customer while serving the interests of the establishment. It is service excellence which gives an organization a competitive edge. Outstanding service makes a lot of money for a hospitality establishment because business is people.

The success of such a commitment to excellence is illustrated in Peters and Waterman's renowned book In Search of Excellence. The intention of a service strategy is to manage the customer's experience. The services that an establishment provides are products, and, like a product which is manufactured, a service has to perform to a measurable standard and fulfil its purpose all the time, every time.

It is not something which only the staff does, either. It requires commitment from the top. In an organization which is committed to a service strategy there are only two types of staff—those who serve the customer and those who help those who serve the customer. It inverts the hierarchical management pyramid where the managing director is at the top and there are levels of seniority leading down to the customer at the base of the pyramid.

Instead, the customer is at the top and full responsibility for the customers and those who serve and help to serve them rests on the managing director on the sharp end. It promotes a 'flatter' management structure, emphasizes team work and makes the chambermaid and the dishwasher as important as the managing director.

Imagine being in a high-class restaurant and just as the meal arrives you notice that the fork has a piece of old meat stuck to it. If that is not enough, the wine glass still has a ring of lipstick. It is hard to feel the same about the food, isn't it? And all because the dishwashers failed to do their job properly, and, worse still, no-one checked the glass and the cutlery when they set the table.

The products which are provided by a hospitality establishment are nearly all service-orientated. The product mix, consisting mostly of accommodation, restaurants, bars and a range of ancillary products which vary with the establishment, have to perform to a level of satisfaction, otherwise the customer will not return. They cannot be good some days and poor on others. Accommodation, restaurants and bars are obvious service products because they are direct profit earners. Less obvious, but just as important to the customer, are the products which indirectly make money by substantially contributing to the customers' service experiences.

Safety standards

Safety does not make any money, but without adequate safety procedures an establishment can lose a considerable amount of money and a hard-earned reputation. Safety for the employees and the customer is a product that performs without it always being seen to perform.

Stock and inventory control

There is nothing worse than running out of a customer's favourite wine, the kitchen running short of eggs, replacement crockery not being there when it is wanted, etc. No-one considers cleaning a profit-maker for a place, and yet it can either earn a reputation for an establishment or ruin one. Most of us expect cleanliness as a norm from the place where we stay and eat. When it is obviously dirty, the establishment has failed to meet our expectations.

Financial planning

Repairs to the premises, the plumbing, renovations to the kitchen and its equipment—there is a long list of things that do not happen or get fixed because there is not enough money—the age-old excuse of management. Do not believe that the customers do not notice, they do. It is not only the fixtures and fittings they see, either, it is the sudden breakdown of a little service that did not happen because a piece of equipment was too old or was not fixed.

Credit control

The places that will not take certain credit cards, or ask for deposits, or insult the customer in many ways simply because someone is too lazy or inefficient to check a credit rating in advance, give reasons for customers to go away and never return.

Proper credit checks are sound business practice, but when they become unreasonable impositions on the customer's patience and understanding such systems are stupid. Attempting to achieve 100 per cent credit control will cost the establishment money. By being diplomatic and sensitive the customer credit control can be enforced, bad debts minimized and customers retained.

Operational systems

Too many of these are designed for the convenience of the staff or management. These include room cleaning which must be done at prescribed times and to hell with the customer who does not want to be disturbed; the tables which have to be arranged for another function while the customers are still eating; a docket system for meal ordering which is designed to prevent items being missed on the bill and petty fraud but which causes a five-minute delay to the customers' meals. Systems are fine as long as they improve the experience for the customer.

Layout appeal and efficiency

Many places seat the customers near to the kitchen so that the staff do not have to walk so far, or close to the windows to make the place look busier than it is. The reception desk is just outside the general office not because it is closer for the customers but because it is closer to the manager's office.

A lot of establishments make their front desk staff responsible for answering incoming phone calls as well as serving the customers face to face.

As a consequence, time and time again customers are left standing and waiting while the phones are being answered—the phone call always taking precedence. In reality, these establishments would be better advised to have the manager and the manager's secretary answer the phones.

Managing the service products

In the course of their stay, customers are part of a whole cycle of activities from the front door through to their eventual departure. Each activity is handled by a different department and the customer is passed from one to the other. Lots of service products are involved, but in far too many places no-one is responsible for making sure that the transitions happen smoothly. The duty manager waits for a complaint, meanwhile assuming that all is functioning as it should. The whole experience for the customer becomes a sum total of a myriad of little experiences.

For all the service products to happen effectively and concurrently to the guest's complete satisfaction, several control factors are necessary:

— There has to be a strategy which identifies when, where and how the service product shall perform.

— There have to be systems with measurable criteria for each of the working procedures involved in providing the service. If a service is to be managed, it must be capable of being measured.

The people providing the service have to be 'people people', those who are interested in others, caring for their welfare and making the comfort and satisfaction of the customer top priority. Procedures are only as effective as the people performing them. The people providing the service directly to the customer must have the support of everyone else. Albrecht and Zemke emphasize that the organization exists to serve the needs of the people who are serving the customer.

Management's primary function is to monitor and maintain the service standards. Management must make sure that nothing and no-one prevents the service product from happening.

In a service organization, management's role is not merely giving instructions, it is to help those providing the service. If there are delays or upsets, what or who is causing them? Is it a procedural problem? Is there a weak link in the staff chain? Is more training needed? Perhaps the person is wrong for that job?

Some consider the service culture to be reactive to customers rather than proactive. This is wrong. Customers recognize that the establishment has to make profit. They look for leadership from the establishment and want it to provide the magic that gives them a quality experience.

With a service strategy, you are involving the customers and the staff so that the strategic service mix works to everyone's satisfaction. It is a process of drawing together the expectations, needs and wants of the customer and the provider so that the customer gets value and the provider gets money. It sounds so simple, doesn't it? Then why does it not always happen?

Part of the answer lies in the arrogance of a large percentage of human beings who are not really interested in other people's thinking. It is a 'We-know-what-is-best-for-you' attitude. Such types are rarely successful in the hospitality business. It results in a general preoccupation by management with putting products in place which they think are for the benefit of the customers, when often they are not what the customer wants or expects at all.

For example, a restaurant put on a special three-course meal for a very low price in anticipation of creating an influx of business, only to be disappointed because the customers did not come and those that did never came back. The restaurateur added more choices, but still failed to increase business.

After two or three weeks of this he finally snapped at a table of uninterested customers. 'Well, what the hell do you want then?' They proceeded to tell him, and he finally realized that he had not been taking notice of what the customers wanted. He had not taken the trouble to review what the customers were consistently choosing from his normal menu. Nor had he ever bothered to talk to his customers about their preferences. The wants of the customer mix should always drive the service strategies. Equally important, though, is to anticipate the customers' wants and occasionally provide something delightful that they did not expect. Michael Hurst experiments with various dishes and consults his customers before including the dishes on the menu.

Secondary services

Effective service products achieve increased business by 'laddering'. This is drawing from the total market a number of people who are transformed from potential customers into advocates for the establishments. The objective of laddering is to identify suspects and target the best prospects (potential customers).

With the help of promotion a percentage of them will become customers. From this point the objective of service products is to provide customers with a quality experience that turns them into regular patrons of the establishment. Consequently, they will soon become firm advocates and go out and,sell' the place to their friends and acquaintances.

Most restaurants provide good food, reasonable service and charge average prices or prices which suit their customer mix. This is called a 'primary service'. Michael Hurst states that it is the small extras, the 'secondary services', which take an average customer experience and elevate it into something beyond his or her expectations.

It may be the special brand of coffee, the bread and shortbread that have been made on the premises, the appetiser at the beginning of the meal which is not charged for. Hurst claims quite rightly that there are many ways of doing things that are better and different which become the main factors in the customers' minds.

The primary service product usually does its job of satisfying the customers without much comment. It is the extras that give the customers something to go away and talk about, giving the establishment the competitive edge.

Planning

Service has to have measurable criteria. It has to have objectives and perform to a prescribed set of rules and standards. Its purpose is to define precisely what will happen to, or for, a customer by when and by whom. Measurement is achieved by deciding the required outcome of the service. The standard criteria are as follows:

Set the service standard objective

What is it you want the product to do to and for the customers? It is the answer to this question which determines the objective. Forget the money objective. That is an overall corporate objective. This is a product objective, and it is its outcome, what actually happens and how that happening is accepted in the minds of the customers which counts. It may take several statements to sum up the outcome that the objective is set to achieve. Remember, for an objective to have meaning it must contain measurable criteria of achievement within a stipulated time frame.

Set the tasks to be done in the time allocated

For example, a restaurant allocates staff numbers by customer numbers depending on the style of service of the establishment. So one waiter may be allocated to fifteen customers. Three chefs may be required to cook for 150 customers. The service standard which is set requires each customer to be served with drinks within two minutes of sitting down, to have the first course on the table within five minutes of ordering, to have the second course on the table no later than twelve minutes, and so on. If it is not being achieved, management must find out why, isolate the difficulty and remedy it. 'Whatever it takes' is the rule that governs the provision of a service standard. The measuring criterion in this instance is keeping account of individual performances and comparing them with the average. Those who lag are trained, encouraged or helped until they come up to the standard required.

Hospitality is team work, people working together to jointly achieve the objectives of an excellent guest experience. A team leader is essential; a catalyst for the smooth functioning of the procedures required in delivering the product. Each person must know exactly what is expected of him or her and be constantly acknowledged as he or she performs. Achievement is a reward on its own, but nothing beats the rewards of money and extra privilege for a job that goes beyond the standard required.

Set quality standards

Not every action or function can be directly translated into money terms or measured by customer reaction. Much of what happens in a service product goes unseen by the customer. As it is the culmination of little things that ultimately counts in the final assessment by the customer, the contributing functions need a points rating system ranging from poor up to excellent. It is surprising how standards are lifted and enthusiasm develops when staff are performing to known criteria.

Measure the level of satisfaction

The desired outcome of a range of service strategies is the extent of the customers' consistent satisfaction. This can be measured in terms of increased sales made, and repeat business, which is the real measure of a product's success. There is another way, and that is to constantly research customer attitudes to find out if the number of complaints are reduced and whether the customers appreciate the various experiences being provided. Guests, in the main, do not mind filling in brief questionnaires, particularly if a prize incentive is offered.

Set a goal for money earned

Whereas the objective is to meet the satisfaction of the customer, money has to be made. At the end of a service period the money required from a product has to be added to make sure that it meets the corporate objectives. A non-profit product such as cleaning can be measured by a points rating system and judged by what it does not cost in terms of lost or disappointed customers.

Analyse costs involved

There is always an accountant adding up the costs of a product. That person has a job to do, which is to make Sure that more money does not go out than is coming in. An accountant performs the function of being management's conscience. A product service has to be cost-efficient, with the customer satisfaction level being measured against the costs incurred and the profits made.

Develop a service strategy

A high-quality service orientation is such a powerful competitive weapon that it will soon come to be regarded as an essential part of business strategy, not a frill or a 'nice-to-have' feature.

Organizations which cannot demonstrate a significant commitment to the needs of their customers will be left further and further behind. Quality of service is now a top management issue. The steps to be taken that provide a sustainable competitive advantage over the competition by using a product-service-orientated approach to marketing are as follows:

— *Establish customer needs and wants.* This is done by market analysis and segmentation. It will lead to a target market whose particular needs and wants the establishment intends to satisfy.

— *Ask the customers.* Nothing beats the simple research technique of talking to a representative sample of customers, existing and potential, and asking for their opinions and advice.

— *Set down objectives for improvements or changes.* Decide the outcome you want from a product or series of products.

— *Identify key strategies.* Decide how you are going to achieve the objectives and realize the outcomes required.

— *Establish measurable criteria for strategy.* If it cannot be measured it cannot be managed.

— *Allocate tasks and responsibilities.* Decide who is going to perform the functions involved in producing the outcome. Choose 'people people', those who can share the 'gift of friendship'. Look for catalysts which lead and encourage a team effort.

— *Train staff.* Anything new requires comprehensive explanation and careful supervision to begin with. Monitor what happens thereafter. Even high quality service can deteriorate into mediocrity if left unmanaged.

— *Remove demotivating systems and staff.* Every organization has a number of systems which are designed for the convenience of operators. Seldom do they help the customer. In fact, most of them will be 'customer-hostile' in the sense that they will create adverse reactions from the customer in many instances.

— *Gain commitment to the objectives and strategies*. Without the active support of all the staff, service becomes a bore and a nuisance. Only by involving the staff totally can this problem be overcome. Communication at all times is critical. Never hold back information. Praise those who are doing it right, help those who do not come up to standard. Always make it a team effort. Lead by example.

— *Make physical changes where necessary*. Any physical object, part of a building, piece of equipment or whatever which prevents a service product from performing properly should be changed, moved or replaced. Never allow a physical problem to be an excuse for lack of service.

— *Experiment with the changes*. Do not go charging in with a whole host of new concepts. Test each one first. Involve both the staff and the customers to see if it will work and perform as expected. When it works to expectations and performs according to the desired outcome and to the customers' satisfaction, then make it happen as a permanent operation.

— *Measure and manage*. Management's role is to monitor and step in to help and train whenever it is necessary. Continue with the measuring criteria laid down. The moment you stop it will start to come unstuck.

— *Ask the customers*. The ultimate test of a service product is its satisfactory performance for the customers. Maintain a regular research programme with the customers so that you are informed of progress at all times.

— *Modify where necessary, measure again*. Not every product will service the customers' wants indefinitely. Conditions change, expectations change, moods and fashions change.

The training strategy

One of the principal laments of managers about implementing a service strategy is about the lack of cooperation and consistency of their staff. 'We tell them how to do it. We spend money on training. We try to motivate enthuse, but in the end we find the staff going back to their old habits and we give up in despair. What's the use? It's a nice idea, but it isn't realistic. People are people.'

One has to feel sympathetic with this lament, which is about as consistent as the inconsistency of hospitality staff's ability to perform consistently. The problem lies with management, and we will come to that in a moment. There is another management attitude which says: 'Our staff know what is expected of them. They don't always do what they should, but they know.' Experience shows that this is a false premise.

The truth from research and a series of random interviews of staff reveals that in most cases they do not know what is expected of them. They may know the rules and they may know the procedures they have been taught, but in the majority of cases they think that what is expected is only to perform to those rules and procedures.

This is an open invitation to rebel. It is human to buck the system, so as human beings occasionally they deliberately flout the rules and procedures just to prove that they are individuals in their own right and not a bunch of robots caught up in a system. After a while, flouting the rules becomes a habit and then they feel a bit guilty. As the guilt rises, so do the defence mechanisms, and then it is someone else's fault, not theirs.

Most service people think that they are doing their job for a remote, cold and uncaring manager, or a bunch of shareholders they will never meet and who have no interest in whether they live or die.

Anyone who works in that sort of environment knows that as long as they do enough to not get fired they will get paid, and that is all that matters. That sort of knowledge takes precedence over any other knowledge because it is the truth.

The answer therefore is to give them responsibility for their customers. When they realize that the people they serve could be theirs for a long time and that their real job is to keep them as their own customers it helps to change their attitude to the procedures.

If, in addition, they are given a financial incentive for every customer they retain, and each time that customer spends money they get a little part of it for themselves and they get praised for their efforts, you have a person who is working for him or herself as well as for you. If the right people are hired, they will know that the procedures are there to help them build their own customer base.

Notice what happens when customers request to be served by a particular waiter that they like. It is a funny type of waiter who is not flattered, and naturally he or she responds with additional, personalized touches of service.

Often a handsome tip is the reward. However, it is better if management supplies the reward so that there is a standard recognition for retaining a customer and providing outstanding service.

This approach does two things. One, it personalizes the service. The staff get to know the customers by name. Two, the customers get service because every person who walks in, phones in or writes in is worth money.

All of a sudden, the staff are scrambling to get to the customers first and claim them for their own! The ones who do not scramble are the ones you do not want. So, instead of management saying that staff are all the same, it becomes apparent that they are not all the same. If you want staff who give service you need to retain the scramblers and keep them motivated.

Some managers may balk at this concept because they think that service people are mercenaries, merely hired for a job. In the case of waiters and commis chefs, they are often hired on a casual basis so that they can be laid on and off at will. And here is the real problem—management's attitude to staff.

Until that changes, and the staff are given individuality and respect by managers as being vital contributors to the joint prosperity of themselves and the property, the customers will be at the mercy of a high percentage of mostly unmotivated and uncaring staff. The staff are an integral part of the product being sold.

Most motivational training is wasted. The staff see this type of training as an insult to their intelligence, and often it is. They think, 'Here we go again.' Most staff want to be nice to customers if they can and they think that they already provide 'service'.

Many of them want to do better, and often they know how it can be improved, but frequently they are restrained or demotivated by systems and uncooperative attitudes born from management which does not respect them as individuals. No-one asks them for their opinion.

All too often there is little management supervision, only authoritarian direction. Systems and procedures are put into place without staff consultation or understanding of the problems that they often pose. Profit and expediency come first and the staff come second. Usually there is no means of measuring service or what the staff do except by casual observations.

As a consequence, most service training begins with the premise that it is the front line 'sales and customer service people' who need to have the right attitude. Wrong. Service is a marketing product which requires strategies that begin at the top, and it is management which has to respect, support and service the front-line people. Training should be conducted around the strategies and involve the people who will implement them, and that requires staff acceptance and commitment to the concept.

A service strategy is required for each product in an establishment's 'product line'. Of course there should be an umbrella strategy for the whole establishment, but as each product is aimed at a segment of the customer mix, each one needs its own strategic plan. With a product like accommodation, the service strategy begins with the initial hotel contact because being welcomed by name is the first service a customer notices. This is before he or she has had a chance to see a room, drink in a bar, anything.

You can build a whole strategy very simply around a smiling, happy concierge by extending the rapport he or she establishes and spreading it throughout the organization. It is so easy. It starts with calling the customer by name and remembering that name and the important details about that person's preferences.

Let us say the customer's name is Mr Smith. The porter carries up 'Mr Smith's bags' and puts them into Mr Smith's room. When the chambermaid comes the next day it is to clean Mr Smith's room, not THE room, but Mr Smith's room. Mr Smith is not just a guest, but has hired his room which can only be invaded with his permission. A different staff attitude emerges. The chambermaid therefore *asks* when it would be convenient to clean the room; it is no longer an automatic function.

With a dinner reservation, the table does not have a 'reserved' sign on it, it has 'Mr Smith's table' written on it. The waiters, everyone, calls him by his name. In turn, everyone in the place wears a name tag so that Mr Smith can return the compliment and call the staff by name.

A side benefit of this strategy is that in a large organization with many people carrying out different functions, it is far easier to build a sense of belonging and being appreciated. In so many places, most people working there do not even know each other by name.

Years ago, James Lavenson gave a speech to the Executives' Club of Chicago and recited many amusing stories about his experiences when he first took charge of the Plaza Hotel in New York. Lavenson made a very strong case for the simple stratagem of calling a guest by his or her name and for the staff to wear name tags. When he moved to his new position things were far from right at the hotel.

There were 1400 staff members, and as he said, 'How would they ever know all the people working there, who were the guests, who was just a burglar smiling his way through the hotel while he ripped us off? I can assure you that in the beginning if he smiled and said "hello" he was a crook. He certainly wasn't one of us.'

Lavenson went on to explain that after the Plaza name tag was born and affixed to everyone's chests:

> Believe it or not, Plaza people began saying hello to each other by name when they passed in the hall or in the offices. At first, of course, our regular guests at the Plaza thought we had lost our cool and that we were having some gigantic convention there. But

> now the guests are also able to call the bell person, the maids, room clerks and the manager by name. And we began to build an atmosphere of welcome with the most precious commodity in the world, our names and our guests' names. When someone calls you by name, and you don't know his or hers, another funny thing happens. A feeling of discomfort comes over you: if he calls you by your name twice, and you know you're not world famous, you have to find out his name. And this is the phenomenon we saw happening with the Plaza staff name tags. When a guest calls a waiter by name, because it is there to be read, the waiter wants to call the guest by name.

There is another very simple strategy that anyone in the hospitality business can employ which does not cost very much money, and that is teaching the staff about the products the place has to offer. If you want the staff to sell they have to know what they are supposed to sell. The additional business created by staff information and recommendations is huge. Familiarizing the staff with the products not only helps the selling process, it also builds a sense of pride in the whole organization.

The word selling implies pressuring clients into buying something they may not want. Michael Hurst does not believe that staff should 'sell', but they do have to inform and advise, and to do this they must have an intimate knowledge of the products they are offering. Informing customers about what is available and asking them if they would like it is not selling, it is first, simple courtesy; and secondly, supplying knowledge which can be gratefully used by the customer to make a decision. James Lavenson reported in his speech that when he took over the Plaza Hotel he made a few calls to the various departments and made casual enquiries as if he were a potential customer. He did this before the staff could recognize his voice over the phone.

Here are some of the examples.

'What's the difference between your $85 suite and your $125 suite?'

The answer was, you guessed it, 'Forty dollars'.

'What's the entertainment in your Persian room tonight

'Some singer', was the answer.

'A man or a woman Lavenson asked.

'I'm not sure/ was the reply. It made Lavenson wonder whether he would be safe going there. Why was it, he asked, that a hotel staff does not act like a family of hosts to the guests who have been invited, after all, to stay at their house?

Lavenson introduced a week of orientation for the staff which included a visit to the nightclub, a night in one of the rooms, just like a guest, and a meal in each of the restaurants. Today, everyone knows who is singing in the nightclub and everyone knows the difference between the $85 and $125 rooms.

In the restaurant, another 'moment of truth' for an establishment is often reached when the customer asks the waiter about the wine. A frequent answer is along the lines of 'Wouldn't know, sir. Don't drink wine myself.' How bad is that? What is the point of a drinks waiter who cannot advise the customer on the choice of wine? Another favourite customer question is, 'What is this menu item? Can you tell me something about it?' How many times have you watched as the waiter frowns, desperately trying to remember something about it and finally admitting with a sense of despair that he or she has never tried it, then adding with a smile, 'But it looks nice!' Waiters are not order-takers. They are there to advise and assist the customer with his or her product selection. How can they do that if they do not know the menu or the wine list? Like Lavenson and the leading operators around the world, Michael Hurst makes sure that every waiter tries every dish before he or she serves a customer. You cannot sell or tell somebody about products that you know little or nothing about. Before the waiters go on the floor the kitchen must tell them about the whole meal and how it has been designed and prepared. If there is something new they must try it so that they can tell the customers. When everyone in an establishment is an expert on its products, sales soar, because if the staff are enthusiastic the advice they give is infectious and the customer gets the message that it could be a fun thing to try. Teaching the staff about products and encouraging them to tell the customers is a very simple strategy for management to use to build a business.

Michael Hurst tells the story about a man who sat next to him on a flight to Denver. Without knowing where Michael was staying, his companion proceeded to sell him on staying at the hotel where he was staying, which happened to be the same hotel. One of the main reasons for his companion's enthusiasm for the place was the special things they did, and the one that stood out most of all for him was the hotel's lemon soap! That is silly, you might think, but it is lots of seemingly 'silly' little things like a special lemon soap that make the all-important points of difference between places to stay.

It is not the large issues that concern the average human being so much as a sequence of seemingly inconsequential small issues. Think of the silly little aggravations that have broken many a relationship or even a marriage, like men who do not put the cap back on the toothpaste tube, or women who shave their legs with the man's razor. It is the little things that can beat the competition. At the Knockomie Lodge Hotel in

Scotland a red squirrel features as the hotel's logo. Not only that, but ceramic figures of the little creature appear in all the nooks and crannies around the hotel, peeking out at the fascinated guests.

On departure, each guest is presented with a small ceramic version of the friendly mascot—a little detail which translates into a 'Wow factor', powerful in the ability to promote positive word-of-mouth publicity and encourage repeat business. Whisky which is specially blended to the specifications of the hotel and labelled with the hotel's uniquely designed label, that is a point of difference. Flowers which are always fresh and imaginatively arranged, that is another good talking point. The flamboyantly dressed, slightly eccentric, but nevertheless efficient and friendly chef/patron sticks in the customers' memories.

John and Mary McMenemie own and operate the charming Knockendarroch House Hotel in the Scottish Highland town of Pitlochry. The Victorian manor has the atmosphere of a large country house and home. There is no bar, guests are not permitted to smoke, lunches are not offered to the passing public nor to residents, and only residents are offered dinner from a limited menu. You may think that the Knockendarroch has not got much going for it and that it is even a little impertinent to call it a 'hotel'. Well, you would be wrong. John and Mary have a very special way of offering genuine, warm, authentic hospitality.

The hotel is very much an extension of their own home. Mary creates superb quality food, drawing on her Irish roots for inspiring recipes. John welcomes the guests in a real, timeless 'mine host' fashion, drawing them into the spacious hall with its roaring log fire. 'We treat our customers as guests in our own home, which the hotel is,' says John. When evening comes and a fine meal has been enjoyed, guests, host and hostess gather in the drawing room to chat, play chess or enjoy a song at the piano from John. Nothing is too much trouble. What the customers need to make themselves comfortable they get.

All the stationery, point of sale materials, menus and children's activity materials play a part in the overall image of the Little John group of family restaurants. The children's menu is available also to senior citizens.

As well as featuring the adventures of Little John the cat, the questions included on the menu's kids' club quiz are intended to encourage youngsters to ask their parents and grandparents for answers. The restaurants themselves feature raised model railways, station signs and other rail memorabilia. Other wall-mounted conversation pieces include adverts for branded goods also taken from the time which many would regard as the golden years of rail.

Michael Hurst makes the point that when we are children we are told to come to the table the moment the food is ready. We sit down to eat. That does not happen in most restaurants. We sit down to wait. We wait to order our food, we wait to order a drink and then we wait for someone to bring it to us. That gives the word 'waiter' a totally different meaning. In too many places it is bad luck if you are hungry, dying for a drink or have children who need occupying to pass the time.

Meanwhile the waiter performs the meaningless task of putting a napkin on our laps. What for? It may be twenty minutes before it is needed, and as you sit and perhaps talk or just watch everyone else if there is nothing to save the useless napkin keeps falling on the floor. A nice thing about Littlejohn's is that the children are kept occupied, there is a source of conversation and plenty of eye-catching furnishings to make whatever time you need to wait fly by. Whitbread's conspicuously successful restaurant division TGI Friday has made a feature out of training bartenders to read the guest's needs to establish what type of experience they want. For example, a group of girls on a night out may be treated to some ice-juggling, whereas less riotous patrons may be offered a matchstick brain-teaser. Here the point of difference is concern with responding, in all sorts of unexpectedly personal and fun ways to the customer who buys your wares.

When customers go to stay somewhere or when they go out to a restaurant, they hope they will be given a bit of fun; maybe entertained, perhaps excited, but certainly they expect to be given some special treatment and be made to feel good.

Mostly it is a distraction they want, a temporary refuge from business, work, home or some situation that they would prefer to put to one side for a while. If you are paying a large amount of money to stay or eat in an expensive place you should be treated as though you really matter. In the best hotels around the world you can get that kind of treatment; however, it is not really dependent upon how much you pay but how much you get in return.

For most people, the places that really stand out are not always the most expensive, biggest or in the most glamorous locations. Julie's Sunset Bar in Clearwater, Florida, is a two-storey shack of a building situated on the coast in a run-down end of the town. Food is simple' surf and turf', steaks and seafood, and the only drink served is bottled beer, driink 'by the neck'. So what makes it special? The atmosphere is electric, full of people of all ages, enjoying the simple, honest good value of the product. The operation is controlled by Julie herself, a colourful character, and service is by young, lively staff glowing with the Floridan sun. All of a sudden the hustle and bustle stop, there is silence as patrons and staff alike stop all activity to gaze in awe at the sensational sunset which has enveloped the sea and the skyline. Julie's Sunset Bar is not expensive, certainly not glamorous, but definitely fun, exciting and the thread from which the fabric of special moments is woven. Fun and excitement, the joys of staying somewhere are provided mostly by people not things. Sure, the marble, the fountains, the imposing atrium rising to the heights above you are impressive and they provide a sense of occasion. But you cannot sleep on marble and you cannot eat the fountain. If you want an imposing and impressive ambience you can visit a cathedral and stand in the nave with its soaring arches, stained glass windows and vaulted ceilings.

The value-added package you buy which offers a free bottle of champagne, discounted restaurant rates and free use of the leisure club is all great. What happens, though-, when warm champagne is brought by a depressing-looking waiter? 'Here's your champagne,' he says, placing the tray on a side table. 'Sign here to say you got it!' The champagne is now flat and so is the sense of occasion. Services performed in a perfunctory fashion with feigned smiles take the sparkle from the enjoyment of an experience in even the most fantastic of places and situations.

It is people who make an occasion special. Which is why the secret of a successful establishment is nearly always its people. Yes, the foyer, the procedures, the efficient service, the value you get, the location, the extras of pool, spa, sauna and massage are all important, but to make the occasion really happen people have to make it happen.

It is the staff with the 'gift of friendship', the charm,

wit and engaging personalities who make an experience memorable. There are plenty of staff who can whiz through the orders and get the work done faster than most, but if they leave a trail of disaster of ruffled guests and irritated cooks behind them, what is the point?

When someone turns up for work and he or she has the flu, a friend or relative has died, or there has been an argument of some sort at home, do not let him or her near a customer! That cloud around the head may ruin the experience for some guest. It is better to pay the staff member to stay at home than to lose a customer.

Michael Hurst hired an Irish lady for a specialized task—to sell Irish coffees. He hired her because of her beautiful accent and her fascinating personality and the ability to spin the most charming tales about the effects the various Irish whiskies would have on the customers. She talked about ancient spells and the drop of magic from old Ireland that was in every nip. It was all nonsense, of course, but the customers loved her and wanted a little bit of the magic to rub off on them. Michael Hurst said she had to sell a quota of Irish coffees to justify her place on the staff, but she had no trouble at all in meeting that quota.

Some in the hospitality industry say that good service should go unnoticed. Although there is a lot of truth in that, it suggests that service is an expectation and that it is only noticed when it is not there. The trouble with a lot of places is that A is more likely to be noticed if it is there. It take-, a lot of hard work for a place to achieve that smooth-running excellence which realizes the customers' expectations.

Exceptional service, that extra something in the way in which a place does things and gives it that competitive point of difference, is usually provided by the personalities of the people who provide it.

Service for the customer begins from the very first contact with the establishment. This initial contact may be with a travel agent. A property cannot directly control what a travel agent says or does, but it can indirectly control it by making sure that the travel agent is armed with information to pass on to the customer. That information has to be more than a description of the property, the number of rooms and the going rates. It must include the points of difference and the benefits, the reasons why the travel agent can recommend it to the enquiring customer. Proper briefing of the travel agent is not just a selling strategy, it is also a service to potential customers via an intermedialy. The handling of an enquiry by an establishment should also be perceived as a service to the customer. Let us take out the mercenary considerations of 'getting-what-you-can' for the room for a moment. Sure, that is part of the business of being in business, and most experienced travellers know that. What most of them want is helpful information so that they make a decision, whether to stay at your place or another place.

For a number of establishments this does not always work the way it should. A ring-around of hotels in London and Manchester once produced some interesting results. Despite the fact that the world was in a recession at the time, in most instances the answer to the simple enquiry about rates resulted in a single reply, 'so much a room'. Nothing more. No additional helpful information, and this from some of the best in the country. In one case the phone just rang without being answered. Those who responded properly to the enquiry handled the situation by first quoting the rack rate and then going on to mention some of the packages they had. Not one respondent added any reasons why the enquiring customer should consider their establishment ahead of the rest.

When this situation was related to some hotel managers the response was mostly a rejection that it had happened. They used an excuse such as: 'must have been busy', 'it was an off night, we all have them', 'probably struck the wrong person', 'I'm really surprised, our people are excellent as a rule.' No one seriously considered what could be done to improve the situation, nor did they admit that something should be done. The moment of truth for customers occurs when they arrive at a property. How much preparation has there been for the guest's arrival? Were they told in advance what to do about parking, for example?

Most establishments are very good at making first impressions when guests arrive. Building appearance, decor, cleanliness, the door person, the reception by the concierge or receptionist and the booking in procedures are normally fine. This is where place's well-oiled machinery goes into operation. There is usually evidence of good training at this point, and seldom does it go off the rails unless a reservation is lost.

For a new customer there is the initial impact of the room—its decor, lighting, size, layout, cleanliness and tidiness, the bed, the smell, the music, TV, mini-bar, tea and coffee-making facilities, bathroom and toilet, linen fresh and crisp, etc.

All of these items make their impression. The customer either feels at home at this stage or wants to run screaming from the building and catch the first taxi out of there. It is a very sensitive moment for the customer and the quality of the hotel is often judged on how that moment is handled.

In a good place the service strategy is to explain how the room works: an induction course on where things are and how they work, such as switches and appliances, then information is given about the facilities and additional services which are available. This is the opportunity for reassurance on the customer's decision. More than that, though, it is the time to establish rapport with the customer and prepare the way for 'selling' other services. Ideally, the person doing the induction should be the continuing contact for the guest during his or her stay so that advice, information and 'fix-it' situations can be readily handled by one person or another designated person when the original contact is off duty. This contrasts with most establishments which divide the hotel into a number of departments working as separate profit-earning outlets without anyone assisting the customer in his or her use or choice. The list of service items that form part of the overall strategy can be extended according to the size and nature of the establishment.

The proximity of a hotel's restaurants to its accommodation should ensure that a very high percentage of guests use the facilities such as fine dining room, bistro, carvery or coffee shop. The problem is, such places are also competing with others in the streets nearby. So it is not enough just to be there. Each hotel eatery has to offer a really exciting benefit to win a share of its own guests and add a number of customers from outside the hotel. Food is interesting and can be fun. Dining should be an important part of the total guest experience of an establishment.

A strategy for this product requires close attention to first impressions, the guest's comfort, familiarity, welcoming staff, easy on the eye decor and style. It should build on tile ambience and quality experience provided by the rest of the hotel. Again, it is all the extra touches - hiring personality people especially that make the competitive difference for the customers.

Details matter, such as having a baby high chair,

cushions for the elderly, music which is used to create an ambience for the place (not merely to fill a sound vacuum), perhaps the smell of freshly ground coffee, newly baked bread and rolls and, most of all, the food quality—all add up to a place being a really great experience.

Getting the fundamentals of food and wine right and served well is basic to the business of a restaurant. It is not enough, however. There are many establishments which do the same. Doing the ordinary things in a better and different way is about style, and style combined with attention to every small need of the guest causes guest satisfaction. The bar facilities, for example. The bar does not have to the guest can have a drink. A service strategy can be developed around it so that it is the beginning of a dining experience, not just a place to wait for guests. For example, while the customers drink, the food order can be decided so that they go to the table as soon as the meal is ready.

Meanwhile, a skilled and personable bartender could be offering cocktails which enhance the anticipation and enjoyment of the food to come. The wine list can be a feature, offering distinctive wines of a specific country or region, wines of selected vintages, or special house wines of the month.

Meals and presentation which exemplify the regional tastes can be a talking point for guests, with gourmet experiences that no-one else offers. Special theme nights and promotions lend interest and excitement to the eating occasions and provide reasons for guest participation.

9

Menu Planning

Menu planning is one of the most important tasks in a foodservice operation and an essential component of the foodservice system. Simply stated, a menu is a list of food items served by any foodservice operation. In more complex terms, menus are statements of the food and beverage items provided by a foodservice establishment, primarily based on consumer needs and/or demands and designed to achieve organizational objectives.

Menus represent the focal point around which all components of a foodservice system are centered. The success or failure of a foodservice operation depends on the menu and how the foods on it are served. It can also determine the degree of profit for an operation. Thus all efforts need to be directed toward menu planning, taking into consideration all aspects of the operation.

Menu planning is the process by which menus are planned, taking into consideration all aspects of a foodservice system. It involves selection of food and beverage items that are acceptable from the point of view of both management and consumers. Careful menu planning will result in consumer satisfaction, employee motivation, and success of the management. The numerous factors that should be considered prior to and while planning menus may be considered from two aspects: (1) the management's viewpoint and (2) the consumers' viewpoint.

Management's viewpoint

Organizational goals and objectives

The primary consideration in menu planning is whether the menu conforms to the goals and objectives of the operation. The goals vary depending on whether the foodservice is institutional or commercial, and they need careful consideration in menu planning. For example, the menus planned for a hospital will be entirely different from the menus planned for a restaurant. The menu should reflect the purpose of the organization and the need for existence of foodservices at that operation.

Budget

Obviously, this is an extremely important factor in menu planning. The amount of money that can be spent depends on the income from food sales and the relative food cost percentage. In turn, the income from food sales depends on consumers' available disposable income (ADI), the location of the facility, the type of service, and several other dependent factors.

Menu planning requires careful consideration of the relative costs of food, labour, and equipment. There are several economic constraints, such as inflation, which have a considerable impact on the available amount at specific times. Commercial foodservices experience more fluctuations in sales/income than do institutional foodservices, where budgets are primarily based on consumer counts for a relatively longer period of time.

On the other hand, institutional foodservices are usually on a very tight budget, and therefore menu planning becomes very critical for this type of operation. This is not to imply that variety and appeal in menus cannot be planned under tight budgets. Careful planning with a blend of imagination, efficiency, and creativity is an important attribute for success in menu planning.

Efficient utilization of all the available resources is essential for success in planning menus.

Depending on the type of foodservice, budgets are normally projected (1) on the basis of estimated costs for serving an actual number of residents, (2) by per capita allowances for the expected number of consumers, or (3) by forecasting the number of consumers during a specific period of time. The food cost percentage is also a very valuable tool in determining budgets. Also, pre-costed standardized recipes, when updated from time to time, help in the calculation of costs to be used in the formulation of budgets.

Menu planning becomes very complex and difficult when a number of high and low cost items are included on a menu and when one or more of the items are offered as choices. Careful screening and selection of items are required in order to arrive at the desired combination that will result in a consistent average consumer check.

Food market conditions

Raw food products, the primary resource of any foodservice are subjected to seasonal fluctuations that have an enormous impact on the demand and supply. Favorable weather conditions may result in overabundance of a product and result in lower prices. On the other hand, adverse seasonal conditions may cause severe shortages of food products and conseq-uently higher prices. This factor is of primary importance when menus are planned, particularly for longer time periods. Fruits and vegetables are the food items most commonly affected by seasonal fluctuations.

Menus are to be planned in such a way as to take maximum advantage of the seasonal availability or nonavailability of the food products. Also, the location of the foodservice operation and its accessibility to the market affects menu planning. Foodservices located in larger cities have less problems in obtaining a variety of food products or their substitutes.

Physical facilities and equipment

The physical facilities and plant of the foodservice and the equipment it contains dictate the type of menus that may be planned and vice versa. Not only the availability of certain pieces of equipment but their number play an important role in the selection of menu items. Based on the facilities and available equipment, it may not be possible to include a menu item or a variety of menu items within a desired period of time.

Sometimes a major piece of equipment may be needed to prepare several items at a time. The proper type of equipment as well as its sequential arrangement in a facility results in smooth operation, with less fatigue for the employees. Such labour-saving devices and equipment as food processors and mechanical slicers, peelers, and corers facilitate menu planning by providing various choices for selection.

Efficient menu planning requires a well-balanced approach toward the utilization of materials, equipment, and employees. Efficient use also results in prolonged life of the equipment. The use of a variety of equipment simultaneously facilitates smooth food production and service operations. For example, deep-fat fryers, grills, and ovens may be used simultaneously to provide a variety of food items.

Trunnions may be used for preparing soups or steamed vegetables, while an adjustable and tilting skillet may be used for a variety of food preparations. Thus, planning helps in air even distribution of load to all available pieces of equipment.

Also, the size and capacity of the equipment available are very important considerations. Using the optimum capacity of the equipment reduces expensive duplication of the preparation process.

A variety of items may be included in a menu by careful utilization of equipment and space. The lack of or an insufficient number of certain pieces of equipment may lead to the complete or partial omission of certain profitable and popular foods. For example, the lack of fat fryers, chafing dishes, or mobile units may restrict the serving of high-demand profitable foods. Thus, menu planning requires a careful assessment of the equipment available, as well as its capability and performance.

Personnel skills

Efficient equipment and its layout will prove to be of little value without skilled employees to handle them. Elegant menu items requiring specific skills cannot be included if trained food personnel are not available to make them. Any temporary or permanent lack of skilled personnel therefore restricts the number and type of menu items. In most restaurants, chefs play an important role in the success and popularity of the operation.

Employees' capability and availability should be considered when planning menus. Some employees may be more skilled than others so that the average level of skills of the employees should be taken into account. Skilled and hard-working employees should be utilized efficiently without overloading them. Frustration and dissatisfaction among employees often result from an unequal distribution of work.

Menu planning therefore eliminates these problems. On the positive side, well-planned menus may become a source of motivation and challenge for the employees. While planning menus, it is desirable to consider the time and labour required for various stages of the food-product preparation. Employee availability during a particular time period also affects the type and variety of items that can be offered. An even distribution of work load helps in scheduling and forecasting the labour costs of each item of the menu.

Underutilization of employee skills may result in higher- labour costs, lack of employee motivation, lower productivity, and/or high turnover rates. Attracting, training, and retaining good employees is very difficult in foodservices and may mean the difference between making or losing money. Selection of menu items that efficiently utilize employee time and skills is therefore necessary.

In other words, the menu items selected should be those that can be produced easily, utilizing the average level of skills of skills of the available workers within a reasonable length of time. Items that require lengthy and elaborate preparation methods and require a high level of skill should be considered for possible elimination or replacement. This does not mean that variety or elegance need be sacrificed in the food items offered.

Another important consideration is the number of employees available for work or the total number of person-hours available. Providing assistance to skilled employees, like a chef, will free their time for use in the preparation of other menu items that perhaps only they can make.

Many menu items cannot be prepared and stored before service, and many items require last-minute preparation, such as hollandaise sauce. Last minute preparation normally imposes a burden on employees at peak service times, and therefore every minor detail should be taken into consideration while planning menus.

At times, permanent or temporary replacement of employees makes it necessary to modify or adjust the menus offered. It is advisable to get as much preparation as possible completed during any slack periods of time with only essential last-minute preparation to be taken care of at a later stage. Since labour costs represent a major item of expenditure in food preparation, careful control of the above-mentioned aspects is necessary.

Types of production and service subsystems

Production types have a great deal of impact on the items that can be included in a menu. Time lag between production and service is very critical. In a conventional food production and delivery system, where foods are prepared, held at serving temperature, and served on the same day, there are relatively many choices that may be included on the menu.

On the other hand, in systems where food is cooked and chilled or frozen, there are severe limitations on the type of foods that can be prepared and served. The amount of time required for service is also very important. For example, in large multistoried hospitals, the time lapse between tray assembly and service may be so long that certain foods such as ice creams or omelets cannot be used.

In some foodservice operations, where fast service is desired, the choices for menu items are restricted. A restaurant with table service will have a different kind of menu than that of a cafeteria. Thus menu choices are also based on the type of foodservice operation.

Consumers' viewpoint

The following factors are directly related to consumer needs and tastes and therefore need consideration when planning menus.

Nutritional requirements

Almost every type of foodservice is starting to put a high priority on meeting the nutritional needs of its consumers. Until recently, institutional foodservices were the only type that were much concerned with nutritional balance in their menus. This may be due to the fact that these operations are required by different agencies as well as by their organizational objectives to provide well-balanced meals to their patrons.

Meeting nutritional needs in such institutions as hospitals, nursing homes, and schools, is extremely important and should be given top priority when planning menus for these facilities.

Commercial foodservices are also now beginning to give nutrition serious thought in the meals that they offer. An essential guide that is necessary for nutritional planning of menus is the table of Recommended Daily Dietary Allowances for different ages and sex groups. These standards have been established by the Food and Nutrition Board, National Academy of Sciences-National Research Council for the maintenance of good nutrition of practically all healthy people in the United States. These allowances, commonly referred to as RDA, take into consideration individual variations among most normal persons living in the United States under the usual environmental stresses. Diets should be based on a variety of common foods in order to provide all nutrients, including those that are not included in the recommended dietary allowances and for which human requirements have been less well defined.

Percentages of the daily RDA values should be taken into consideration when planning nutritionally well-balanced menus. Certain federal and state agencies require that the menus planned for certain institutions meet RDA values, as in the case of the school-lunch program, where the provision of one-third of the RDA per day Is required. RDA values are very helpful in the calculation of nutrients and in planning menus. RDA values are updated on a regular basis and are changed to meet the most current requirements. RDA values are used by many foodservice managers, particularly those in hospital foodservices for the calculation and labeling of nutrients in diets.

On the basis of RDA, United States Recommended Dietary Allowances (USRDAs) are defined; they are primarily based on the average requirements, without taking into consideration the age or the sex of the individuals. USRDAs are used primarily for nutritional labeling.

Nutritional labels are printed on food packages and give information pertaining to calories per average serving; the amount of carbohydrates, proteins, and fats; and the percentage of nutrients provided in significant quantities by the specified normal serving of that food. USRDAs are often confused with RDA values, but there is a considerable difference between the two. In foodservice management, the RDA is used for menu planning, while USRDAs are helpful in purchasing and receiving of food, and in labeling menu items.

The growing nutritional concerns among many consumers have resulted in careful assessment of the menu items and portion sizes served by many institutional and commercial foodservice operations. This warrants careful review of the portion sizes and the percentages of the RDAs derived from them while selecting menu items. The salt, sugar, fiber, and overall carbohydrate contents provided by menu items also need careful assessment when planning menus. For certain specific nutrients, such as sodium, there are guidelines for recommended lower and higher limits of safe intake.

A variety of foods, when properly used, will provide most of the necessary nutrients. Related to the nutritional contents of foods in menu planning are consumer preferences of foods. Certain foods, such as liver and organ meats, may be rich in nutrients but may not be liked very well by the average consumer. Thus, nutritional content alone does not guarantee a popular menu.

When planning menus based on nutritional requirements, consumer needs and wants discussed earlier should be taken into consideration. These needs will vary based on several factors, age being an important one.

Menus for children require special consideration. The nutrient content of meals provided by the school-foodservice menus is restricted by the requirements of the National School Lunch Act, which gives guidelines for the nutritional adequacy of school lunches provided for primary and secondary school children, as well as some children in permanent-care facilities. The school lunch program is administered by the United States Department of Agriculture (USDA), which provides a cash reimbursement per lunch when requirements are met by the foodservices.

In addition to cash reimbursements, USDA commodities are donated through state de partments of education, since student participation in such lunch programs varies from school to school. Local commercial foodservice operations, as well as snack bar and vending machines, have an impact on the students' decision to participate in the school lunch programs. Menus for school lunches have to be very carefully planned with a view to the heterogeneous nature of the school population.

Generally, these menus have to be planned well in advance, since they have to be publicized through various sources. The Type A lunch basically consists of the following meal components: (1) main dish, (2) vegetable, (3) salad, (4) bread item, (5) dessert, and (6) milk. A quick, nutritious meal can also be provided by the following permissible variation which consists of (1) protein-rich sandwich (2) salad or raw vegetable, (3) fruit or cookie, and (4) milk.

Many restaurants and fast-food chains are providing nutritive meals a well as suggesting ways through which adequate nutrition can be obtained by selecting certain menu items. Since children and the elderly are among the growing categories of their consumers, the nutritional quality of their meals is of paramount importance. Providing nutritive foods by careful menu planning becomes absolutely necessary for hospital patients and nursing-home residents. Such careful planning is even more critical for nursing-home residents, since long-term planning has to be made and pleasing this category of consumers becomes a real challenge.

Menu planning for this group of consumers is not only based on nutrition, but also on food preferences. In planning menus it is essential to consider the nutritional requirements of all the categories of consumers. Closely associated with the selection of the items based on their nutrient contents are the different food groups, the most important of them being (1) meats, (2) fruits and vegetables, (3) milk and milk products, and (4) cereals and breads. The food items or choices selected should be such that all the food groups are included in one meal, if possible. This will indirectly ensure the nutritive content of the meals, although this may not be a very accurate way of estimating it.

Many foodservices provide the caloric and nutrient contents of the menu items and also express those values in terms of the percentages of the RDA. There are several ways of computing the nutritional values of the food items selected. One of the most common and economical way of estimating the nutrient composition of foods is by using the values from food composition tables.

The U.S. Department of Agriculture (USDA) has published various handbooks and tables which can be used in the calculation of the nutrient values of the foods. The USDA "Handbook No. 8" and USDA "Handbook No. 456" are indispensable references for anyone involved in menu planning, since they contain tables that provide the nutrient compositions of hundreds of foods in various forms expressed on the basis of commonly used portion sizes. These publications are updated from time to time so that new foods and cut-rent nutrient values can be added.

Menus should meet the nutritional needs of the patrons as well as those requirements set by federal and state agencies, wherever applicable. Nursing homes and health-care facilities are required to meet certain requirements in order to qualify for state or federal aid. Residence halls, day-care centers, and other foodservices where quality food items are served should consider serving nutritionally well-balanced and wholesome meals.

Although institutional types of foodservices are more particular about meeting nutritional requirements, there are many commercial types of foodservices as well as franchises that have begun to put nutrition labels on their foods so that the consumers may be made aware of the nutritive value of the foods they select. This type of information is definitely needed and will prove helpful in at least two ways: (1) by providing the amount of the recommended daily dietary allowances provided by each meal and thereby helping in food selection, and (2) by reducing the misconception that foods provided by that foodservice operation are devoid of nutrients or are loaded with calories.

Some foodservices are advertising or are listing the special types of foods offered by them, such as those containing low fat or low salt. This attracts the undecided consumer and leads to greater consumer satisfaction. Restaurants and other commercial foodservice operations offering balanced nutritious foods may prove to be valuable outlets for providing balanced diets to selected segments of the population. Inclusion of salad bars, fruits, and vegetables provides for nutritious meals as well as for making menus more appealing. At places, particularly foodservices in industries, where workers may consume the main meal of the day, it is extremely important that the foods selected for menus be rich in nutrition.

Food habits and preferences

No matter how sophisticated food preparation methods are or how attractively foods are served, a menu is of little practical value if the foods in it are not liked by the consumer. In menu planning, food preferences and habits play a very important role.

Currently, this factor is largely underscored by many foodservice operators primarily because of the following reasons: (1) food preferences are intricately related to several factors and are very complex, (2) data are lacking on food preferences, (3) simple methods for evaluating food preferences are lacking, (4) the study of food preferences requires expertise in several disciplines such as psychology and the behavioral sciences, and (5) the potential uses of food preferences in the management of the hospitality industry are not very well defined. In order to comprehend fully the intricacies involved in food and foodservice preferences, it is necessary to analyze all interrelated aspects.

When a menu is presented to a consumer, there are a variety of factors that act simultaneously prior to the final selection of the menu item. "A person prefers to eat what he/she likes and likes to prefer what he/she eats" summarizes the complex nature of the food preferences. Managers in the hospitality industry should recognize that all consumers have a great deal of previous knowledge and experience of food (no matter how limited that may be), which makes them highly critical of food compared to other services or products.

Food preferences may be defined as the selection of food items from choices available among acceptable foods. Patterns of food selection may emerge as a consequence of temporary or permanent food preferences. Food habits may be defined as the way in which individuals, in response to social and cultural pressures, select, consume, and utilize portions of the available food supply.

Food preferences are based on sensory, social, psychological, religious, emotional, cultural, health, economic, preparation, and other related factors. Food habits and food acceptances are learned, acquired, and finally become a part of oneself. They become a very strong form of individual self-expression. Several influences start acting on one's food preferences at birth and continue to operate throughout life.

Intirinsic factors

These include certain influences directly associated with food such as appearance' colour, odor, texture, temperature, flavor, and quality. The manner in which food is presented, the way food is arranged on the plate, and the temperature at which it is served, all have an impact on food preferences. Standardized large-quantity food production may lead to a different food preference ranking than if similar foods are prepared at home.

Variability in these intrinsic factors affect food preferences.

Extrinsic factors

Extrinsic factors include the direct external factors that can affect food preferences as follows:

1. *Environment*. Food preferences are affected by the environment in which it is served as such areas as homes, restaurants, and clubs. A good example is the hospital environment, which has a marked effect on the selection of food. On the other hand, the effect that a candlelight environment in a restaurant has on food preference compared to that in a fast-food restaurant is obvious.
2. *Situational expectation*. The quality of food one expects is a function of the situation in which it is to be consumed. Food is expected to be good when it is associated with social, ritual, or religious occasions. Thus, the food served at a banquet or wedding party carries with it the expectation of something outstanding, in keeping with the occasion itself.
3. *Advertising*. It is evident and has been proven by many studies that advertising can influence one's attitude toward food. Many foodservice operations use this vehicle for attracting consumers. Also, the consumers are tempted to try new food when it is properly advertised. Many places advertise the specialties on their menus.
4. *Time and seasonal variations*. Food selections appear to be somewhat immune to the influence of certain natural phenomena such as seasonal variations, outdoor temperatures, and the day of the week. However, the availability of certain seasonal foods, particularly fruits and vegetables, affects their selection. For example, watermelons are generally

preferred during the hot summer months. On the other hand, hot chocolate is not a summer favorite. Other factors such as the hours of meal service, the length of the meal times, and the selection of food as close as possible to the meal times may also have an effect on food preferences.

Biological, physiological, and psychological Factors

These factors are each broad in scope but are grouped together here since they are closely interrelated. Physiological disorders can have a profound effect on food preferences by changing the appreciation, perception, or appetite toward food. These changes are often associated with psychological influences commonly related to physical well-being. Age and sex are major demographic factors that influence food preferences. A good example of this is the higher acceptance and preference of "fast foods" by the younger generation.

Personal factors

The individual and personal attributes that affect food choice are as follows:

1. *Level of expectation*. This has been shown to have an definite effect on food preferences and selection. For example, patients in hospitals have a low expectation regarding hospital food. When these patients find the food better than they expected, the preference ratings are favorably affected. On the other hand, the level of expectation is much higher when dining at a restaurant. If the food is of lower quality than expected, the ratings can be adversely affected. This phenomenon coincides with the sociopsychological theory that the lower the level of expectation, the more easily satisfied the person is; and that people perceive things as they expect them to be, rather than as they are.

2. *Priority*. This factor is indirectly related to the level of expectations. Airline foodservices or hospital foodservices are good examples of the consumers' priorities to reach their destination or recovery and well-being, rather than to have outstanding gourmet meals. Thus, other aspects are more likely to be critically evaluated than food.
3. *Familiarity*. The conditions under which a person initially experiences food has an impact on acceptance behavior. Earlier studies have shown that familiar terms on menus produced controversial results. Some research has shown that menu acceptance is enhanced by the use of familiar terms, whereas others have indicated that interesting or descriptive menus may increase food appeal and selection.
4. *Influence of other persons*. Friends, relatives, and family members can influence food preferences. Even those being served on a cafeteria line can influence the food selection of a person behind them in the line. Individuals have been found to accept food advice best from those they consider friends or professionals. As can be expected, parents are most influential in the introduction and acceptance of foods by children.
5. *Appetites, moods, and emotions*. These represent a complex intermingling of preference factors. A careless server may be spared for bringing cold food to the table when one is in a good mood; the same may not be true if one is in a bad mood. Preferences for similar foods vary based on moods. Moods are unpredictable and are constantly changing, which causes problems in planning. Moods and appetites are also influenced by physiological disorders, as well as such factors as satisfaction or dissatisfaction with work and salary.

6. *Family unit.* A mother's educational achievements and her employment status are some of the items associated with this type of influence on food preferences. A young family is more concerned with economizing than a couple between 45 and 60 years of age, who are primarily concerned with reducing calories, cholesterol, and salt in their diet.
7. *Educational status.* Degree and type of education affect food preferences and selection. Nutrition education also influences food preferences, but nutritional knowledge or education alone does not ensure an adequate diet or the correct selection of foods.

Socioeconomic factors

Socioeconomic factors operate when one is following set food patterns or is altering them temporarily or permanently to meet economic limitations. Abundant evidence exists in both developed and developing countries to demonstrate that food choices are related to income. During such short-term crises as illness or unemployment, people tend to cut back on the money they spend on food and drinks. Food can also contribute to one's sense of security by retaining past habits and resisting any change in them. Food preferences can be a means of demonstrating group acceptance, conformity, and prestige.

Cultural and religious factors

Cultural and religious motivations for food preferences are transmitted from one generation to another. Various religious restrictions have resulted in stable and rigid food preferences. For example, Muslims and Jews restrict the use of pork and pork products. Religious beliefs affect food preferences, which become rigid food habits and influence vast segments of the population.

In foodservice menu planning, recognizing these population groups and their food preferences is crucial. Differences in food preferences are obvious among cultures in different parts of the world. All these factors should be taken into consideration in menu planning, regardless of the type of foodservice. Food preferences have to be considered very carefully to avoid individual bias. These can be avoided by using informal and formal methods to analyze and study how the consumers in an operation react to various menu items that are served.

Informal observations in the dining room and in the cafeteria line, comments made by the consumers, leftovers, and the extent of food wastes provide valuable information on food likes and dislikes. Formal types of surveys can also be conducted using different methods.

Various types of questionnaires may be designed to suit specific foodservices by including pertinent questions. The results of such studies are very useful in planning menus. Food preferences of the consumers should be assessed periodically, in order to consider changes in technology, food availability, economy, and consumer food habits. Consideration of food preferences becomes more critical in planning menus for a longer period of time.

Menu items have to be rotated so as not to repeat food items, particularly those that are not well liked. A possible solution to food dislikes may be to include choices among menu items. A way of ranking food preferences may also be developed and when choices are provided, foods can be selected in such a way that similar ranked items are included on the menu as choices. This will facilitate an even selection of items from choices provided in the menu. Choices should be carefully weighed before inclusion, since forecasting production becomes more complex with the number of choices added to a menu.

Food characteristics

Probably the most important factor to be considered in menu planning's the food itself characteristics of foods, which include their organoleptic properties, play an important role in their acceptance. The most important aspects related to food characteristics are discussed below.

Colour

Interesting and coordinating colour combinations are very desirable and help in the acceptance of food and to an extent (indirectly) in stimulating appetite. Planning and arranging foods so that there is a good colour combination, whether on a plate, tray, counter, or salad bar are very important aspects of menu planning. Even a small garnish, like a parsley twig or a cherry, can make an enormous difference in food appearance and its acceptability, Colourful foods have eye appeal, which can lead to their selection. Colour also emphasizes the variety available for selection.

When planning menus, different coloured items should be included, and too many items with similar colour should be avoided. In some printed menus, the visual aspects of the foods are enhanced by providing colour pictures. Bright and desirable food combinations add to a menu's attractiveness, while dull colours may convey a sense of blandness in the food. Thus, a consumer will often select food first by its eye appeal and thus colour is a very important aspect that should be considered in planning menus.

Colours also have a psychological impact on consumers. Red, orange, peach, pink, brown, yellow, and light green are considered desirable colours for foods. Purple, violet, dark green, gray, and olive are less desirable as colours for foods. Artificial colouring may be added to enhance the colour of foods as long as it is safe and does not impart any undesirable taste or bitterness.

Generally, food colours that are natural are preferred. Fruits and vegetables, in all their variety of forms and shapes, add to the colours of the items included in the menu. Garnishings, plate decorations, and attractive counter displays add to the colour of the foods and should be considered when planning menus.

Texture and shape

These characteristics of foods also affect consumers Preferences. Certain foods are preferred because of their hard texture and some because of their soft texture. A desirable combination between the soft- and hard-textured items on the menu is essential. The impressions of the texture and shape of a particular food are formed even before tasting it. Texture can best be detected by mouthfeel. "Soft," "hard," "crispy," "crunchy," "chewy," "smooth," "brittle," and "grainy" are some of the adjectives used to describe food texture. A variety in texture in foods is highly desirable. Certain food items go well with a difference in texture. Soups are preferred with crispy crackers, soft-textured potatoes go well with chewy steaks and casseroles are desirable with crisp vegetables.

Normally, consumers do not prefer all item" on the menu to be chewy or soft; therefore, it is important to consider the texture of the food items. Foods in different colours and shapes add to the attraction of the menu as well as to eye appeal when the foods are served. Vegetable and fruit carvings provide interesting shapes and can also add to food appeal.

Special equipment can be used to dice, cut, or carve products into various shapes and sizes. Carrots, for example, may be cut in squares, strips, circles, balls, screws, and other interesting shapes. Mixed vegetables are another good example of interesting shapes, since they not only provide colour but also add to the texture and enhance the attractiveness of the food when placed on a plate. Even if similar products are included in the menu, shape breaks the monotony of having a single texture of food.

Consistency

Consistency refers to the degree of viscosity or density of a product. Like texture, consistency provides for variety among the menu items. "Runny," "gelatinous," "pasty," "thin," "thick," "sticky," and "gummy" are the most common adjectives used to describe consistency. These terms are most often used for sauces and gravies. Food items on a particular menu should have varying consistencies. Too many runny items on the menu will not only affect the flavor of the food but it will also be hard to keep these items together on the plate without intermingling them. As a rule, items that have a hard texture should be complemented by items having a thin consistency. Relatively hard textured meats go well with thin gravies while nuts in thin items add a desirable combination of textures.

Flavor

The flavor of foods is a very important consideration when planning menus. Simply stated, foods can have sweet, sour, bitter, or salty flavors, which can be present alone or in combination. In addition, there are various off-flavors or undesirable flavors specific to foods.

A desirable blend of flavors is essential for creating uniqueness in the menu. The predominance of any one flavor is often undesirable. A contrast in the types of flavors and their intensity adds to the acceptability of menu items. Bland foods may be made more appetizing by adding pungent sauces or a blend of sweet and sour flavors may be added to a menu. Pickles and mustards add to the flavor of the foods when used in proper quantities. Too many pungent items or sweet items are not desirable. The right combinations of spices and condiments are therefore essential in order to develop the right kinds of flavors. Frequent taste testing and standardization are needed in order to achieve the desired flavor combinations.

Examples of desirable combinations of flavor are sweet and sour pork, curried chicken with rice, lamb with mint sauce, sauerkraut and Polish sausage, chicken with orange sauce, and broccoli with hollandaise sauce. Flavors can also be masked or enhanced by adding contrasting items, as in the case of liver and onions, vanilla pudding, and curried eggplant. Some recipes call for the addition of certain natural or artificial flavor enhancers, which, as the name indicates, enhance the flavors present in foods rather than provide their own flavors. A combination of strong- and mild-flavored vegetables also is desirable in menus. Broccoli, cabbage, and onions provide strong flavors and therefore should be complemented by mild flavored vegetables.

Method of food preparation

Consideration should be given to the method of preparation in menu planning. There are several ways food items can be prepared, and a variety in the methods of preparation is desirable. Some restaurants are limited or known for a certain type of food preparation, but most foodservices have the option of preparing foods in many different ways. These methods include frying, baking, broiling, boiling, steaming, grilling, braising, or a combination of these methods. In each of these types of preparation, there may be variations based on the sauces or gravies used or the equipment used, such as flame-broiled chicken with barbecue sauce or roast duck with gravy. It is very much advisable to group by method of preparation all the recipes offered by a foodservice operation. Then it will be easier to select the items for preparation as well as to avoid items that are similar in preparation.

From the management point of view, it is essential that there be a uniform distribution of the methods selected for food preparation. Optimum use of employee skills and equipment demands that there be a balanced distribution in preparation methods. A fried item on the menu may tie up the deep-fat fryer or the skilled cook, thereby limiting the possibility of including other food items similarly prepared. Predominant use of a single preparation method is not desirable. For example, too many fried items on the menu—even with variability in the types of foodd—is undesirable and unappetizing. Also, from the nutritional point of view, many consumers may dislike fatty foods and/or may prefer steamed items. A balance is therefore very desirable in the methods of food Preparation so that a variety is provided.

Serving temperature

This is probably the easiest part and least complex component in planning menus based on food characteristics. Temperatures for food preferred by individuals vary with age and other personal factors. Both hot and cold foods are desirable items to be included on the menu. A chilled gazpacho appetizer is desirable with hot entrées, a cold salad may go well with hot bread, or a cold sandwich may be more desirable with hot food items.

Similarly, cold desserts are preferred after hot entrées In planning menus, these factors should also be taken into consideration. There is no strong evidence that season or weather will have an impact on the selection of particular temperatures of food, but it may be desirable to include a lemonade or sherbet on a hot day. Similarly, hot chocolate may be preferred on a relatively cold day.

The seasonal availability of foods will also affect their inclusion on menus. Strawberry milk shakes, watermelons, and peach desserts help provide the feeling of warm or hot seasons.

Presentation method

The final appearance of food—whether on a plate, cafeteria counter, serving tray, take-out package, buffet table, or a display case—is a very important aspect in the final selection of the item. This should therefore be taken into consideration when planning menus. Consumers buy with their "eyes."

A three-dimensional appearance of the food adds to the attractiveness of the menu whether on paper or in actuality. Flat food items on the plate, regardless of their taste, are unappealing and to a greater extent, undesirable. Similarly, all tall food items on the plate are unappetizing and do not contribute to a contrast and sequence in arrangement. A meat chop with a whole baked potato, a dressed whole tomato, a rectangular cornbread piece, and cut celery stalks on a plate are very unappealing, regardless of their colours or flavors.

Menu patterns

A menu pattern is the outline of food items and choices to be included in each meal. Menu patterns are based on the types of foods to be included on the menu, taking into consideration all different factors. Menus may be divided based on the patterns into three principal types.

Non-selective menus

This type of menu is set and therefore does not provide any choices among food items offered. Institutional types of foodservices would normally have a set menu pattern although some commercial operations may also opt to have set menus, particularly if their specialty is based on one or limited food items.

Set or non-selective menus are most suited to situations where the consumer is unable to make a decision as in the case of children, the elderly, or patients; or when there is limited time available for service as in the case of banquets or foodservices at parks and tourist attractions and sports arenas. In some operations, production costs, the type of delivery service, available equipment, and personnel skills may make it necessary to have set menus. Set menus facilitate easy production forecasting—saving management time and reducing waste to a certain extent.

Planning set menus is relatively difficult since such factors as variety, nutritional quality, and consumer satisfaction have to be considered simultaneously among choices available for use, which in certain situations may be very limited. Consumer dissatisfaction may result if the set menus are not carefully planned. These types of menus are generally used in hospitals, nursing homes, banquets, and schools. Plate waste may be indicative of the popularity and consumption of these menus. Sometimes these menus are also referred to as simple menus, since they do not provide for choices and are simple in nature. Since these menus are set, there is less potential for accommodating different categories of consumers, their food habits, and preferences.

Selective menus

These menus provide two or more choices for each meal and choices may also be provided for each course of the meal. These menus have relatively more flexibility and provide sufficient choices to fulfill food preferences of most of the consumers. Selective menus are used most commonly in restaurants, fast-food franchises, and cafeterias. Evidently, these menus result in greater consumer satisfaction than the set menus. Since there may be numerous choices involved, a well-balanced selective menu is very difficult to plan. Forecasting demand and consequently production, are very difficult mainly because of the uncertainty in grouping choices.

Food-preference ratings for food items may help in ranking foods and providing combinations. The process of selection by the consumer leads to more contacts and interactions with the personnel, which may be desirable. Thus, a person in a cafeteria line, restaurant, or hospital will get an opportunity to interact with those providing service. Also, this interaction facilitates selling of the items by helping in the selection of the choices as in the case of a food server in a restaurant.

From the management point of view, this type of menu is difficult to plan and serve. Increased production imposes a load on the equipment and personnel which needs careful planning. Also, more production and service equipment is needed. This type of menu may include several choices among appetizers, soups, salads, vegetables, entrées, desserts, and vegetables. The number of choices available for each type should be decided on in advance and are better planned by setting up a menu pattern. Efficient portion-control methods are also needed to control costs when this type of menu is used.

Partially selective menus

This type of menu provides choices among entrées, vegetables, or desserts but not the other menu items. Partial-choice menus may provide answers to some of the problems inherent in the two types of menus discussed earlier. Several types of foodservice operations use this type of menu. Most often, the choices are provided among entrées. Menu planning is facilitated by planning all other items and then selecting the partial-choice food items. It not only makes the forecasting easier but also helps in planning production. Where there are limitations on the kind of equipment and the availability of skilled personnel, the partial-choice menu may be more suitable.

Menu cycles and cylce menus

"Menu cycle" refers to the time period for which menus are planned which may range from a few days to several weeks. It is advisable to have menu cycles based on odd-numbered days so that the serving of similar food items on particular days of the week is not repeated.

The term "menu cycle" is often confused with another term "cycle menus," which refers to a set or different sets of carefully planned menus that are rotated at fixed intervals of time. Menus are planned for various periods ranging from two weeks to several months and are rotated at the end of the selected period. Thus, the cycle is repeated at a fixed period of time.

Typical menu cycles in foodservices are based on a three- or four-month cycle, mostly in accordance with the seasons. An advantage of using cycle menus is that they provide for changes based on seasonal variations. A set of menus may be planned for each season and repeated at a set period of time, which provides for the inclusion of seasonal foods. Within each set cycle, the menus can also be rotated.

The length of the cycle should be selected very carefully, since the entire rotation is based on the cycle. The cycle has a beginning, middle, and an end period. The food items selected should be adequately balanced throughout this cycle. The cycle may be "short" or "long. " Short cycles may be of three weeks' duration or less and may be repeated at least four times per season. Separate cycles may be planned for each season. Thus, threeweek cycles may be planned for fall (September, October, and November); winter (December, January, and February); spring (March, April, and May); and summer (June, July, and August). Long cycles may range over an extended period of time, such as six-week cycles within a year or more.

Cycle menus are commonly used in institutional foodservices, particularly hospitals and nursing homes. Where consumers are likely to utilize foodservices for a short period of time, such as in hospitals, shorter menu cycles are very appropriate. On the other hand, cycle menus may cause problems and may create monotony due to repetitions. The advantages of the cycle menus may be summed up as follows:

1. If menus are carefully planned, cycle menus reduce the need for frequently planning menus, which avoids this tedious procedure and also frees much needed time for other management functions.
2. The frequent use of menu items in the cycle helps in standardizing production and service procedures.
3. The work loads of the employees and the equipment used may be evenly distributed on a long-term basis and can be balanced uniformly.
4. Food purchasing and inventory control are facilitated, since purchase orders are easy to make and the inventory can be controlled accordingly. Also, well-planned and formal methods of food purchasing may be utilized since the long-term needs are known.
5. Production forecasting and control becomes relatively easier.
6. Comparative evaluations of the cost of production can be made between menu cycles as well as between set periods within the cycles.
7 It is easy to make changes and troubleshoot any problems.

On the other hand, there are several disadvantages associated with the use of cycle menus. The greatest problem stems from the fact that the food may become monotonous due to the lack of variability over a period of time. Also, if the cycles are not very carefully planned, the errors or problems keep repeating. Shorter cycles may result in too frequent repetitions and monotony. If the cycle is too long, planning and management may become too difficult and complicated.

Therefore, the length of the menu cycle is extremely important and should be carefully assessed before and after its implementation. The first cycle of the newly planned menu should always be regarded as a test period and adjustments should be made after careful assessment based on the problems encountered and/or observed deficiencies. Frequent adjustments may be necessary in the subsequent cycles. New food items, when possible, should be included in the menu cycle to break the monotony. Adjustments should also be made for the food costs based on inflation and other economic conditions. If not, an expensive item may keep rotating in the cycle thus imposing an additional burden on the available budget. Cycles should be adjusted or arranged, keeping in view forthcoming special occasions and holidays. Once the cycle menus are carefully planned and evaluated, they become established and provide all the above-mentioned advantages.

Mechanics of menu planning

Menu planning is one of the most important responsibilities of management. Thus the person(s) planning menus should be aware of all aspects of production and service and must be well experienced. Since all foodservice operations are different in some respects, it will be necessary for a new manager to understand the situations and any problems at the new foodservice facility regardless of his/her previous experience. Much can be learned from the successes and failures of past menus. In health-related foodservices, menus are checked and/or planned by dietitians. It is advisable to have a group meeting for menu planning so that different ideas can be explored. Consideration should also be given to invite those in charge of purchasing and production to these meetings, which should be planned at a convenient time and location, well ahead of time, with no distractions or interruptions. Sufficient lead time should be allowed for scheduling food ordering, production planning, and employee scheduling. Some of the reference materials that should be readily available for menu planning include:

1. Standardized recipe files, showing in detail method of preparation, portion sizes, portion costs, and nutrient content
2. Copies of previous menus, if available
3. Cookbooks
4. Pictures of prepared foods, If available
5. Food preference data, if available
6. Market statements
7. Consumer comments, if available
8. Food delivery schedules
9. A comprehensive list of menu items, preferably with their prices
10. Food sales record
11. Production records
12. Professional and trade journals
13. Organizational manual
14. Other pertinent publications

Since most of these items are readily available in the foodservice manager's office, it may be advisable to have the menu planning meeting in there. Copies of these materials may also be placed in the library or meeting room. Although not all of the above-mentioned references may be needed at one time, those listed provide important information for menu planning.

Consumer preferences and comments should be analyzed and reviewed first and, if possible, before the meeting. It is also advisable to arrange the menu items in categories based on one or more of the following attributes: cost, nutritional value, possible choices, colour, seasonal availability, texture, and flavor. There are certain computerized programs that can categorize menu items based on the above-mentioned attributes and also provide a ranking among the menu items.

To start the process of menu planning, it is important to have several blank menu forms for use, as they are extremely helpful. These menu forms should be based on the menu patterns and the number of choices planned for each meal. Careful planning of these forms will avoid a lot of inconvenience. Several copies of these blanks should be made available since the process may involve several trials and errors. These forms may be printed in regular size papers or incorporated on a large blackboard. Erasable ink, chalk, and pencils will be needed for use in the planning session.

A typical menu pattern should be outlined on the basis of which menu forms can be designed. A menu form should therefore include meal pattern(s), number of meals, days of the week, and types of food items. When planning menus, care should be taken to avoid food leftovers as much as possible. In cycle menus, it will be difficult to utilize any leftovers until the cycle is repeated. It is advisable to keep a record of the leftover items and consider that when planning menus. The leftovers are also indicative of the popularity of those items or the preferences for those types of menu items.

The next aspect that should be considered in menu planning is which meal or type of food should be considered first. There are certain food items and meals that have priority and therefore should be considered first in planning. It is advisable to follow a sequence every time a menu is planned. The steps in menu planning, which have proven successful, are the following.

Step 1. Entrées, or main courses, of meal selection for entire period of menu cycle

This would be, in most cases, dinner entrées, meat items, or their alternatives. These should preferably be selected first because (1) other food items for each meal are selected to complement the entrée choice, (2) they are often the most expensive items on the menu, (3) good balance among the menu items may be maintained by planning food items that complement the entrée, and (4) their cost will be Indicative of the average meal price that call be expected. It is also recommended that the entrée selection be based on the cost of the item, maintaining a good balance between the high- and low-priced menu items. This balance should bring about an average price of these items on it day-to-day basis. This primarily depends on the type of foodservices and what is desired to be an average daily meal check for that type of facility.

If the menu pattern does not provide for choices, a weekly menu should be planned using different entrée items from meats or meat substitutes, such as beef, chicken, fish, pork, and organ meats. Care should be taken to see that the same type of meat is not repeated on the preceding or succeeding day of the week, even if the preparation methods are different. For example, use of a casserole with ground beef should not be followed by hamburgers. If there are several choices provided for the same meal, combinations may be selected on the basis of preference ratings.

BREAKFAST
Juice or fruit
Hot or cold cereals
Meat or meat alternative(s)
Bread w. butter or margarine
Hot and/or cold beverages
LUNCH
Soups or appetizers
Entrée
Vegetable and/or salad
Bread w. butter or margarine
Dessert
Hot and/or cold beverages
DINNER
Appetizers
Soups
Entrée
Salad
Potato, rice, or pasta
Vegetables
Bread w. butter or margarine
Dessert
Hot and/or cold beverages

Fig. 1 A typical menu pattern

Food items with similar or close ratings to each other should be included in choices in order to avoid selection of only one popular item when placed against relatively less popular items. Variety should be considered when providing more than one entrée choice on the same day. Barbecued beef, turkey divan, and cheese omelet; or fried chicken, roast beef, and fish are good examples of variety among choices. Even when choices are provided, care should be taken to see that there are no repetitions on preceding or succeeding days. For example, fried fish and fried chicken, or curried veal with rice, and a carrot-and-rice casserole should preferably be avoided as combinations even though they are somewhat different. Similar variations in preparation methods should be provided for various days of the week. Also, items with similar garnishes and/or gravies should be avoided. It should also be considered that there are limited items to which garnishes or gravies are to be added since they are an added labour cost.

Another fact that should be taken into consideration Is the texture of the selected entrées. For example, it is not advisable to provide casseroles as the only choices on a particular menu. Soft- and hard-textured entrées should be offered so that there are enough variations to suit the demand of the consumers. Foods that are fried, baked, broiled, pouched, and steamed should be evenly distributed on the menu. Also, choices should include highly seasoned and relatively less seasoned items in order to provide variety. Gravies or drippings may be added to improve the flavor of the entrées or other menu items as well as to supplement their nutrient content.

Step 2. Entrée selection for second most important meal of day

In most cases this will be the entrée for lunch, except in the case of certain foodservice operations where the elderly or the employees are served. In these cases, lunch is the most important meat of the day. Most people prefer salads or light meals for lunch, and therefore these should be included on the menu. If choices are provided, there should be a balance among these items. In the final selection of the items, all aspects discussed in Step 1 should be taken into consideration. Variety among type of meat, preparation method, texture, and colour, should all be considered. Also, a balance should be maintained by selecting high-cost and the low-cost entrées. For example, if a high-cost entrée was selected for dinner, a relatively low-cost entrée may be selected for lunch, and vice versa.

Step 3. Starchy food selection

Starchy foods such as potatoes, rice, pasta, and yams, should be selected to complement the entrées, since they will provide variety in colour, texture, consistency, shape, and flavor. These starchy foods should be coordinated with the entrée If the entrées are relatively dry, moist and creamed dishes should be selected; on the other hand, if the meats have drippings or juice, bland foods such as mashed potatoes should be included to complement the flavor. Creamed or steamed items provide moistness when included with entrées that tend to be dry. Care should be taken to see that there are only a limited number of starchy items on the menu. It is quite possible that the entrée may be a casserole with starchy foods like rice or potatoes; under these circumstances, this step should be totally excluded from the planning process. From the nutritional point of view this step should be very carefully controlled since starchy foods are often laden with calories. When the main entrées are low in calories, these foods provide a very good variety and may be used as "fill-ins." It is also possible to include one such item in the overall combinations provided in the menu. This is the step where the judgment and experience of the menu planner(s) are needed.

Step 4. Vegetable selection for lunch and dinner

Vegetables should complement the entrée items and should be selected on the basis of colour, shape, size, texture, preparation method, and flavor. In addition to contributing nutritive value, vegetables play a very important role in making the total meal attractive and appealing. The versatility in the types of vegetables that can be planned add to their desirability. Their colours, texture, and preparation methods provide for various possibilities and alternatives for the menu. They may be served as whole, halved, quartered, sliced, diced, cubed, julienne, or carved into attractive shapes.

Carrots, broccoli, peas, cauliflower, beans, and other vegetables provide rich colours and interesting combinations. They may be prepared by using various methods such as steaming, baking, and sautéeing. They may be creamed or added with other gravies. Various sauces and seasonings go very well with vegetables. When more than one choice is provided, texture should be considered, and alterations should be provided between the soft and hard-textured vegetables.

Contrast in colour, shape, and preparation methods is essential when choices are provided or when more than one vegetable is included in the menu. Vegetables provide attractive colours when foods are displayed, particularly on a cafeteria counter.

Flavors should also be considered since some vegetables are pungent and have strong flavors as compared to others. For example, vegetables belonging to the cabbage group or onions are strong flavored and so should preferably be used with vegetables that are relatively less strong flavored. Also, the vegetables served should be based on the entrées of the day.

Highly seasoned entrées should be complemented with mild-flavored vegetables and vice versa. These vegetables complement the flavors provided by the entrées, such as in the case of liver and onions and stuffed bell peppers with ground beef.

From the nutritional point of view, vegetables are a very important food group and more than one type of vegetable should therefore be included in any one menu. A menu that provides for dark green or deep yellow vegetables daily ensures a high content of certain required vitamins. Vegetables should be cooked for the least possible time or served raw in order to preserve their nutritional content.

Step 5. Salad selection

Salads may consist of one or more combinations of vegetables, fruits, meats, fish, cheese, and gelatin molds. They may be accompanied by different kinds of dressings and garnishes. As in the case of vegetables, salads also add colour, flavor, and texture to the meal. In the selection of salad items, entrées and vegetables for the meal should be considered in order to avoid any type of repetition. All aspects should be taken into consideration; for example the meat in a salad, even if in small quantities, should be different from those selected for entrées The same rule applies to the vegetables and fruits used in salads. The temperature of the items also plays an important role. Chilled salads complement hot salads and this variation in the serving temperatures adds to the variety and appeal of the menu. Salads may also be selected as the main item of the meal. If choices are included, there should be at least one large salad, and there should be a variety in serving sizes of the salads. A small size three-bean salad may be preferred with a filling entrée or a large salad may be desirable with a sandwich. Some salads such as tuna-bowl salads or meats, vegetables, and cheese salads become popular attractions and specialities of an operation.

In general, if salads complement the entrées, smaller serving sizes are usually adequate. Salads also contribute greatly to the overall nutritional value of the meals, and this fact should be considered when planning menus. Although salads do not require elaborate equipment for their preparation, a good deal of hard labour is involved in their preparations, preparation, and arrangement.

Step 6. Soup and appetizer selection

Like salads there are numerous types and kinds of appetizers and soups from which to choose. These items precede entrées or the main item of the meal. As is evident from their name, appetizers are for stimulating the appetite. Soups, to a great extent, serve the same type of function as appetizers. Since these foods are included to "whet" the appetite, it is essential to select recipes for soups that would increase the appetite for the main course of the meal. Soups and appetizers can be light or heavy based on their ingredients. A light appetizer should therefore be planned when heavy and filling entrées are offered and vice versa. Light entrées or sandwiches may be complemented by heavier soups.

Leftover vegetables, juices, and drained syrups from canned foods may be effectively utilized in soups. Soups for the succeeding meal should be planned with consideration of possible leftovers and their utilization. However, costs should be considered in utilization of the leftover items. It will be necessary to determine whether leftover vegetables would be more profitable as an accompaniment to entrées or as ingredients in soups. There are various spices, condiments, and garnishes that are used to complement appetizers and soups.

As in the case of other menu items, it is necessary to plan appetizers and soups in such a way that there is no repetition with other items that may be on the menu. Creamed soups should not be served with creamed entrées. Fish chowders should not be included when other fish dishes are on the menu. The temperature at which soups are served is very important, since the preferences for temperature vary from one consumer to another. Maintaining proper temperature requires equipment and labour, which should be considered in menu planning.

Step 7. Dessert selection

Since the bulk of the menu items for the meals have already been selected, it should be easier to plan the desserts. It is always preferable to keep the dessert selection to the end. Desserts are very important since many patrons look forward to desserts, which not only add a final touch to the menu but also provide a lasting impression of the meal.

Careful planning is therefore essential, as a well-planned meal may be spoiled by an unappealing dessert. It is primarily the taste of the dessert that is important rather than the quantity. A tasty small serving of a dessert is sufficient to leave a lasting impression of the meal.

Desserts may consist of fruits (whole, part, or combination), cakes, pies, cheeses, puddings, ice creams, and cookies. Many interesting combinations are possible with desserts. Since there is a lot of concern regarding their caloric value, it is important to consider that factor in planning. As in the case of other menu items, a light dessert should be planned with heavy meals and vice versa. There should be no duplication with any of the foods already included in the menu. The colour, consistency/texture, and shape should be considered. The intensity of sweetness of the dessert should also be considered. A hot, spicy entrée may be followed by an intensely sweet dessert, or a hot meat item may be followed by ice cream.

Sweet and soft desserts also go very well with filling entrées. Entrées and desserts are usually the main items that the food patron considers when selecting items from the menus, and so they should be planned very carefully. When choices are provided among desserts, consider the type of dessert, as well as its consistency, texture, colour, and flavor. A pie, cake, and pudding are good combinations when choices are provided. Appearance of the desserts is very important when they are displayed on the dessert cart or in display cases. Nuts, condiments, and syrups add to the appeal of the desserts.

Step 8. Bread selection

Breads can be of many different kinds and shapes. Their preparation methods and final texture also vary considerably. Breads complement the entrée item and should be planned accordingly.

Among the many varieties of breads are yeast, quick, sweet-dough, sourdough, flat, and several other specialty breads. There are several types of foreign breads that are especially good with foreign entrées. The serving size of the bread should vary with the type of the entrées included in the menu. Since most of the breads are eaten with butter, greasy items should be limited when breads are provided. Bland types of breads may be included when spicy and/or juicy items are on the menu. Breads may also be used in entrée items such as cheese rarebit on rye bread. In these situations bread duplication should be avoided.

Step 9. Beverage selection

This is probably the easiest step in menu planning, as there are several hot and cold beverages that are usually included on the menu. Since most of the beverages can be made relatively easily and frequently, or are readily available for serving, less effort is needed in their planning. At many places the list of beverages is standardized. Selection is more difficult for alcoholic beverages. Seasonal availability and variations should be taken into consideration in planning beverages. Beverages may be selected from alcoholic or nonalcoholic beverages, carbonated beverages, fruit juices, lemonade, coffee, milk shakes, hot tea, iced tea, and various types of milk products. Herbal teas are also becoming popular.

Step 10. Breakfast-menu selection

Breakfast items are relatively simple to plan. Normally, there are fixed breakfast items that need to be included on the menu, although, variations in the method of preparation are desirable. In institutional types of foodservices, breakfast is important. Breakfast items should be such that they can be prepared easily on short notice. Several choices may be included since preferences vary and there are standard foods desired for breakfast by many consumers. Juices, cereals, toasts, eggs, sausage ham, and biscuits are among the popular breakfast items. Too much duplication and repetition of the items should be avoided as much as possible.

These steps outline the recommended procedure for planning menus. The horizontal and vertical lines of the menus should be checked and rechecked. It is also advisable to plan the menu in two different sessions, one for planning and one for finalizing menus. It is also important to consider all aspects before the menu is finalized. A trial menu may also be offered for the first few weeks, particularly if the foodservice facility is new. It may become necessary to modify and make changes In the planned menus. Enough flexibility should be built into the menu to accommodate future changes and/or unexpected conditions. A final checklist is highly desirable for every type of foodservice operation.

Computers in menuplanning

With the development of computer technology as well as the availability of several types of computers, more and more foodservices are utilizing these instruments for various aspects of management. Several types of computers and computer programs are available for use by foodservices.

The menu-planning process becomes extremely simplified if a computer is used. Final judgment should depend on the management rather than the computer. It should be remembered that computers respond only to the information fed into them and so accurate input of information is vital for the success of computer menu planning. By using computers, menus may be planned on the basis of data on food preferences, food characteristics, production time, labour needs, nutritional quality, overall costs, selling prices, inventory control, and forecasting. Careful programming to include all of this information as well as the handling of data is necessary; this requires both skill and experience.

The major advantages Of using a computer for menu planning are listed below.

1. *Storage of a voluminous amount of data.* Inventory records, lists of recipes and Ingredients, cost of Ingredients and prepared menu items, serving sizes of menu Items, nutritional and food preference data may all be stored in the computer and recalled for use in planning menus.
2. *Financial savings.* If properly used, computers may save significantly the costs incurred in planning menus.
3. *Calculations using the stored data.* Using a computer, it is relatively easy to calculate the cost of the menu items, or the nutritional value of the menu; both procedures would almost be impossible to do by other methods in a limited amount of time.
4. Selection of menu items or choices at random, if a sequential rating/ranking is provided.
5. Avoidance of human bias related to use of menu items and to employee scheduling. Employee complaints and dissatisfaction can frequently be eliminated by using computers in planning.
6. Recommended dietary allowances provided by meals can be very easily calculated by computers.
7. Cost of the items, food cost percentages, selling price, percent profit, and other such calculations can be easily made.

8. Forecasting can be done by using stoied data.
9. Popularity of the menu items can be calculated from consumer demand data.
10. *Use in problem solving*. Graphs, charts, bar diagrams, pie diagrams, and tables are easier to Interpret than raw data.

The use of computers as well as the type of computers to be used is a decision of the management and must be based on several factors. The fact remains, however, that computers are becoming very population and, based on the complexity of the foodservice operation, they should be utilized in menu planning.

Menu format

The menus planned have to be rewritten in two different types of formats, although the menu items themselves will remain unchanged. The two different formats are written (1) for foodservice personnel and (2) for consumers. Menus written for foodservice personnel are supplemented by such pertinent technical information as recipe file number, name of the recipe, production schedule, equipment usage, and preparations schedule, etc.

In many foodservices, this information is included on production sheets. Simple names of the menu items are included in this format, with which all foodservice personnel are familiar. From the consumers' point of view, menus are designed to "sell" and therefore are described to attract consumers' attention. The descriptions are planned to create an appeal for the items served.

Since the purpose of the menu is to communicate with the consumer, a good menu format is one which is effective in communicating the message to the intended consumer. This requires very careful selection of words, and it should be remembered that words have different meanings for different people. The target group of consumers should be envisioned while writing menus.

A well-planned menu is of no value until the consumer "buys" it in all respects. The terminology used in menus should be such that the menu items are described as accurately and honestly as possible. Overemphasis or masking of descriptions may create a negative effect. It is advisable that nothing be left for consumers to assume, since the consumers are likely to avoid unfamiliar or unclear items on the Menu.

"Chefs Delite" or "Fisherman's Catch" with no adequille description of the items leaves it lot to consumers' imagination and may adversely affect a good-quality product. Interesting or attractive terms should also convey ail accurate description of the menu item. There are several foreign terms that are used in menus, and those should be followed by descriptions. It should be noted that when foreign foods are included, the cooking methods or concepts related with that food arouse interest and, hopefully, a desire to try or select those food items.

It may be difficult to accurately represent salads in written menus, since there can be numerous varying ingredients and it may be hard to come up with a representative term. Every effort should be made to describe the contents.

Terms that are unfamiliar or nondescriptive will be a continuous source of problems for the management since the consumers will always be asking questions. This will delay the service, particularly in it cafeteria line. If the person serving is unable to provide an instant answer to question" on the menu, the consumer may be tempted to avoid the item and it may affect the reputation of a restaurant. All these expensive delays can be avoided to an extent by careful planning of the menu format. Pictures are sometimes more effective than written descriptions.

Menu design

Menu design primarily depends on the type of the menu and foodservice facility. Menus that are "á la carte" allow for the selection of food items by the consumer from a list of foods presented on the menu with prices. "Table d'héte" menus offer complete meals at a fixed price. There may be choices provided in one or more categories. There are different sets of menus in the hospitals for regular meals as well as for modified diets.

Some menus are printed in such a way that more than one copy of the menu is produced when the consumer makes his/her selections. Patients are asked to indicate their choices in advance and copies are used on the tray assembly line, record files, and production. Cafeteria and fast-food restaurant menus usually consist of a listing of items on a menu board or printed sheets.

Menu design needs careful planning since it is almost the first thing the consumer sees and it may easily be the source of a first impression of the foodservice facility. The outside cover tells a lot about the facility, since the design, colours, and the quality of the paper provide an overall impression of the restaurant.

Menus with spilled foods and soiled paper are not only indicative of the poor management of the facility but also the type of consumers visiting it. The design and colours of the menu should reflect the type of the foodservice facility.

A well-planned and designed menu is expected at an elegant restaurant. Cafeterias and stands may display menus on boards at the entrance or the back wall of a counter. Lighted, boldly printed or electronically displayed menus are essential for drive-in facilities. The letters, whether in printed or displayed menus, should be of such a size that the menu can be easily read. Dark printing is also needed in restaurants that have candlelight or softer lighting in their dining rooms. Penciled-in changes are not desirable since they cannot be read easily. It also is advisable to provide black-and-white or preferably coloured pictures of the main menu items. Some restaurants prefer to have two different sets of menus, one with prices to be given to the principal host and one without prices to be given the rest of the customers in a party.

Many places prefer adding special clip-ons to the menus. The important items or specialty of the day can be conveniently added by using clip-ons without changing the main menu. The sequence in which the items are listed on the menu is very important and affects selection from the menu. An easy way to list the items is to follow the sequence in which they are to be served. In other words, menus should effectively communicate with customers of all categories and all age groups.

Foreign languages may be used to describe menu items if the facility caters to an international audience or is located near or in airports or seaports. It is also advisable to have special menus printed for those with poor eyesight. The size of the menu itself should be such that it can be easily handled. Too small a menu with items crammed on it is undesirable.

On the other hand, too large a menu creates problems in handling and unfolding. Creativity in menu design pays off by providing a positive image of the restaurant. Some people even collect menus as souvenirs. Menus may also be printed on placemats, napkins, matchboxes, electronic billboards, and handkerchiefs. Good-quality durable materials should be used for menu printing. It is preferable to have washable or easily wipeable materials for menus. It is also advisable to outline the specialty or the nutrient content of the menu items.

Menus should always be updated and kept current as to the food items offered and their prices. Too many hand-written changes on the menu give a poor impression. Ingredients should be listed, if possible, particularly those ingredients—such as monosodium glutamate (MSG)—that may cause allergy or sickness in specific individuals. Special items, such as the low-calorie or low-sodium foods, should be specified on the menu. The menu should also include information pertaining to the facility such as phone numbers; address; location of other chains or restaurants; hours of operation; special events; map of the area; and credit card, check, or cash payment policy. In the case of elegant restaurants or those at historic sites, it may be advisable to include a short history or theme of the restaurant. If special items or antiques are on display in the facility, some description of them should appear on the menu.

10

Pricing Strategies

The balance between price and value largely determines the success of an establishment. With a hotel, it is the room rate which sets the pricing levels for the rest of the hotel's products. Hence price is part of positioning. For example, one expects to pay more for a stay at a high-class, five-star hotel than at a budget lodge. Price helps to determine the customer mix and, conversely, whatever customer mix is targeted by an establishment will determine the price. Recent years have proved that the hospitality industry is a fiercely competitive one and sensitive to economic conditions; consequently the relationship between rates and occupancy has to be very finely tuned.

The rack rate is the regular published room rate. In a perfect market, the rack rate is set as a result of cost-plus pricing, which is based on a simple sum:

Operating costs + Capital recovery + Profit + Forecasted number of customers = Price

Rarely is there such a thing as a perfect market. Therefore the rack rate in many instances becomes a sort of starting price for negotiation, or the price that management would like to achieve throughout the year and at all times during the week. However, the fluctuations in demand dictate that different rates apply at different times of the year, week or even day.

— *Target profit pricing is* where the hotel endeavours to determine a price based on average occupancy which will provide an adequate return.

— *Perceived-value pricing is* where an establishment sets a price based on the value or benefits being offered. This pricing strategy is generally aimed at a specific customer mix.

— *Going rate is* based on averaging, keeping pace with the competition.

— *Price ranging is* employed by nearly all hotels. It is setting a high price for the best suites or rooms ranging down to the cheapest rooms, with each drop in price representing a consequent drop in size, views, facilities and extras.

— *Value-added pricing is* where extras are discounted and coupled with a going rate to provide an attractive package offer, often referred to as a 'product'.

When customers ask the price of a room, the room rate can cover:

— room only

— room and breakfast

— room and all meals

— room plus all recreational facilities

— room plus free enticements, such as champagne, opera tickets, shopping vouchers and so on.

The purpose of a value-added pricing strategy is to make direct comparisons with competing properties difficult while making the offer appear to be worth more than is being charged.

— *Price skimming is* a strategy adopted by new

properties with a well known brand name, a grand facade and a high-profile positioning. From the outset they charge a high price for their rooms and other products because they have a new, exciting, prestigious image which usually attracts a high-flying, 'nothing-but-the-best' style of customer, called in marketing the 'early adopter'. This strategy is maintained for as long as the property holds its position, and it is called 'skimming' because it is taking the cream of the market at the time. However, when other, newer properties are built, and as the facilities become less of a novelty, prices are gradually reduced.

Management usually has a policy on pricing which varies from being rigid to totally flexible. The objectives are usually survival, profit maximization, market share, quality leadership and capital recovery. However, price changes can be forced upon a property by competition. A close competitor can 'steal' guests by offering better deals.

Market conditions—an economic down-turn, for instance—can force every property into a price-cutting war. The market and demand for accommodation will set the price ceiling and an establishment's costs will set the floor for prices. The price ceiling is the maximum price people are prepared to pay in a given market environment. The price floor is the lowest price a property can charge without losing money. Somewhere in between is where competing properties struggle for market share.

Price is a value-for-money equation which potential guests have to deliberate over before making a decision. In some markets, setting a rate is almost a daily decision as rivals have the option to raise or lower rates with every enquiry.

Demand differential pricing strategies

In most city markets, there is, an over-supply of rooms for the majority of the year. Special events and seasonal demands are the only occasions when all rooms are filled. The marketing challenge therefore is to fill as many rooms as possible in the seasonal gaps of market demand. Price and perceived value becomes a significant strategy in this situation. On different days and at different times of the year, a room may be hired out to guests at rates which can vary considerably. Similarly, the rate will vary to attract specific customer groups, such as tour wholesalers, large companies, conference organizers and frequent travellers. This is demand differential pricing.

Holiday packages

Holiday packages are products which the property markets as its own, such as a three-day stay at the property combined with sightseeing tours or a special interest package which takes in sporting or cultural events. These are products that can be advertised, promoted to corporate clients, sold direct to customers or marketed through other tourism-related companies.

Cooperative rates for tour/travel/airline/wholesalers

These are special, discounted room rates which are negotiated with tour wholesalers so that they can market their own holiday packages. Wholesaling rates enable an airline, for instance, to market a product which entails a stay of so many nights at the property as part of a total number of benefits or events for the airline to package and offer as an attractive value-for-money holiday to their customers.

Most large travel agents and transport companies package holidays in this way. From the establishment's point of view, the discount is offset by the volume of business it receives.

Weekend rates

Business people and conference organizers tend to plan their use of the property's facilities for working days. Therefore most properties find that they have excess capacity over weekends. Weekend rates are discounted offers designed, to attract people to stay on over a weekend or to attract local people to indulge themselves. They can also be marketed in conjunction with transport operators to get the domestic market to have a 'short break' package enjoying the luxury of staying at the property.

Business rates

The business traveller is the most frequent user of hospitality and is therefore the target of nearly all properties. To attract their business, special incentive rates are generally negotiated. The additional attraction is usually the use of special business services such as secretarial or 'person Friday' assistance, fax facilities, computers, photocopying, meeting rooms, video-conferencing and, in some cases, language translators.

Frequent user rates

This is a strategy designed to encourage people who regularly use hospitality products to stay regularly with the property and build credit points which either reduce the rate over time or provide the recipient with a free stay after so many bookings. Usually called a 'Guest Loyalty Scheme', the rate is created mainly to attract the business person to become a loyal client. Another form of the same strategy is an offer to stay another day for free. The Hilton has an offer which is promoted as 'Another day another dollar', meaning that for just another dollar the customer can stay the extra day.

Corporate rates

Large companies, or companies with a high usage rate of

hospitality facilities, are targeted and offered a low rate for continued custom, and special deals are often included for the use of other hotel services.

Another variant of this strategy is to enrol them in a special club which provides not only discounted prices for every facility at the property, but also discounts with participating stores, airlines, hire cars, theatre bookings and any other attraction the property can negotiate which is likely to appeal to the corporate customer.

Family rates

'The children stay free', is one type of offer which is a strategy that many properties employ to attract family customers. Another is an offer of a free child-minding or nanny service. Special rooms arranged for the family to be together in a suite or adjoining rooms is another variation of the strategy. These types of products are frequently sold to use the excess capacity over weekends or for seasonal business periods.

Conference rates

Professional, trade, business or social groups which hold conferences, training seminars, celebrations, special sporting or cultural events hunt for the best value they can get. Most properties 'bid' for this type of business and have a negotiable rate which has a floor value to the property (which means it recovers costs and retains a bare minimum of profit).

Most properties offer an all-inclusive price with meals and use of other facilities. Often the objective is to confuse the issue with add-ons so that price comparison with other properties becomes difficult. Some places negotiate with suppliers to help them with special prices to win the deal. A transport element and programme for accompanying persons in the offer is not uncommon.

Up-grading

Some high-profile hotels do not like discounting because it may harm their prestige image. Instead, when they are in a competitive situation they upgrade favoured clients from, say, a normal room to the executive floor so that they can provide added benefits at no extra charge. Or they include business facilities for free. They are, in effect, giving away some of their profits, but they are not seen to be discounting and are thereby preserving a claim that they do not have to reduce their prices to win business.

No frills rates

Another form of discounting is a published 'no frills' rate involving basic accommodation. This is a last-resort pricing strategy for large properties, but a common strategy for properties struggling to be competitive in other ways. For budget accommodation the 'no frills' approach is central to the concept and its apparent success. There are other variations on the foregoing strategies. All of them have the same intent, which is to win business at all costs, especially during difficult times or during off-season periods.

Selling up and selling down

Various customer mixes perceive different values for different benefits they receive. Many establishments have price levels for each segment (top rates for business people, low rates for families). This can result in a disparate customer blend which harms the image of the place.

A 'get-what-you-can' price strategy therefore can lead to a loss of regular patronage. However, even the best hotels sometimes resort to a sell-up, sell-down pricing approach, sometimes called an 'open-door' strategy, as opposed to the 'closed-door' strategy reflecting a policy of price rigidity. The 'foot-in-the-door' strategy is when an enquiring customer asks about rates. The potential guest is given a number of alternatives, ranging from the very low to the highest price.

The client often will choose the middle price, not wanting to look cheap or too extravagant and seeking the best value. It is then, suggested to the client that for only another small amount of money he or she can get some added benefit, like a king-sized bed or a room overlooking some geographical feature. This is 'selling up'. The 'face-in-the-door' strategy is the opposite. The price quoted is the highest. Often this will be accepted; if it is not, other alternatives are offered until a price is reached which is acceptable. This is 'selling down'.

A market penetration pricing strategy is used when a hotel sets lower than usual prices because it wants to capture market share. This is a pricing strategy that will achieve much-needed cash flow at times. It would also make sense if the establishment wants to introduce a new product and needs to gain quick recognition and win some early sales.

Pricing impacts on other products

A price strategy will impact on other elements of the marketing mix, depending on the corporate goals and the marketing objectives. Long-term discounting, for instance, must have an effect on product quality decisions.

Management needs to have cost and profit predictions that will reflect the consequences of price strategy decisions. Whereas room rates set the overall position of an establishment, it can have different pricing strategies for each of its products. This approach can be used to put value back into a room rate which is perceived to be very high. Product-line pricing can be used to offer customers a choice of values. Hence, as well as an expensive, fine dining restaurant, it has a low-priced coffee shop. Or a cocktail lounge, a medium-priced lounge and a public bar. This way, everyone can find their own price level without feeling that they are being 'bled'.

The other strategy is to maintain a high value-for-money room rate and recover profits from its other products and services. Incentives can be offered, such as off-season rates, early booking discounts, preferred customer discounts, or special offers tied with a sales promotion.

Restaurant pricing strategies

A hospitality establishment is no different from a retailer when it comes to making offers. Everyone likes a bargain, which is why sales promotions and premium offers usually attract additional customers, or bring regular customers into the establishment more often. Therefore the same types of strategies used by the large properties can be adapted by other hospitality businesses.

The principles do not vary, but some businesses are perceived in a certain way by their consumers and therefore sensitivity to market demand has to be recognized. For example, a restaurant which has the same prices for dinner, lunch and weekends is being a bit hopeful, and certainly inflexible. At different times of the day customers want different types of eating experiences. The luncheon period is normally patronized by business people who want a quick, light meal with a minimal amount of alcohol.

A restaurateur could stipulate that his or her kind of place does not cater for the crowd, which is fine, but he or she could be missing out on business. More importantly, he or she might be forgetting that the same luncheon customer is also a potential dinner, snack or even breakfast customer. Michael Hurst, the guru- of the restaurant business, changes menu and price structures according to the demands of various customer needs. Hence there is a lower-priced lunch menu and an 'early birds' menu (which is half of the dinner price) which caters for those who want to eat before going on to a function, party or the theatre. It also appeals to retired people looking for a cheap, good-value meal.

During the dinner session, full prices apply because this is the time of greatest demand. Then he has a supper menu for late eaters or those who have come from their evening's entertainment. A varying level of prices and menus makes sense because it is maximizing the use of the staff and the premises.

